Party Conflict and Community Development

Party Conflict and Community Development

Postwar Politics in Ann Arbor

Samuel J. Eldersveld

Ann Arbor
The University of Michigan Press

Published in the United States of America by
The University of Michigan Press

1998 1997 1996 1995 4 3 2 1

A CIP catalogue record for this book is available from the British Library.

Library of Congress Cataloging-in-Publication Data

Eldersveld, Samuel James.
Party conflict and community development : postwar politics in Ann Arbor / Samuel J. Eldersveld.
p. cm.
Includes bibliographical references and index.
ISBN 0-472-09562-5 (alk. paper). — ISBN 0-472-06562-9 (pbk.: alk. paper)
1. Ann Arbor (Mich.)—Politics and government. 2. Political parties—Michigan—Ann Arbor. I. Title.
JS546.A77E42 1995
320.9752′56′09045—dc20 94-36793
CIP

Paperback ISBN : 978-0-472-06562-2

To the political party and community leaders and the public of Ann Arbor who gave so generously of their time to me and my students leading to the completion of the research necessary for this study.

Contents

Introduction

Political conflict is central to democratic belief and practice. Democracies emerged from political struggle, and their institutions were founded on the principle of the legitimacy and necessity of political opposition. The right to oppose, the tolerance of dissent, the clash of divergent ideas, the sharp contest for political office, the open competition between parties for the control of government—these components of the democratic creed have been fundamental in free societies, and in our American society. However, there are many American cities where the "nonpartisan" concept of government somehow invaded people's minds and supplanted the idea of party conflict. This is not true for Ann Arbor, Michigan. Ann Arbor has partisan politics and party conflict.

This is a study of that system of partisan politics in one American city, Ann Arbor, in the period following World War II, from 1945 to 1990. It seeks to describe and analyze how that system evolved and how it functions, particularly how partisan government contributed to the development of that community. The book emerged from over ten years of research conducted with my students on many facets of Ann Arbor's political life since the war. They tracked the careers of more than three hundred persons who ran for city office. Interviews were conducted with mayors, city councillors, and department heads. The students completed extensive surveys of party activists, interest group leaders, and samples of the Ann Arbor public, more than once; students at the university were also interviewed. They analyzed the coverage of the campaigns in the *Ann Arbor News* for the past forty-five years. And they helped secure accurate data on the vote cast in each election, on the city's annual budgets, and on a variety of historical facts about Ann Arbor's postwar politics. Our purpose in all this was, first, to describe carefully political organization, leadership, and decision making in Ann Arbor. Second, and more important, the aim was to analyze the role of party competition in the achievement of an effective and attractive community in postwar America.

The focus of the book, thus, was party government—that is, the evolution of a partisan system, its survival, and its functional relevance for Ann Arbor's development. As a city with partisan elections and government, Ann Arbor is somewhat special, certainly in a minority among U.S. cities. In Michigan, no other city its size has a partisan government. Only ten small cities in the state, besides Ann Arbor, are partisan election communities. In the United States less than 30 percent of cities with a population of twenty-five hundred or more have city charters providing for this type of government.[1] Historically partisan government for cities has been frowned on in the United States by the reformers, particularly after the turn of the century, because local party "machines" were seen as corrupt, inefficient, and detrimental to proper community development. Ann Arbor never succumbed to these reform arguments. It opted for party politics in and by a council-administrator system, with a city council elected by wards in partisan elections. It is this distinctive system on which we concentrate in this study.

Scholars differ as to the importance of a city's political system in determining a city's progress and development. The social structure, the nature of the population, the industrial and business environment, the financial resource base—all these are obviously of considerable importance in understanding a city. The question is whether politics is of secondary or primary importance, and whether political forces work together with these social and economic forces to promote or hinder a city's proper growth. The argument over this has continued for some time. One scholar of the American city argues that external controls and constraints on cities mean that "political variables no longer remain relevant to the analysis [of] local policy."[2] A comparative scholar of cities claims: "Political variables have relatively less direct and independent impact than socioeconomic variables . . . somehow the nature of the socioeconomic environment seems more important than the nature of community politics in shaping community policies."[3] They argue in essence that the nature of local government—who controls city hall, who wins city elections, how city campaigns are conducted, who is politically active and who votes in the city—is really marginal or irrelevant to city development.

There are scholars, however, who disagree. Here is a sampling of their positions:[4]

> "The obstacles in the way of solving city problems are mainly political." (Banfield)

> "Resource capability contributes relatively little to the variance in policy development." (Eulau and Prewitt)

> "A fairly general consensus has emerged concerning the importance of linking urban leadership . . . to policy outputs." (Clark)
>
> "It is not plausible to regard the decline of some of our cities . . . as the irreversible result of economic processes." (Gurr and King)

Such scholars emphasize that the political process in a city is important in understanding how the leadership responds to the needs of the city population. What is critical is how these needs are transformed into the proper decisions, then the implementation of these decisions so that the proper development occurs. The political process in a city varies in certain critical ways—it may be centralized or fragmented, competitive or consensual, led by able leaders or headed by incompetent ones. These differences may play a major role in the direction the city takes. As two European scholars put it, "policy outputs do not spring automatically from the socioeconomic structure."[5] They are the result of "political" decisions. As March and Olsen (1984) state; "The organization of political life makes a difference."[6]

For a community to develop to the maximum of its capabilities, I propose that there are certain requisites. First, it needs a set of governmental institutions which facilitate the articulation and final determination of the goals for the city's development. Facilitation is enhanced by centralized and focused responsibility for decision making, not by divided control among political leaders or between administrators and politicians. Also needed is a deliberative arena where competing proposals can be responsibly advanced and debated and finally resolved. The system also needs an efficient bureaucracy effectively supervised by an administrator who is subject to ultimate political control.

Below the governmental level, there is a need for a political group infrastructure which is interested in and knowledgeable about city affairs, representing diverse social group interests, and involved at this group level in the debate over public policy. These groups need linkages to governmental leaders as well as to the public. Competing political parties and partisan elections is one such infrastructure (as in Ann Arbor). Theoretically, one can argue that alternative types of interest group infrastructures could provide effective linkage. But democratic theory has always emphasized the importance of two or more parties competing effectively in elections. Democratic theory argues that such party competition leads to more responsible leadership, policy innovation, representative government, and citizen involvement in politics. The pressure of competitive politics forces leaders to listen to citizens and, when necessary, to compromise with each other. This is, of course, the theory!

Aside from functional institutions, communities require a certain type of political leadership if they are to develop well. Effective political management depends on the credentials of those elected or appointed to city office. These credentials include a certain political competence, experience, and knowledge of city affairs, plus considerable previous exposure to the public life of the community. Apprenticeship in the political and civic organizations that invest time and attention to public issues is useful. But the attitudes and beliefs of leaders are particularly important—above all, their commitment to development goals, and to the democratic process by which these are decided and implemented, and their sense of responsiveness to citizen opinion.

The crux of the development process is sound decision making by community leadership in the planning of development and in the management of financial resources. The institutional context may appear congenial to effective government. The leadership may be carefully recruited and properly credentialed. But if development goals are to be achieved, the city's leaders need to make rational decisions, first, in the mobilization of resources and, second, in the proper utilization of resources to achieve their goals. Elites have great discretion in both senses, securing income and expending income. Good government depends on both.

Finally, in all of this we need a public attentive to the political process by which development is achieved—a public that believes in its community, accepts the need to progress toward its goals, monitors the performance of leadership, communicates its ideas to leaders, both at election campaign time and between elections, and maintains links to the leaders it has placed in public office, through the parties and political interest groups. There must be a solid public base for political leadership if a community is to thrive. In the last analysis, a coherent political culture has to develop; that is, an accepted set of political beliefs and behaviors, at the mass level as at the leadership level.

These requisites provide an outline of the theoretical argument of this book. We look at Ann Arbor from 1945 to the present. We focus on institutions (governmental, party, and interest groups), political leadership, the management of resources at the elite level of the city, and the attitudes and behavior of citizens at the mass level. Our hope is to shed light through our analysis on the role of politics in the postwar development of this community.

The thrust of this book is that politics *has* made a difference in Ann Arbor. Ann Arbor is considered by many to be an attractive city—in the provision of basic services, in the availability of social, recreational, and cultural amenities, in the investment in economic development. Ann Arbor has had (and continues to have) its problems, to be sure, similar to those of other cities: problems in rational planning, in adequate service delivery, in dealing with crime, in traffic control, in private and public housing, in parklands and recreation development. On the political side, there have been concerns about voter apathy, fiscal strain, the quality of leadership, and the effective representation of citizen opinion. In recent years, leaders have debated over what to do about the welfare and rights of the city's less-affluent members. Despite these problems, however, Ann Arbor has a strong reputation, even receiving an All-American City award in 1967. Social and economic change has taken place in this city as the community of Ann Arbor has developed its own special character. Innovative policy decisions over the past forty-five years have made Ann Arbor what it is today. The point is that it need not have happened this way—Ann Arbor could have become a second-rate or third-rate city. But it did not. Why not? The analysis and argument here is that the nature of Ann Arbor's political system has been very important—above all, its competitive party system and the way that system functions at all levels of political life.

The Data

One must take a fairly long time perspective in studying a community. We look here at the last forty-five years of Ann Arbor. During that time, the city has developed tremendously, and progressively. Its physical and social and political character have changed—its territorial boundaries, its population size and complexion, its social problems, its social group interest structure, its financial resource base, and its culture, particularly its political culture. In 1945, Ann Arbor's politics was quite different than it is today. Many innovative policy decisions have been adopted, often bitterly argued, that have made Ann Arbor what it is today. We hope to describe these 45 years of Ann Arbor's politics, and in the process test our theory that politics has made a difference.

The data for this book are of different types, collected carefully and laboriously by my students and myself over many years. They are not as complete for the entire postwar period as I would like, but they are rather unique. Our data files now include the following:

Fairly complete information on the background of candidates for mayor and council since 1945

The votes cast for all candidates for city office, and for proposals

Analysis of the *Ann Arbor News* campaign coverage during this period
Sample interview surveys of the Ann Arbor public in 1981 and 1984, and of the leadership of the Republican and Democratic parties in 1980, 1982 and 1986
A study of Ann Arbor's interest group leaders in 1983
Surveys of student political attitudes and participation in politics in 1985 and 1987
A budget analysis for each year since 1945.

Other special studies and reports are also utilized. Further, several comparative studies have been done of cities in the U.S. and in Europe. Where possible and when these comparative data are relevant, we will present them in order to place Ann Arbor in a broader and more global perspective.

This book has been written from two perspectives, that of a participant in the politics of this city and that of a student for many years of political elites and local government in the United States and elsewhere in the world. The vantage point of the participant, as a former mayor (Democratic) with long involvement in the politics of Ann Arbor (since 1946), has provided, I think, certain helpful insights and precise knowledge about Ann Arbor's political life. The vantage point of the scholar of comparative politics has contributed an understanding about how political systems differ, how cities differ, and how one must connect local and system context to an understanding of political behavior, of leaders, and of publics. I cannot escape from this dual set of perspectives. I hope that I have subordinated the first perspective to the second. I have tried to present the data, the analysis, and the interpretations as a detached scholar studying a particular political community over time. I have revised this book a dozen times, on the urging of colleagues, to make it more detached and scientific. I hope that it is. But if occasionally evidence of personal engagement with the locale emerges, I hope it will add to the value of the analysis rather than detract.

Obviously, I am indebted to many people in the collection of these materials about Ann Arbor. Without my students, much would not have been accomplished. Without the cooperation of the respondents in these studies, I would have had to speculate much more than I did in this book. And some old data, very fugitive and difficult to track down, given me by Democratic and Republican friends, were extremely helpful. My department of political science and my college (Literature, Science and the Arts) bore the brunt of my expenses for preparing materials. My academic colleagues advised me (particularly Lawrence Mohr,

John Jackson, Thomas Anton, and Arthur Miller). Many political leaders provided helpful information; three in particular advised me on parts of the manuscript: Albert Wheeler, Robert Harris, and Eunice Burns. I received help as well from city employees and administrators. The city clerk's office, Herbert Katz particularly, assisted me often. My friend Guy Larcom, city administrator from 1956 to 1973, was a wise counselor. And my special research assistants, Nancy Webster, Joel Bloom, Shen Mingming, and Judith Kullberg helped me greatly. Several secretaries worked on this manuscript: Judy Fogle, Holly Bender, Thelma Perry, Kris Moga, and Tanya Hummels. However, none of these persons is responsible for my interpretations; the mistakes are all mine. I will try to list in the appendix my students who were most active in this research, but there were others I am sure I will forget whose contributions were very useful.

It is difficult to do such a study as rigorously as one would like to, and to conclude with findings in which one has complete confidence. Among my difficulties: (1) The data we needed for the past forty-five years were not perfectly available nor retrievable. Information disappears; people throw data away. Precise data on even the budget process in early years, for example, were hard to find; party platforms were very fugitive. (2) Not all people were available to be interviewed, and not all who were would talk freely. Hence, the roles of certain actors and "hidden influentials" were difficult to ascertain. (Even sitting as mayor in City Hall, I had difficulty being certain who listened to whom and what the motivations of certain councillors were.) (3) The forces responsible for historical movements are hard to document precisely (for example, why has voting turnout declined sharply in Ann Arbor from the 1970s to today? A big question and hard to analyze definitively). What forces, economic or political or social, were important in explaining the alternation of Democrats and Republicans in office? These and many more types of questions are difficult to analyze conclusively, with the best of data. Politics in a community are particularly elusive to analyze. If we had periodic surveys of the public and leaders over the past forty-five years, we would have much more confidence in our conclusions, but such systematic data were not collected until 1980. Nevertheless, many data of different types are available, and we shall evaluate our theories in the light of the available evidence.

Conclusion

Our research on local government in Western democracies reveals that in the U.S., as in Europe, municipalities have been forced to assume more responsibility for public sector services and expenditures than ever before. Central governments have devolved more tasks on them, either by directive (Europe) or by abdication of financial support, or both (U.S.). Thus, cities in Western democracies seem today to be more than ever the focus of responsibility as well as concern.

The recent reports on the financial plight of U.S. cities are indeed gloomy. The National League of Cities in 1991 revealed that revenues were less than expenditures in 61 percent of the cities, that 48 percent had cut services, 59 percent had laid off employees, and 71 percent were less able to meet financial needs in 1991 than in 1990.[7] Mayor Raymond Flynn of Boston, President of the U.S. Conference of Mayors, said there was "a growing crisis in hometown America . . . something is very wrong." The mayors' conference asked President Bush for $35 billion in immediate aid, but was ignored.[8] In 1988, Mayor Ed Koch of New York expressed the concern that the "urban agenda" was unimportant to people, especially to federal authorities: "I sense that the spirit and imagination of American politics have, once again, somehow disengaged from city life."[9]

A basic question is posed quite frequently these days: Can the city provide good government in America, government that is effective and responsive to citizen demands and needs? If so, under what conditions is this possible? Much of the recent scholarly writing answers this question in the negative. Many scholars are very skeptical of the capacity and will of city governments to deal with their problems. One scholar calls his book *The Decline of Urban Politics* and claims, "The very heart and soul of local politics has surely died."[10] Another observer states his position as a dilemma: "Most cities find themselves literally too small to handle their policy problems, but politically too weak to resist trying."[11] Those who study cities outside of the U.S., in other Western societies, also express disillusionment. One recent analysis argues that there is a "complex syndrome of conditions" in cities in contemporary systems which is part of "urban decline": a declining industrial sector, decaying housing and infrastructure, growing poverty, fiscal strain, and social stress. Linked to these are technological change, residential mobility, population decline, and inadequate tax resources.[12]

These examples of alarmism and pessimism in recent writing make the point clearly. Cities everywhere are presumably in trouble. And yet, many authors refer to another phenomenon—the "regeneration" of cities—to the possibility that cities can overcome their difficulties, that they can cope with their problems and develop despite their limitations. It is contended that while there are constraints, there are also opportunities.

Well-developed and well-governed cities are central for the wealth and happiness of our nation, for all of us. In a real sense, the city is the locale where human beings struggle for the fulfilling life. And as the federal government provides less and less help for American cities, how do urban elites deal with their problems, their conflicts, and their needs, and manage effectively what resources they have to not only survive, but also prosper? That is the key question of the 1990s. Ann Arbor's experience is instructive.

CHAPTER 1

The Two Images of Development in Ann Arbor

How and in what directions a city develops is a complex, multi-faceted process. It includes and is related to population and territorial change, economic growth (or stagnation), improvement (or decline) in social relations in the community, change as a cultural market, and change as a polity. All these types of development usually occur simultaneously, quickly or slowly, successfully or poorly, at the leadership level and at the public level. If coordinated well, by some design, an attractive community can emerge to fulfill the needs of a majority of the citizens. This by no means happens always. A breakdown or disjunction in the achievement of developmental goals often occurs. What causes such failure, and what produces success, has long been a question over which scholars have argued.

Along the route to success or failure, every community has to make decisions, explicitly or implicitly, about its goals for development. Obviously, every community has to provide basic services for its population (water, sewers, light, police and fire protection, garbage and trash collection, adequate roads, traffic lights, and such). Beyond the provision of these basic functions, there are many other options. Should the city invest much (or little) in parks and recreation? Should it feel it has a major (or minimal) responsibility for downtown development? Should it expend great (or no) effort in attracting industry, and if so, what types of industry? Should it welcome people of diverse racial and ethnic backgrounds or try to exclude them? Should it provide human welfare services for its population or decide these are not the proper responsibility of the city?

The "development dilemma" that confronts American cities is often seen as a conflict between responsibility for encouraging economic development and for meeting social welfare and other human service needs. It is contended that these two images of development collide and that it is difficult to have both. Scholars have debated this question with considerable intensity. The issue is usually put in zero-sum terms,—that is, you can't have both economic development *and* policies that are redistributive. Therefore, economic interests must prevail. Thus one scholar argues: "The interests of local government require that it emphasize the economic productivity of the community . . . . [This] requires that local governments concentrate on developmental as against redistributive objectives."[1] Others disagree with this position, arguing that both objectives are necessary and/or are possible.[2] This is indeed the type of dilemma that may dominate the planning and actions of American cities. It is seldom a conflict of the same dimensions in Western European democracies, where extensive social welfare systems are in place as a result of central government policy decisions. Such social welfare programs are administered primarily at the local level, or certain programs are explicitly outside the province of local government.

The development of Ann Arbor in a very real sense illustrates the development dilemma. It confronted these options with what may be called two images of development. The history of the community in a major sense is how sequentially and eventually in tandem these two images were implemented. In the succeeding analysis, the pursuit of these two visions in what Ann Arbor should be will be described. This will be followed by a discussion of how the party system has contributed to the achievement of these visions.

The Early Image of Development in Postwar Ann Arbor

In 1945, Ann Arbor was a small city of a little more than 40,000 population and six square miles in area, less than one-fourth the area it includes today. University enrollment on the Ann Arbor campus was only 11,847, one third of its present enrollment. There were only slightly more than 9,000 paid subscribers to the *Ann Arbor News* in the city. Ann Arbor's politics was completely dominated by Republicans in 1945 and well after that into the fifties. Of the fourteen council members (from seven wards), only two were Democrats, and that was only because the Republicans generously refused to oppose them in the fourth ward. William E. Brown, a businessman, had been elected mayor in 1945, without opposition; in fact, only in three wards was there an opposing candidate for city council. The Democrats put up few candidates for council seats in those days and received a grand total of 477 votes in 1945, 174 votes in 1946, 110 in 1947. The Republican percentage of the council vote ranged between 75 percent and 95 percent. But the total vote for both parties was extremely low, a turnout of 8.3 percent of eligible voters in 1945, 2.5 percent in 1946, 13 percent in 1947. It was government by conservative consensus, then, and most of the public withdrew from politics. Possibly this was because city government was basically a service-producing administration, not innovative, not very controversial; hence, the public was very complacent. The total General Fund budget in 1945 was $743,000, a per capita cost of $17. Clearly this was government at minimum cost, with minimum political confrontation, and minimum public involvement.

Ann Arbor did not remain that way for long. On April 16, 1945, just before the end of World War II, Mayor Brown presented a communication to the city council that was, on the one hand, the signal that a new era of development was to begin, and, further, illustrated the thinking by Ann Arbor's leaders as to the nature of development, that is, their view of the early image of development. The mayor's message read in part, as follows:

> Gentlemen:
>
> The war has brought to Ann Arbor numerous problems which cannot be solved without the support of this body . . . . In 1920, after the last war there were in Ann Arbor approximately 5,000 homes. In 1945 . . . there are approximately 7,700 . . . . I have been also informed that there are approximately only 300 building lots available for small home-building . . . . The University will soon take more property, meaning that there will be even fewer homes available . . . . The demand for homes after this war will be much greater than after the first world war.
>
> Several other factors . . . make action necessary to remedy this alarming situation. I have talked to the officers (of six large firms) regarding their post-war employment . . . . These men expect to employ . . . 45 percent more people in a normal post-war year than in a normal pre-war year . . . . And what about the returning serviceman and his desire for a home? It has been said that the University of Michigan expects to have a student attendance of possibly some 18,000 . . . . It is apparent that we are faced with a lack of homes, a lack of lots on which to build, and an ever increasing population.
>
> The point I wish to make is that something must be done about enlarging our city. We must find a way to take additional land into our corporate limits so that Ann Arbor can retain its place as the number one Michigan city in which to live. If this problem is not intelligently handled, we may expect that uncontrolled communities will spring up on our outskirts.
>
> The financial condition of the city . . . [is] excellent. Its bonded indebtedness has decreased . . . to only $598,000. The deposits on hand (cash surplus) have increased to approximately $460,000 . . . . Whether we like it or not, it is my opinion that our savings of the past

ten years will have to be spent, and more too, if we are to do only the things that are absolutely necessary . . . . I am sure we will accomplish [our] ends . . . if we give unselfishly of our time and always work for the good of the community.

Very sincerely yours,
W. E. Brown, Jr.

This document is significant because it laid out some of the early goals of city development as well as the strategies: expansion of housing, planning for population influx, catching up on capital improvement needs neglected during the war, annexation of new land, working with the university and the business establishment, and increasing tax revenues. Above all, the focus for this agenda for development is clear: territorial, industrial, economic, financial change.

It became clear also that the regents of the university were involved in postwar planning and aware of the pressures of new situations, the need to build residential halls, and therefore, the need to work cooperatively with the city. As a result, the regents in March 1946 adopted a resolution presented to the city council on April 4, 1946, in which they stated they were aware of the financial situation the city faced. The resolution reads as follows:

Whereas 1. The student population has increased to 14,400 and will continue to grow,
2. The city of Ann Arbor has not found it possible to expand the city limits to produce additional revenue to meet the increasing costs,

Be it resolved that the Board of Regents of the University of Michigan suggest to the Common Council of the City of Ann Arbor that the water and sewer rates now being paid by the University be

TABLE 1.1. Basic Indicators of Change in Ann Arbor 1945 to 1960

	1945–50	1950–60	Total 15-Year Period
Population increase	9.1%	39.6%	52.3%
Area (sq. mi.) increase	19.7%	105.5%	145.9%
University enrollment increase	64.4%	26.3%	105.1%
General fund budget increase (constant dollars)	$29.0	$154.6	$230.7
Per capita budgetary cost increase (constant dollars)	$5.90	$30.40	$36.30

Source: City Budget and Reports of the Registrar of the University of Michigan.

studied with the intention of increasing the payment being made for these services.

And be it further resolved that the administrative officers of the university are directed to continue to work with the proper city of Ann Arbor officials in studying appropriate ways of solving common university and city problems.

Thus was laid the foundation for university-city-business collaboration on many aspects of development.

The period from 1945 to 1960 was a decade and a half of tremendous growth for the city. The change was slow to develop up to 1950 (except for university enrollment), but the following decade was indeed a take off period for change. Note the indicators of change in table 1.1. As Mayor Brown indicated, the university enrollment would increase at once, and the city's population would then follow, requiring a larger city. One of the early decisions was that the city would seek to annex adjacent areas, persuading the residents in adjoining townships to agree to annexation by a policy that no city services would be provided to unincorporated areas. This policy was a key factor in city growth (tables 1.2 and 1.3).

A study of budgets in this early period (which we will analyze in detail in a later chapter) reveals that development was indeed taking place. The total general fund budget almost doubled in five years and tripled again in the next ten years, to 1960 (in actual dollars). If we control for inflation (and use constant dollars), there was an increase in the general fund from $1,378,000 in 1945 to $4,558,000 in 1960. Per capita costs jumped from $31.40 to $67.70 for the general fund alone. Many of these new allocations went to departments that had minimal outlays in 1949, such as planning and parks and recreation (see table 1.4).

Other departments were increasing also. The police department budget rose 249 percent (in constant dollars), garbage collection from

TABLE 1.2. Population and Area Growth, 1950–90

	Population	Area (sq. miles)	University Enrollment (Ann Arbor Campus)
1940	39,676	6.1	11,874[a]
1950	48,251	7.3	19,448
1960	67,340	15.0	24,229
1970	100,035	23.3	37,396
1980	107,969	23.5	35,670
1990	109,252	27.4	36,306

Source: U.S. Census, County and City Data Books and City Reports.
[a]Figure is for 1945.

1950 on when the city shifted from private collection to a city run operation had a budget increase of 225 percent. The total general fund budget increased 231 percent. The allocations for the new development thus were above the norm. The major point is that there was early planning, funds were allocated for that purpose early, and the city's leadership supported new development fairly consistently during this early period. In many other cities of similar size, the attention to the planning of development was largely neglected. Few committed even $1,000 to planning. Ann Arbor made a $7,500 commitment already in 1945 and gradually increased that commitment to over $50,000 by 1960.[3]

How did Ann Arbor finance these skyrocketing developmental

TABLE 1.3. Changes in Socioeconomic Characteristics of Ann Arbor's Population

	1950	1960	1970	1980
Race				
White	94.2%	93.5%	91.0%	85.1%
Median Family Income				
Actual dollars	$3,881	$7,550	$12,819	$25,202
Constant dollars (1967=100)	$5,251	$8,512	$11,675	$10,203
Increase in constant (dollars by decades)		+62.1%	+37.1%	−12.6%
Education				
25 and older who had college education	35.0%[a]	38.7%	46.8%	56.2%
High school graduates	66.8%	72.5%	82.9%	90.6%

Source: U.S. Census, County and City Data Books.
Note: Median family income data are for 1949, 1960, 1969, and 1980.
[a]The 1950 census did not provide the exact percentage of those 25 and older with a college education. This is an estimate.

TABLE 1.4. Budgets for Selected Departments, 1945–60

	Budget Outlays			
Department	1945	1950	1960	Increase 1945–60 (corrected for CPI)
Planning				
Actual dollars	$7,500	$9,700	$50,700	311%
Constant dollars	$13,900	$13,500	$57,100	
Parks and Recreation				
Actual dollars	$54,400	$60,000	$342,600	282%
Constant dollars	$100,900	$83,300	$386,300	

Source: Ann Arbor City Budget documents.

costs? Primarily by increasing property tax revenues as a result of higher property assessed valuations. The period of massive federal and state revenue sharing had not yet begun, and the property tax rate remained fairly constant during this period (actually decreasing from 11.94 in 1950 to 9.16 in 1960). So the alternative was obvious. Aside from mobilizing funds from city fees, fines, and special charges, there had to be an increase in assessments. And that occurred, as the summary in table 1.5 reveals.

Linked to these changes, were three other changes occurring from 1945 on: annexations, population increase, and a building boom. There was new construction of residential dwellings as well as commercial and institutional buildings. The permit data in the file of the Ann Arbor Building Department include complete records for the past 35 years. They do not provide complete data before 1955. They do indicate that before 1950, the city authorized permits for new residential units, estimated at between 200 and 400 units a year. After 1950 the building boom set in, and from 1955 on, permits were given to build from 700 to 1,000 new residential units (single-family and multifamily) annually. This continued to 1960 (and construction activity was even more intensified in the next decade). The total value for all construction (residential, commercial, and institutional) averaged $20 million a year in the period from 1955 to 1960—about 60 percent of it residential, of which over half was for single-family dwellings.

In studying this early period just after the war, it becomes clear that a concern for the proper development of the city was shared by many city officials, businesspeople, civic leaders, and the university's officers. The early push for cooperative efforts (stimulated by the regents, resolution in 1946) continued. It led eventually to imaginative, systematic, and detailed planning during the period from 1950 to 1960. Guy Larcom's appointment as city administrator in 1956 was a primary stimulus.

TABLE 1.5. Property Assessments in Early Years in Ann Arbor

	1945	1950	1960	Increase 1945–60
Property Assessed Valuations (in millions and adjusted)				
Actual dollars	$53	$63	$216	308.0%
Constant dollars	$98	$87	$244	149.0%
Per capita assessments (constant dollars)	$2,227	$1,810	$3,640	63.5%

Source: Ann Arbor City Budget documents.

A study of this early postwar period reveals that crucial premises for city development achieved a certain consensus among the city's leaders. A summary of these basic premises may be helpful:

1. *Industrial growth of a particular type was necessary, would be encouraged, would be controlled, and would be tailored to the special characteristics and advantages of Ann Arbor.* The university was recognized both as the central attraction for the particular types of industry wanted and as a partner of the city in bringing the right type of industry to the city. Bent Nielsen, in an excellent review of this early period, has described this decision well: "As far back as 1957 there was a realization on the part of the local leaders that Ann Arbor's continued prosperity would depend upon a balancing of residential and university growth with new industry"—not "indiscriminate industrial promotion but rather to attract industry appropriate to the local environment." He said the university's highly technical research facilities and its personnel trained in these high-tech fields was a major asset which should be used in the attraction of new industry.[4] Illustrative of the implementation of this premise is the decision by Parke-Davis to construct a $12 million plant. The arrangements for this were worked out in a three way agreement between Parke-Davis, the city, and the university: the university agreed to sell Parke-Davis sixty acres, the city agreed to provide a $500,000 worth of utilities, and the university and Parke-Davis agreed to pay a prorated share of the cost of the utilities. Other such agreements followed, Bendix soon thereafter deciding to locate on land near the university's north campus.

2. *While city leaders recognized the inevitability and the need to increase in size, the basic policy adopted was that no extension of city services would be provided to unannexed areas.* Annexation meant the payment of city taxes, and only after annexation would there be the provision of city services. On that basis, Ann Arbor grew from seven square miles in size to over twenty three square miles, all of it between 1950 and 1970. Not only were rural areas annexed, but also another city—East Ann Arbor (in 1956). This policy was firm, but was applied in an enlightened way. A good example is the long negotiations that finally led to the creation of the Greater Ann Arbor Research Park (GAARP) in the early 1960s. The chamber of commerce and the city worked closely on this, together with the township. A two hundred-acre parcel of land two miles south of the city limits was identified as an excellent site, but the problem was that the site was not contiguous to the city and would need to be annexed if the site were to be properly developed. Arrangements were made for annexation, and the city agreed to install

streets, sewers, and water mains necessary to attract new science-based industry and developed a plan for delayed payments of these costs, recouping its outlays as the land was sold by the GAARP. The economic development committee of the chamber of commerce played a major role in this plan, working with the university and the city as well as with the research industries that purchased the land. Thus the annexation policy was not breached, but adapted to creative economic planning.

3. *Implicit in both the aforementioned developmental perspectives was that the city and the university would work cooperatively*. This understanding goes back a long time, but has been particularly evident in this postwar period. It is partially a consequence of the involvement of university professors in city politics. Of the eleven mayors since 1945, five have been associated with the university; many others have sat on council and run as candidates. More important is the awareness that proper city growth is vitally linked to university interests and, hence, university executive officers and planning officials have worked closely with the city. This was evident already in the 1940s and 1950s. In approaching industries that might be brought to Ann Arbor in the early 1960s, the president of the university took a personal role, as did other university officials. Very soon thirty seven science-based industries located in the city, fourteen actually started by university personnel.[5] A final point is that the university, though a tax-exempt institution, has offered to make a substantial contribution to the cost of public utilities and improvement related to its own interests. From an early beginning of congenial relations and close cooperation, the university has generally continued to consult with and work with the city's officials.

4. *Another key principle basic to the city's development has been the idea of long-range and multiprogram planning*. Guy Larcom, the city's administrator for almost twenty years, laid the groundwork for this plan, which operated with a conception and prediction of what the city will be like and what its needs will be in the distant future. The illustrations of economic planning referred to already suggest this approach. Another example is in the development of the city's infrastructure. For example, when Ann Arbor built its new sewage treatment and new water system in 1965 (committing $6 million), the city was anticipating what the 1985 needs of the population would be. When in 1963 the city negotiated with Detroit Edison for its properties along the Huron River, it was projecting the need to protect these areas and the hope that eventually they could be converted to the recreational use of the city. Larcom put it this way in 1965:

> The government's job has been to project the expansion of the city in terms of population and area and the impact on city development, utilities, and services . . . . Growth must be met by positive, affirmative action that . . . anticipates and avoids many of the products of growth . . . . It would be an irresponsible administration that [ignored growth] and then tried to catch up with the consequences.[6]

To Larcom and to other early city officials, a city plan had many components or subplans, very interrelated: plans for land development, parking, traffic, parks and open space, central business and downtown development, central campus, thoroughfare, university medical center, and others. This conception of long-range and multiprogram planning dominated early thinking at city hall, and to a great extent is still today central to discussions about city development.

The continuity of support for Image One functions such as planning, parks and recreation, refuse collection, police, fire, and other services can be demonstrated in various ways. One way is to look at the increase in real (constant) dollar allocations after 1960, shown in table 1.6.

The decline in 1980 in support for these departments was mild and only temporary. If we compare the key developmental and service departments in the 1960 and 1990 budgets, we see no diminution in support for these basic functions. Police, fire, planning, parks and recreation, and garbage collection collectively controlled 43.6 percent of the 1960 general fund budget of a little over $4,000,000. In the 1990 budget of over $56,000,000 they controlled 49.3 percent. The council thus maintained-even increased-its proportionate support for these basic functions.

The Second Image of Development: Responses to the Problems of Minorities and the Needy

What one notices in these early premises or approaches to city development is the heavy emphasis on what might be called four key aspects of

TABLE 1.6. Budget Allocations for Three Selected Departments, 1960–90

	Constant Dollars Outlays (in thousands)			
Department	1960	1970	1980	1990
Planning	57.2	163.9	107.6	111.5
Parks and Recreation	386.3	1,107.9	912.6	955.1
Police	733.0	2,278.0	2,434.0	2,889.0

Source: Ann Arbor City Budget documents.

the functions of government: industrial or economic development; provision of key governmental services; planning of a solid infrastructure; and budgeting for recreational and cultural amenities. What seems to be missing in the early days of developmental thinking is a concern for social welfare and humanitarian needs. Gradually an awareness of the human relations problems in Ann Arbor and the need for new housing led to the evolution of a new, or supplemental, image of development. This occurred from the mid-1950s on, and was incorporated in governmental policy in 1957 and expanded subsequently.

The second developmental perspective that emerged was at first quite controversial, even rejected, but subsequently accepted. This image or vision of development emphasized a concern for the social welfare and humanitarian needs of the public. It argued that it was a proper developmental goal, and that it was the proper province of city government to use resources and energies to provide assistance to the more disadvantaged sectors of the population, the socially and economically deprived. In a sense, those arguing for this second image of development were facing up to the development dilemma very early in Ann Arbor's history. They were in effect not denying the importance of such issues as economic planning, capital improvements, and provision of basic services, but rather arguing that such developmental goals did not require all attention and resources. The city could help the poor, those discriminated against, and the deprived. This second approach to development gradually was persuasive.

The minimal interest by city government in social welfare and selected problems is clear if one studies the period immediately after the war. There was a token sum of $600 in the early budget earmarked for the "poor," but poverty and the lack of low cost housing and similar provisions were not seen as the real problems. This is not because there was no expression of concern by outside voices: By the early 1950s, some people were worried sufficiently that the platforms of the political parties reflected this in the planks which were adopted. In 1952 both parties advocated a study of "the housing problem." The Republicans proposed "the formation of a commission for a long range study and action program to provide adequate housing for all people." The Democrats in addition proposed a study of areas of racial and religious friction by a "civic unity committee or commission." The previous year, the Democratic candidate for mayor, Lewis Reiman, and Karl Karsian had proposed a human relations commission. Further, when the Ann Arbor City Charter Commission met in 1954, it was urged by Democrats (particularly Albert Wheeler, who would later become mayor) to include a housing and a human relations commission in the new city charter.

Very little, if any, action was even considered to deal with the treatment of minorities, particularly blacks. The discrimination against them was blatant in the forties and fifties, particularly in housing and employment. As a relatively recent *Ann Arbor News* story cites, "For many local blacks . . . Ann Arbor is home to some ugly memories."[7] Emma Wheeler, former president of the local National Association for the Advancement of Colored People, put it this way: "People who come here now don't realize what a struggle it was in Ann Arbor. Thirty or thirty-five years ago it was terrible." Her husband, Professor Al Wheeler, illustrates with the story of how he sought to buy and finance a house in those days. He and his wife had only half the price of the house and "couldn't borrow the rest of the money from anywhere else in this city, including the University of Michigan." Through the Civic Forum, a small group of black men who organized in the late 1940s, and eventually through a recreated NAACP (from 1954 on), the movement to ameliorate these conditions grew. Liberal whites also became involved, and the Democratic party began to take the position that the city council should act. But nothing happened under the Republicans. In the 1957 campaign the Democrats made the adoption of a human relations commission a key issue. They drafted an ordinance, published its salient features in the *News*, and promised to make such a commission the first order of business if they won the election for mayor. They won the mayor's seat in 1957, but since the Democrats had only three seats on council in 1957, they had to persuade some Republicans to support such a commission. After much controversy they did and the commission was created June 3, 1957.

The Human Relations Commission as created had limited powers. It was restricted to receiving and investigating complaints of discrimination, holding hearings on such complaints, and engaging in mediation of conflicts. Its goals and purposes were defined as:

To investigate problems and situations of discrimination
To disseminate information and educational materials
To address and recommend to the council the appropriate steps to deal with conditions which strain human relations
To promote mutual understanding and respect among all racial, religious, and nationality groups
To aid in seeing that no person in this city is deprived of equal services furnished by the citizens of Ann Arbor by reason of discrimination on account of race, color, creed, national origin, or ancestry.

The city council created a commission of ten members. After more controversy, the Democratic mayor appointed as commission chair the

Rev. Henry Lewis, rector of St. Andrews Episcopal Church. The appointments were designed to make it a multireligious, biracial, bipartisan group of commissioners. The majority of the commission members were dedicated to positive action against discrimination, as their accomplishments later revealed.

Urban renewal became the next critical issue in redistributive development, emerging in 1958 and provoking controversy. The history of this effort illustrates the problems with mobilizing public support for such an issue and how a plan was finally developed and given preliminary approval, then scuttled by the veto of a Republican mayor. The idea of urban renewal surfaced in Ann Arbor early, shortly after the U.S. Congress passed the Urban Renewal Act of 1954. The Republican city council in January 1956 approved a request to Washington for $28,000 for planning an urban renewal project. Nothing was done, however, until after the 1957 election. In May 1957 a federal urban renewal official from Chicago came to encourage the city to develop a proposal and to apply. In August 1957 a preliminary plan was given approval by the federal government. The basic concept that emerged was complex. The area to be renewed included seventy four acres of property in what came to be known as the North-Central area. The plan called for the rehabilitation of residential and commercial structures, including the replacement of seventeen residences definitely, and another twenty possibly if repair costs were not exorbitant. New single-family, two-family, and multifamily housing was to be constructed, which meant that approximately thirty families were to be relocated. The junkyard was to be eliminated, playground facilities were to be expanded, and certain traffic diversions were to be made. Further, public improvements in curbs, gutters, storm sewers, and street widening were also planned. The net project cost was $1,641,354, of which the federal government would pay two-thirds and the city, after credit for land donations and improvements, would pay only $225,248 in cash.

From early 1957 to mid-1959, this plan was the focus of controversy. At least three different citizens committees were created to participate in developing the plan and in persuading people to support it. The city's planning department conducted a survey of the area and helped put the plan together, with the city administrator in charge of overall coordination of preparations. Politically prominent Republicans and Democrats worked hard on the proposal and assumed major roles in planning and in mobilizing public support. Professor A. D. Moore, a longtime Republican councillor, chaired a large citizens committee. Earl Cress of Ann Arbor Trust, and Lawrence Ouimet, a former Republican councillor also were deeply involved, as were black leaders Russell Howard and

Richard and Rosemary Blake. Cress put together an ingenious plan for creation of a nonprofit development foundation, as well as a profit corporation, that would subsidize, for those with inadequate means, the difference between the economic rent and the rent they were able to pay. This was necessary for the thirty families for whom relocation housing would be required. Over $50,000 was subscribed to this nonprofit development foundation in a short period of time, with the mayor and Cress, as well as other prominent persons, collaborating in their appeals for support. The city council eventually approved this approach.

The opinion of families and businesspersons in the urban renewal district were split on various aspects of the proposal, but the relocation of families was a major concern. The two most prominent black ministers, the Revs. C.W. Carpenter and Lyman Parks, took different positions. Tumultuous hearings and public meetings occurred several times. The plan was revised in late 1958 in response to this protest, on the basis of a Republican proposal in council in July 1958. In August the federal officials gave preliminary encouragement to the revised plan. A new citizens committee called the Plan Standards Committee then progressively helped formulate the details of the new proposal. The city council forwarded the revised plan to the federal government, which approved it tentatively in April 1959 subject to final local approval. Then the 1959 election occurred Mayor Cecil Creal, the Republican candidate, was elected, and almost immediately vetoed the council's approval of the plan. To many this was a tragic end to a worthwhile and humane proposal that was supported by a bipartisan coalition of distinguished leaders and had widespread citizen support. But certain of the conservative forces in the community won out. Creal was their champion. The Republican council in the last analysis did not override his veto.

In the meantime the Human Relations Commission was gradually getting support, notably from the Republicans. In 1960, Mayor Creal told the council: "We must cooperate with the Human Relations Commission and do all we can to supplement these ideas and programs"[8] A full-time director was appointed, the commission was expanded in size, and both parties approved increased appropriations for it. But not much money was allocated in those early days—only $525 in 1958 and $2,275 in 1960. Conservative opposition to the commission had largely dissipated, and by 1964 the Republican party platform could state:

> Every person regardless of race, color, or religion must be offered an equal opportunity to . . . employment . . . the home off his choice . . . the best education available and the full personal respect that he merits. We urge that the total community assist in

> making the Fair Housing Ordinance and the work of the Human Relations Commission effective tools in furthering the goals of better human relations.

It is one thing to set up a commission; however, it is another to demonstrate that change occurred, linked to the actions of that body. One bit of evidence that development might have been occurring is the number of complaints investigated. These attested to the existence of the problem and its persistence over time. From 33 per year in the early years up to 1963, the number increased to 75 by 1965, declined in the late 1960s to between 20 and 30, then increased again in the 1970s to a high of 117 in 1974, and since then decreased to between 20 and 30. Even today the commission (now the human rights section of the personnel department) investigates complaints.

The commission developed a sometimes good, sometimes poor reputation over the years. Its history turned out to be a hectic one, as it was attacked politically from both left and right. It is impossible here to review that history in detail. It is important, however, to note some of its accomplishments. The philosophy the HRC formulated was that of "reaching out into the community to help people resolve problems" while stimulating discussion of human relations issues. While this seems passive and innocuous, in fact the commission was very active and even confrontational. It investigated and confronted the city police, the sheriff's department, the public schools, city hall, the county, the university, realtors and landlords, and business firms. Even though it had no power to issue cease-and-desist orders, or to subpoena, or to seek civil injunctions, it was quite effective. It investigated several hundred complaints of discrimination and brought a resolution to many of them. It played a role in promoting the idea of a housing commission and it was instrumental in the adoption of the fair housing ordinance of 1965. Among other accomplishments, the commission:

Pressed the school board to hire nine black teachers and administrators

Persuaded two trade unions representing electrical workers and plumbers to take on two black youths as apprentices

Helped create a committee in police-community relations

Sponsored several hundred discussion meetings in private homes on problems of discrimination

Sponsored a summer camp for children of low-income families

Sponsored a cooperative occupational training program in the public schools

Created an employment placement service with the assistance of the Chamber of Commerce to help blacks find jobs
Located emergency housing for the poor
Initiated a resolution, adopted by the city council, establishing a city affirmative action program for the employment of blacks, after which the council eventually approved a 9.2 percent "quota" for blacks
Helped establish human relations offices in the public schools and university
Sought financial support for a black theater for teenagers.[9]

Clearly the commission developed into an agency that worked hard to deal with human relations problems and made significant contributions. In its twelve years after 1957, it may have saved Ann Arbor from its own violent black crisis.

Precise evidence as to what was happening to discrimination is difficult to secure. Two early studies, in 1956 and 1964, indicated that progress was slow and much had to be done. While 9 percent of city employees were black (compared to 6 percent of the population), most of these positions were in Public Works. Employment of blacks at the hospitals was high, increasing from 21 percent of this labor force in 1956 to 29 percent in 1964. At the university the proportion was 4 percent (aside from the hospital employment), 7 percent in Ann Arbor's schools, but only 2 percent in the business and manufacturing firms studied. In fact, the conclusion of the study by the Washtenaw Conference on Religion and Race in 1964 was, "No plan for improving negro working conditions in Ann Arbor will succeed without the participation of the local business community."[10] By 1967 an investigation revealed that sixty one blacks held positions in city government, 12 percent of city employment, but thirty nine of these were lower-level garbage collection positions. The university proportion had increased to 5 percent for nonacademic and nonmedical employment.[11] It was late, and somewhat ironic, that on Sept. 29, 1969, the council approved a 9.2 percent "quota" for blacks for city employment.

Other important actions occurred in the areas of human rights and justice. The 1960s became a period of tumultuous protest in Ann Arbor, on the campus and in the city. The Students for a Democratic Society (SDS) was formed by activist Tom Hayden in Ann Arbor in 1962. The issues of racism, housing, poverty and the Vietnam War mobilized the students and citizens. Both Republicans and Democrats advocated a variety of proposals, among them open housing, fair employment, assistance to young people and establishment of a youth commission. Republican Mayor Wendell Hulcher addressed the city council, saying: "These are unparalleled times . . . . Extraordinary action to eliminate the root causes of unrest is mandatory . . . . To accomplish long needed change we must put our money where our mouth is."[12]

"Fair housing" or "open occupancy housing" legislation was finally adopted in 1963 after much party conflict on the issue. Republicans had opposed it in 1960, 1961, and 1962, being much concerned about the priority of property and contract rights. The 1963 council ordinance was limited in its applicability (applying only to those rental properties with five or more units), and the pressure continued for full coverage, which was adopted in the fall of 1965.[13] It was at that time also that Ann Arbor adopted its first public housing in Ann Arbor, a special feature of which was the location of the units in scattered sites to avoid segregation. When the Democrats won control of local government in 1969, they also changed the status of the Human Relations Commission, making it part of a separate Department of Human Rights with real power: subpoena authority, cease-and-desist orders, power to seek injunctions, and power to fine violators. The new ordinance sought to broaden the jurisdiction of the department to the schools and the university, included sex discrimination in its mission, and increased the scope to public accommodations and employment. The city council also adopted a new, strong, affirmative action program which was subsequently implemented and resulted in minority-group members heading the Departments of Housing, Human Rights, Model Cities, and Personnel.

The other major development in the 1970s, and up to the present, was the decision by the city council to take seriously the poverty problems and social welfare needs of the community. Under the Republicans, there had been some expression of concern, but virtually no significant budgetary allocations. When Democratic Mayor Robert Harris assumed office in 1969 (with an 8 to 3 council majority), he proposed at once to take action on his three priorities: civil rights, civil liberties, and the war on poverty. After careful study, a variety of human resources outlays were budgeted, beginning with over $40,000 in 1970 and increasing each year until 1975. After a six-year period during which support for such expenditures evaporated, they were resumed in 1981, as Democratic pressure on the council mounted, and it has continued to the present. In 1988, $560,000 was appropriated for a wide range of services, including shelter for the homeless, crisis help, food for the needy, community centers, and assistance for elder citizens and persons with disabilities. These have continued, with some changes, to the present. A detailed analysis of the budgetary history of these programs and of the support for human relations will be made in a later chapter.

It took a long time, therefore, since the 1950s before Ann Arbor's budget came to include sizable allocations for human resources and human relations development. After 1970 the city's leadership took these needs more seriously. Today there is a separate department in the general fund budget called community development, for which $2,282,000 was budgeted in 1990 and $2,730,000 in 1991. There is evidence that to this day, certain types of development problems persist: the need for affordable housing, the conditions of the poor, continuing signs of racism, and discrimination against other disadvantaged groups. But there is a better awareness by the public and its leaders of the existence of these problems, their complexity, and a willingness to work on them. The challenge continues to be one of adequacy of financial resources. The conflict remains between economic development and its priorities on the one hand, and the priorities, of the poor and needy, on the other hand. City leaders have demonstrated in the past that such conflict can be managed, bridged, and compromised, and it is hoped that the city will be able to resolve this basic conflict in the future. In the meantime, the two images of development that have been pressed by both parties over the past forty years have resulted in a city that has made much progress, through a development that is both humane and economic.

The Overall Composite Picture of Postwar Development

It makes sense to conceive of Ann Arbor's postwar development as occurring in three major stages chronologically: 1945–60, 1960–70, and 1970–90. The first stage consisted of a five-year "predevelopment" period when, in a sense, we were organizing for the change that was to occur. Then in the decade of the fifties we see a period of massive change on a variety of fronts. The second stage during the sixties, built on the first, maintaining the high commitment to the early goals and a movement toward some new directions in policy around the end of that decade. The third stage, which really encompasses the past two decades, 1970–90, included a variety of specific changes, but the overall pace of development was slower. In certain respects, the city's growth was stabilized in functional terms while the fiscal problems continued or were even accentuated.

The accompanying table presents a set of indicators which seek to provide an overview of development for these three stages (table 1.7). Certain features in this picture stand out. The pace and magnitude of change was obviously much greater before 1970 than after. By 1970 the city's population reached a plateau of 100,000. The same was basically true for territorial expansion and annexation; university enrollment actually declined after 1970, as did median family income. The great increase in property assessments (in constant dollars) had occurred by 1970 and was much less (37 percent) after that year. It is true that new building construction continued after 1970, yet the greatest proportion of residential construction (64 percent of the total number of units built in the 1955–90 period) occurred by 1970.

One should not jump to the conclusion that Ann Arbor's development stopped in 1970. In two senses this was not the case: The development of the community in terms of improvement and strengthening of basic services, the provision of more attractive parks and recreational facilities, industrial and economic growth, maintenance and improvement of the city plant and sewer/water infrastructure—all these have been well financed and supported after 1970. We have called these the first image of development, which guided the city in the early period

TABLE 1.7. The Composite Picture: Major Indicators of Development by Stages

	1945–60	1960–70	1970–90
Demographic and Spatial Trends (increase or decrease in each)			
Population	52.3%	48.6%	9.2%
Area (sq. miles)	145.9%	55.3%	17.6%
Univ. enrollment	105.1%	54.9%	−2.9%
Median family income[a]	62.1%	37.1%	−15.5%
Educational level[b]	8.5%	14.4%	9.3%
Fiscal Trends[c]			
General fund budget increase	230.70%	134.90%	33.40%
Per capita cost—general fund budget increase (Actual $)	$36.30	$39.34	$23.73
Property assessed valuation increase	149.00%	61.10%	37.40%
Tax rate—actual increase or decrease (in mills)	$−2.78[d]	$+5.44	$+3.13
Development in Construction[e]			
New residential/commercial/ institutional construction total value	$178.6	$336.3	$421.1
Average per year	$35.7	$33.6	$22.2

Source: U.S. Census, County and City Data Books and City Reports.
[a]Figures are for 1950–90, with percentage of change in constant dollars (1967=100).
[b]Figures are for 1950–80, for percentage of population completing high school.
[c]General Fund figures in constant dollars (1967=100).
[d]Figure is for 1950–60.
[e]Figures are in constant dollars (1967=100), in millions, for 1955–60, 1961–70, and 1971–89. Construction permit data not available before 1955.

from 1945 to 1960. This conception of development continued to play a significant role throughout the entire postwar period. Some basic data on expenditures by departments can demonstrate this clearly (table 1.8).

It is clear from these data that as the general fund budget declined proportionately, so did the basic developmental department allocations. Planning and parks allocations were particularly cut in the seventies, but there was a resumption of support in the eighties, although not at those earlier levels prior to 1970.

The second image of development which was launched in a sense in the late 1950s, became a significant secondary vision from 1969 on. Human relations began to receive important financial support in the sixties and human services did after 1970. A simple recapitulation of the actual allocation for human relations/rights and human services in the city budget documents this clearly. These are given in total dollars budgeted by time periods (in constant dollars), as shown in table 1.9.

The pace and chronology of budgetary allocation for economic, service, and infrastructural development, therefore, was quite different than for human relations and human services. Table 1.10 summarizes

TABLE 1.8. Trends in Departmental Outlays over Time (Percentage Increase/Decrease)[a]

Department	1945–60	1960–70	1970–80	1980–90
Police	249%	211	7	19
Fire	171	145	26	3
Garbage[b]	225	175	63	6
Planning	311	187	−34	4
Parks and Recreation	282	187	−18	5
Total General Fund Budget Change	231	135	3	29

Source: Ann Arbor City Budget documents.
[a]Percentages based on comparison in constant dollars (1967=100).
[b]Began in 1950.

TABLE 1.9. Human Relations and Services Budgets by Periods, 1945–90

	Actual Outlays[d]			
	1945–60	1960–70	1970–80	1980–90
Human Relations/Rights	4,632	398,970	475,464	210,060
Human Services	43,782	69,854	399,996	969,812
Total	48,414	468,824	875,460	1,179,872

Source: Ann Arbor City Budget documents.
[a]Expressed in constant dollars (1967=100).

the differences. Image One development was well under way in the fifties, achieved major funding in the seventies, and still received large sums thereafter. Image Two development began to get funding after 1960, but 80 percent of its budgetary support came after 1970. As a proportion of the budget, human relations and human services funds were small. As a commitment to the humane component of development, they were significant.

One major aspect of development from 1950 on has not yet been discussed. That is the political change that was occurring. As the city moved toward 1960, and beyond, the party system in Ann Arbor was changing radically. The confluence of this political mobilization, rebuilding, and revitalization with the two images of development outlined in this chapter is a major focus of this inquiry. In succeeding chapters, we shall analyze that confluence in detail.

TABLE 1.10. The Differential Pace of Allocations over 45 Years for the Early and Later Images of Development

	1945–50	1950–60	1960–70	1970–80	1980–90
Image One Functions (Selective)					
Planning	2.1%	7.2	25.6	36.3	28.8
Parks and Recreation	1.9	7.4	20.4	32.1	38.2
Police	1.9	7.0	16.3	34.2	40.6
Image Two Functions					
Human Relations/Rights	0	0.4	36.7	43.7	19.3
Human Services	2.5	0.5	4.7	26.9	65.4
Total Image Two Functions	1.4	0.5	18.2	34.0	45.9

Source: Ann Arbor City Budget documents.

Note: Refers to the proportion of funds allocated to a particular function in a particular time period as a percentage of all funds allocated to that function for the entire 45-year period.

CHAPTER 2

Political Institutions in Ann Arbor: The Model of Party Conflict

For a city to develop properly, it needs a good institutional environment as well as a supporting set of cultural beliefs and practices. That is, if development is to be carefully planned and effectively carried out, political institutions will play a critical role. Development decisions do not just happen; they are made in political arenas and by political leaders with public acceptance. Actually, the institutions as they evolve are part of the development process, while they are also the context within which development occurs. The institutions affect the society as well as reveal the values of the society.

A considerable body of recent literature emphasizes the "relative autonomy of political institutions." The argument is that in contrast to early scholarship, the emphasis is now—and should be now—on politics as playing an independent, controlling role in society, not as merely being responsive to social forces. Legislatures, courts, and political groups are "political actors in their own right," and these political institutions must be seen as affecting the distribution of resources as well as the power of political leaders and their preferences, choices, and values; thus they are important as autonomous forces in the life of a community. This approach has been called the "new institutionalism."[1] Of course, political institutions need strong supporting political cultures. Institutions depend on these cultures as well as help to evolve them. Our discussion here begins with this basic set of assumptions.

Institutions can either hinder or facilitate a city's development. Some requisites for effective political institutions are: (1) the focusing of responsibility for decision making in a single, authoritative body, rather than a dispersed, multicentered decisional process—there must be a leadership body with the power to act; (2) rational allocation of functions between bureaucrats and elected leaders, so that administrators work with elected councillors and implement decisions made by politicians, to whom they are ultimately responsible; (3) provision for an official, public forum for regular and open deliberation and debate, where there is opportunity for advocacy of proposals and counter-proposals by individual citizens and interest groups; (4) good linkage structures between city hall and the public, particularly party organizations and/or interest groups which can articulate and represent public opinion on the problems of the city and the proposals advanced to deal with them. Institutions should provide the effective channels for policy discussion as well as provide constraints on how decisions are to be made. They should make it possible for leadership to act, but also force leadership to be responsive. They should play an integrative role for the community while also protecting the values of opposition, competition, and dissent.

Not all cities meet these requisites. In some cities, leadership decision making is hampered by the fragmentation in authority—there is often no one central decisional body. In fact in the nineteenth century, one of the favorite forms of city government in the United States, the commission form, was defended because it dispersed the leadership structures of cities. Today there is often a sharp conflict between mayor and council in some cities because the decisional power is bifurcated. Further, one does not always find city bureaucracies with a clear line of responsibility to a central elective body, nor is the city council in many cities the open, competitive, deliberative body it should be. Finally, we often find very weak linkage structures in cities. In short, the institutional conditions in many cities are inadequate for effective politics.

Ann Arbor, on the other hand, has evolved over the past forty years a viable set of political institutions. They meet quite well, though not perfectly, the criteria for effectiveness specified above. In this chapter, we shall discuss these institutions and processes and the rules of the political game associated with these processes in Ann Arbor. That is, we shall discuss the structure of city government, the general nature of political party organizations and the major interest groups, and the norms of the political games in Ann Arbor. In subsequent chapters, we will analyze specific institutions in more detail. Our focus is on these institutions, processes, and norms as they are linked to the development of the city—how they have been, and are, instrumental for the achievement of change in postwar Ann Arbor.

The City Hall Institutions

Ann Arbor has had four charters in over 150 years: 1833, 1851, 1889, and 1956. The city has experimented over the years with a variety of governmental arrangements. It has varied the number of wards, the number of councillors, and the types of officials to be elected—city clerk, treasurer, assessor, constables, justices of the peace, even "overseers of the poor!"[2] It also has changed the powers of the mayor, the legislative responsibility of the council, and the roles of boards and commissions. The 1956 charter builds on earlier versions, but it also rejects certain features of the 1889 charter. Its concept of government is quite clear.

First, Ann Arbor has a council-centered government in the sense that final decision making authority rests in an eleven-person council (mayor and ten councillors). The council has budgetary control, wields ultimate control over the bureaucracy, has the primary appointive power under the mayor's initiative, and holds all other legal powers of the city. Second, in 1956 the power and status of the mayor was reduced, although the mayor still can play an important leadership role. The mayor, as the presiding officer of the council, has veto power. The mayor also has appointive power (with the council). Third, the city administrator supervises (but does not alone hire and fire) administrative officers, is on indefinite tenure, and is immediately subordinate to the council. There are other special features, such as the status of the planning commission and department, but these are not primary. The pivotal center of government consists of the council members who are elected by wards in staggered terms every two years, plus the elected mayor, who also serves two years.

In the history of Ann Arbor's charters, it is interesting to note that the city changed from a system in which the mayor, though not as strong as in other cities, had considerable powers. The 1956 system made the mayor weaker and the council stronger. The present charter states, "All powers of the City shall be vested in and exercised by the council." The clause stating that the mayor "supervises" the departments, which one found in the earlier charters, has been deleted. Instead, the 1956 charter states that "it shall be the duty of the City Administrator to direct, supervise, and coordinate the work of [the departments]." But the council retains the power to hire and fire. The 1921 charter commission stated the concept well, if simply: "[Our] idea of government by the people [is] that the people elect a limited number of representatives, give them power to act, and hold them strictly responsible for results."

The chronology in the adoption of the latest charter is important to keep in mind. The issue of reform surfaced early, in 1948, when a citizens committee for charter revision made a report. This report stated:

> Responsibility for municipal administration is loosely held in numerous citizen boards, commissions and council committees. Municipal

> board members, although mayor-appointed and council approved, are appointed for long and overlapping forms and are responsible to no one once they have been appointed. Thus many of the important decisions on how our city departments operate are made by boards whose members are neither elected themselves nor responsible to elective officials.[3]

By 1950 serious questions were being raised by leaders and citizens about the adequacy of the old 1889 charter, particularly about the efficiency of a system with bifurcated authority between mayor and council, plus the administration of departments by commissions or boards. In 1950 the Democratic platform called for a movement by both parties to work for charter revision. By 1952 the platforms of both parties included references to charter reform—the Democrats for an "overhaul of the city charter," the Republicans for a "continuing study of the city charter." The Democrats made reform one of their major issues, and they were joined by community groups such as the League of Women Voters. The *Ann Arbor News* put the issue to candidates at elections, pressing them to take positions. Gradually the Republicans began to accept the idea of reform, although the mayor was still skeptical in 1951 and said Ann Arbor "should not throw the charter out because of a few changes." But his Republican colleagues began to support major revision of the charter, then in 1953 he did also. The council had already decided in June 1952 to call a special election for April 1953 to permit voters to decide on the issue. The voters responded with a strong (90 percent) affirmative vote. In June 1952 nine charter commissioners were selected. This was a prestigious group, five from the university (three law professors, a professor of sociology, and the wife of a professor of Botany), and four from the city (three businesspeople and an attorney). Professor Robert Angell chaired the commission. Its proposed charter was adopted about two years later, in April 1955. The elections were quite decisive, 75 percent of those voting (8,755) approved. Thus was established the form of city government that has survived until now and which was a major forum and mechanism for the decisions leading to Ann Arbor's development in the succeeding years.

In adopting its charter, Ann Arbor rejected certain key recommendations of the Progressive Movement which had been pushing for reform of city government: a city manager, nonpartisan elections, elections at large. Instead they opted for a city administrator (with reduced managerial powers), partisan elections, and a ward system. The basic form adopted was council-manager, in contrast to the mayor-council or commission forms. (fig. 2.1). But it was a council-manager system with

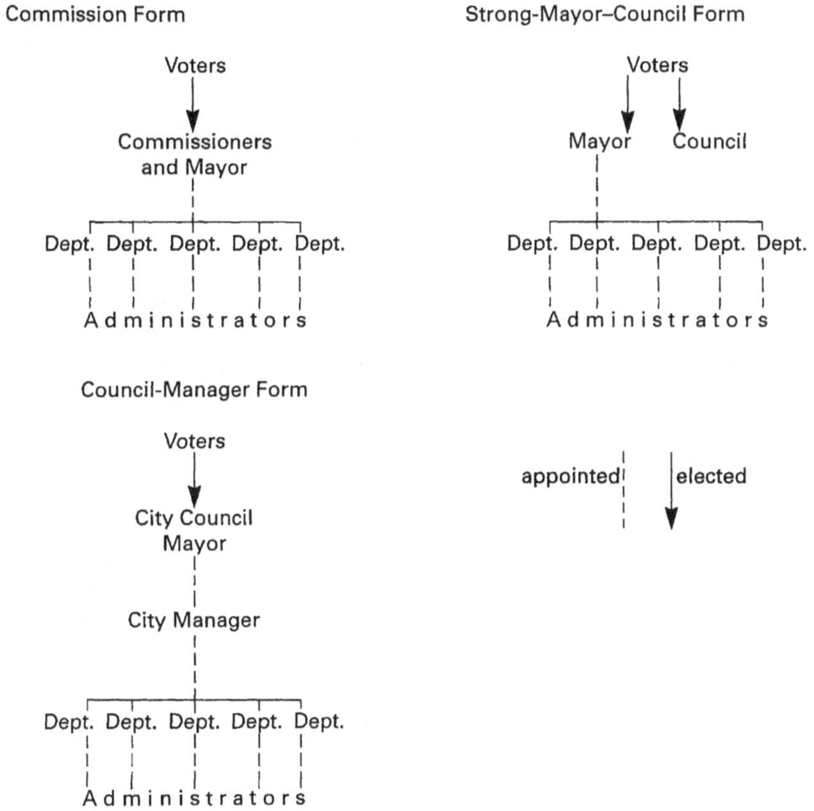

Fig. 2.1. The three basic forms of local government in the United States. Under the Weak-Mayor Council Form the council shares the appointive power with the mayor as well as administrative surveillance of city operations. Under the Strong-Mayor system council does not have such control. (Adapted from Arthur W. Bromage, Introduction to Municipal Government and Administration [New York: Appleton-Century-Crofts, 2d ed., 1957], 218, used by permission.)

particular features. The system replaced was a complex hybrid with divided authority, called the "weak-mayor-and-council plan."

To deal with the problem of divided and irresponsible government, the manager plan was adopted in 1956, but called the occupant of the position an administrator, who was directly responsible to the council for the supervision of city departments. He or she was to be called the administrative agent of the council. The administrator had limited control over the hiring and firing of personnel. One exception to his or her authority was provided for—the planning director was made responsible to the nine-member Planning Commission appointed by mayor and council. The administrator was given considerable control in the budgetary process. The charter specifies that if the budget presented by the administrator is not adopted by the second Monday in May, it automatically goes into effect. Changes in the proposed budget require seven votes to be adopted.

All lines of responsibility and control in Ann Arbor's government lead to the city council. The ideas of separation of power and divided government, of checks and balances, which we find at the national and state levels of government, and to some extent in some cities, are not present in the Ann Arbor structure of city hall institutions. It is our argument that this streamlined charter reform in 1956 greatly facilitated developmental planning. The council, mayor, and administrator became partners in development, not rivals, and they made the decisions under the final authority of the council.

The Political Party Institutions

Unlike many cities, Ann Arbor has partisan government and strong party organizations. Indeed, one can say that just as the system is council-centered it is also party-centered. Some cities have governments which are run by what have been called executive-centered coalitions (or a boss-controlled machine), or by powerful economic elites, or by a pluralized set of special interest groups which control particular parts of city government or particular types of decisions, "a system dominated by many different sets of leaders."[4] None of these descriptions fits Ann Arbor. Rather, Ann Arbor has a fourth type—a party-competitive system in which partisan leaders confront each other and make decisions in a single decisional arena: the city council. Conflict between the political parties is a dominant feature.

The partisan election system dates back to the early days of Ann Arbor in the nineteenth century, and it has been a partisan system ever since. Attempts to switch to a nonpartisan system were unsuccessful when the proposed charters of 1917 and 1921 were soundly defeated by the voters (by more than a 60 percent negative vote in April 1921). The new charter in 1956 reconfirmed the desire for a partisan election system.

Ann Arbor had two strong parties through most of the nineteenth and twentieth centuries. In the 1940s, however, it became virtually a one-party Republican patrimony. Certainly by the time World War II ended, the Democratic party was in a shambles. Data over time suggest the depth of the Democratic party's decline and subsequent recovery (table 2.1). In 1947 the Democrats reached their low point—no candidate for mayor, one councilor elected (unopposed by Republicans), and a total of 110 votes for the party. The details of the postwar reconstruction of the two-party system are described and analyzed in the following chapter. Here we concentrate on the building of the party structures.

It was in the immediate postwar period that the reconstruction of the Democratic organization began. Three changes occurred: (1) State-level Democratic leaders met and decided to rebuild the party and run G. Mennen Williams for governor against Republican incumbent Kim Sigler in 1948 (Williams won); (2) As part of the Democratic strategy of top-to-bottom state party reorganization, the liberal Democrats took over the Washtenaw County party, culminating in August 1948 at the county party convention (Later that year the liberals unseated the Ann Arbor city chair and replaced him with the author in a close election); (3) The local Democrats began to articulate, and carry out, plans for building a new city organization, from the top down, by precinct and ward, recruiting new staff, training them, developing careful cross-referenced files, selecting candidates carefully, and running better campaigns than in previous years. This tedious process resulted in the immediate increase in the size and proportion of the Democratic vote. It culminated in a mayoral victory in 1957. This process of party building led to, or at least paralleled, the rise in the number of seats contested, the increase in the opposition votes, and the increase in voting turnout. By 1957 all seats were contested by the Democrats, they secured 46 percent of the council vote and 53 percent of the vote for mayor, and held three of eleven seats in 1957 (five of eleven in 1958).

There was, then, the convergence of several developments, triggered by party organization building: a combative, cohesive opposition (Democratic) party came into existence; the Republicans responded by strengthening their organization; elections were contested more completely; better candidates confronted each other in the campaigns; in terms of issues the campaigns were more adversarial; voting turnout increased. Political competition became closer as political conflict was more structured.

The long-term consequence of this change was the development of

TABLE 2.1. Decline and Reconstruction of the Democratic Party, 1937–58

	1937	1943	1947	1951	1958
Democratic Vote in Council Elections	48%	25%	5%	27%	49%
Council Seats Held by Democrats	47%	20%	20%	13%	45%

Source: All references to voting in Ann Arbor elections are based on Election Reports of the Ann Arbor City Clerk's office.

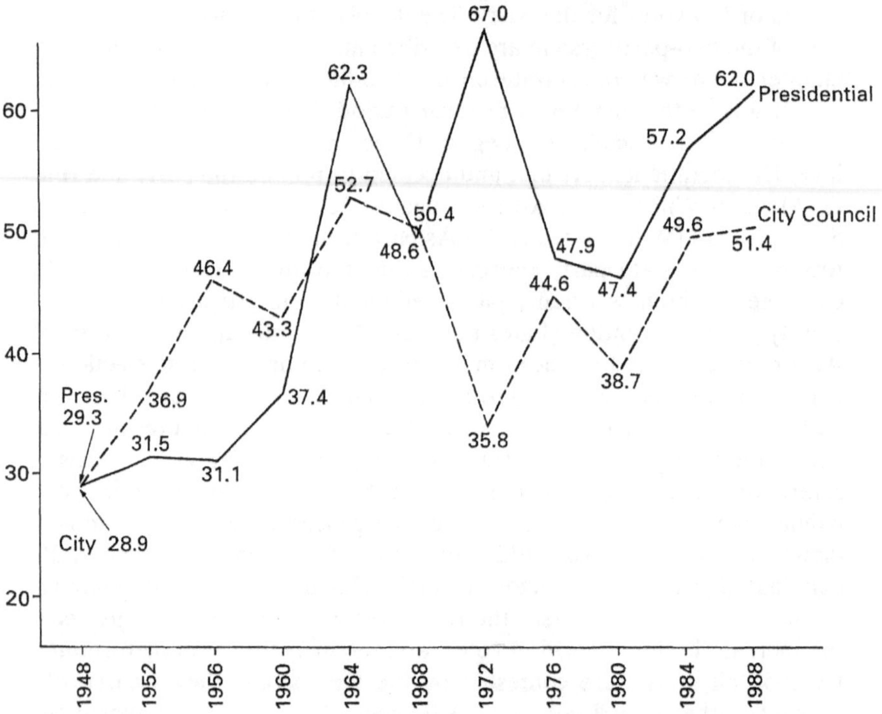

Fig. 2.2. Growth and fluctuation in Ann Arbor's Democratic vote, 1948–88. In the 1980 presidential election, John Anderson's Independent Party secured 15 percent of the total vote in Ann Arbor. In the Ann Arbor city council election of 1972, the Human Rights Party secured 24.4 percent of the vote; in 1976 3.3 percent. From Election Reports and Documents of the Ann Arbor city clerk and Washtenaw county clerk.

a truly two-party system in Ann Arbor (which we will describe more fully later). It also led to an increase in voting turnout from 13 percent in 1947 to 31 percent in 1957 and to over 40 percent in the 1970's. The Democratic percent rose steadily, with occasional declines, from its low of 4.9 percent in 1947 to an average over 50 percent in the last ten years. (See fig. 2.2.)

The competitive relationship between the two parties as well as the patterns of alternation in party power over time define the context in which city governance occurs. One should note that three major patterns occur: (1) strong (dominant) control of the city council by one party, including the mayor's position; (2) strong (dominant) control of the council by one party, but the mayor is with the opposition party; (3) close two-party competition in the council, with mayor of either party.

The type of city government varies by these patterns, and also, by which party, Republican or Democratic, is actually in the majority. The relevance of party control will be examined in a subsequent chapter.

Partisan conflict, thus, has been central to the political life of Ann Arbor, although intermittently there has been one-party dominance. For many years now Ann Arbor has had partisan elections, partisan campaigns, partisan council deliberations. This is a major key to understanding Ann Arbor's political system and process. And this is quite different than in the majority of cities. A 1965 study of eighty-two California cities found that 40 percent were very harmonious, 36 percent had only irregular conflict episodes, and only 24 percent had "conflictual decisional structures." All these cities were nonpartisan. Hence, Ann Arbor is apparently in a small class of its own.[5]

Since 1957, Ann Arbor has operated under a much more competitive party politics which potentially and periodically is explosive—a system of adversary politics. Two parties, the Republican and the Democratic (except for a brief three-party period from 1972 to 1977) have been contesting shortly and durably for control of city council. Anyone who keeps abreast of Ann Arbor politics, particularly anyone involved in city campaigns for council or mayor, is conscious of the adversarial nature of politics there. Every Monday evening at 7:30 at City Hall the party battle is formally joined, the conflict sometimes only latent, sometimes manifest. The great majority of council decisions may be harmoniously arrived at, and unanimously decided. The big issues can be divisive and confrontational.

A Partisan Conflict Model for Ann Arbor

The emergence of this type of truly competitive partisan system in Ann Arbor in the fifties and the maintenance of that system into the nineties has been central to the city's development. But why is this so and how is this so? The rationale for such a party conflict centered system needs discussion and explanation. First, it is important to have a perspective about conflict.

Scholars have for years differed over the virtues of political conflict—over its inevitability and its value. Some political scientists and sociologists feel conflict is unnecessary and negative, at best only to be tolerated. Others see positive aspects. But the tendency often is to be critical of political conflict these days. As Robert Dahl put it, there has developed a "stability fetish" among scholars, emphasis being placed on a *stable* democracy and seeing "conflict and change" as "menacing the foundation of existing democracy itself."[6] Among those, besides Dahl, who see virtue to conflict, there has been much argument over the function of conflict. Some scholars defend conflict as necessary for the achievement of consensus. To the German scholar Dahrendorf, this was wrong. He contended that while conflict may lead to system maintenance, its real value is that it leads to social change. Conflict for him is a precondition for changing the system for the better.[7] Above all, it is argued that if one is interested in a politics of "compassion," a politics of conflict and competition among leaders and groups is necessary.

The position we argue here is that political conflict has a critical relevance for local government. Conflict and competition among political forces, between political structures as parties, and between elected political leaders in electoral democracies can lead to elite awareness of community problems, can force leaders to listen to the "noise" at the mass level, can force them to develop legislation to deal with human needs—in short, can make political leaders more responsive.

Next, it is necessary to specify the conditions or requisites for such a partisan conflict system to be effective in the development process. The first requisite for partisan politics to make a difference is structured, genuine, *competition*. As V. O. Key argued, nonpartisan and disorganized political life, that is, personalized factional politics, is dysfunctional.[8] There must be party groups (or other political groups) with public visibility which contest elections regularly, presenting their candidates and issues to the electorate, and challenging each other effectively. That is, one-party dominance will not do—65 percent, 70 percent, or more control by one party. The competition does not have to be extremely close, but there has to be the expectation on the part of the public that there is a reliable, credible party as challenger. Second, organizational strength and *cohesion* for the parties is necessary. There must be a cadre of activists and workers who constitute a regular, mobilizable fighting force on whom leaders can call for support and to whom they are responsive. If parties are to play a role, several studies suggest that *alternation* in power periodically is productive of responsive elite behavior. That is, the turnover of leadership (or as Pareto said, the "circulation of elites") is closely linked to policy change. Even the genuine threat of turnover, the real possibility of it, the tension this induces, has an impact. With such alternation we can get policy *innovation,* particularly during the honeymoon period in the first year following the taking of power by the new leadership. The new governing majority can make new proposals which after a time lag are manifest in different types of outcomes, such as, but not limited to, different regulatory decisions and different budget allocations.

Several factors determine whether such policies are truly innovative and are effectively put into action. One requirement is *ideological* distinctiveness. The party in power must represent a different policy orientation from its predecessor. That is, the replacement party, the new majority, has to stand for certain other goals, objectives, value priorities than the party it has defeated. In addition, the new party must have a perceivable *mandate* (its victory should be seen as substantial) and *mobilization potential,* the ability to marshall its forces so effectively, or to persuade enough members of the opposition, that it can pass its policy preferences through the legislative chamber and have the bureaucracy implement them. Subsequently, if the newly adopted policies are to prevail over any period of time, what is needed is continuous *monitoring* of policy implementation, and persuasion and *pressure* on decision makers, so that eventually there is a *conversion* of the opposition to the acceptance of these new positions. If policy programs are to endure, the original opposition must be gradually socialized to the acceptance of the new programs, so that even after electoral defeat, subsequent policy decisions and subsequent budgets will reflect a developing consensus that the "new" programs are indeed necessary and appropriate.

There are differences of opinion on these elements of this party conflict model, but the basic thrust of the model is probably accepted—that is, accepted as a model, but for some scholars rejected in reality. The size of the party victory mandate and how much competition are debatable points, as is also when the policy innovation can and will occur: in the honeymoon period or after the party has been in power for some time. But essentially the basic components of the model as presented in table 2.2 find wide currency in the literature, and we will employ the model in our study of Ann Arbor.

One should notice in that connection that there are alternative outcomes or effects, depending on the direction and strength and lasting nature of the factors and relationships. If any of the explanatory forces is not really present, the probability that political change can be produced by the functioning of the party system diminishes. Other community forces will then have to play the game, if change is indeed to occur.

There are scholars who are much more concerned with political cooperation than conflict and who develop models under which cooperation and consensus can occur.[9] Our basic position is that Ann Arbor's experience demonstrates that we should focus on how political conflict is organized, how it can generate innovative alternative leadership and policies, how it can mobilize public support, how it can survive, and how it leads to good public policy. Above all, our focus is that truly competitive, well-organized conflict, particularly under a two-party system in a city like Ann Arbor, can be functional to progress not necessarily because it produces cooperation, although this often does ensue. Convergence in the basic values and ideologies of political elites and activists is highly unlikely; hence, the maintenance of party conflict structures over time is indispensable to progress. Party conflict may lead to compromise and cooperation, but often not. If not, party conflict can still transform a community. So far as political compromise is concerned, party conflict between strongly opposed forces often originates the process which leads to cooperation. As Heclo and Madsen put it; "Compromises do not gravitate from a political center as much as they are forged from political opposites."[10] When compromise emerges, it is after political conflict processes have set the terms of debate, determined the nature of the debate, and provided the context for a mediation of conflicting forces leading to a creative solution.

TABLE 2.2. A Proposed Model for the Impact of Party Conflict

Explanatory Forces	Possible Outcomes
1. Party competition—genuine, repetitive, durable	1. New policies
2. Supported by Institutionalized Party Organizations that are relatively cohesive and durable	2. Substantial changes in the level of support for old policies
3. Generating Rival sets of party workers and supporters	3. Negation of (veto of) old policies
4. Who are ideologically distinctive and hold at least some divergent policy objectives	4. Leading to a new "policy orientation" for the government
5. Leading to Elections that are closely enough contested that no party's leaders can be ignored	5. With wide community support (or opposition)
6. Eventually leading to alternation in party control of the government	6. And developmental consequences for the system
7. With victories substantial enough to permit the presentation of new policy initiatives	7. The eventual Emergence of new demands and opposition forces that sustain the competitive party system or lead to its transformation.
8. Subsequently, sufficient pressure, monitoring of performance, and conversion of the opposition to assure some convergence toward, and acceptance of, new policy orientation	
9. Alternatively, Strong opposition that resists new policy orientation, forces a revision or a stalemate, until a new election	

The process by which creative solutions on policy are arrived at has been the object of much reflection and research. The special Ann Arbor context—that is the gradual emergence over forty years of a competitive two-party system—provides an opportunity for us to study that process. We would suggest several factors here that are critical to understanding whether party competition has an effect, in leading to a compromise or a new policy direction. The first is, the electoral support for the opposition party and its number of seats on council. Second is the simple fact of who controls the mayor's office, irrespective of the size of the electoral majority. Third is the existence of a credible policy program by the opposition, and one which, fourth, commands considerable public support. Implicit is a fifth condition—the realistic possibility of electoral reversal. Whether a creative compromise occurs is often contingent on the mutual respect by the leaders of one party for those of the opposition, a respect for sincerely, intelligently held positions, and constituent backing. Then there is the factor of values and value conflicts. Compromise that does not require change in basic beliefs is possible, but when absolutistic value positions are involved, even the most pragmatic politician often will refuse to cooperate. These theoretical questions and concerns underlie our research here. We hope the discussion of party conflict will shed some light on the extent to which our propositions are tenable.

Other Features of the Ann Arbor System

The other three significant components of the Ann Arbor political system have to do with the relationships and strategies of the top elites (mayor and councillors) and the public. These linkages are heavily emphasized and sometimes criticized as too deferential. Ann Arbor elects councillors by wards, hence, there is a certain parochialism in the debate over policy. Neighborhood politics is what preoccupies politicians often. People want development decisions, zoning actions, and resource allocation decisions to be made in response to neighborhood preferences. Neighborhood groups are better organized politically than ever, and an active, aroused neighborhood group cannot be ignored by a political leader without considerable risk. Added to that are the many community wide interest groups which can be deeply involved in policies, sometimes with very specialized policy interests, sometimes in a whole range of policy areas. The chamber of commerce and other business groups, the great variety of liberal activist organizations, civic groups, church groups, ethnic and racial groups—many of these are, or can become, deeply involved. We shall present data later on the political beliefs and

		Degree of Party Conflict	
		High	Low
City Council Status	Council Central	Adversarial, Programmatic Politics (Ann Arbor)	Council-dominated Consensual Politics
	Council Weak	Personal-Rivalry Politics	Boss-controlled or Patrimonial Politics

Fig. 2.3. Two key dimensions in types of city governance: party conflict and council centrality.

activities of these groups. The group memberships of members of the city council, for example, have changed radically over the last thirty years to reflect the interests of these groups in city affairs and the mobilization of these new groups by political leaders.

Finally, we must remember that in Ann Arbor, city elections are a central arena where the political drama occurs. This is not necessarily true in many cities—those where there is no real party competition at all, or where the key policy decisions seem to be unrelated to election results. In Ann Arbor, city elections each April are important because they determine the structure of party control, and, hence, the direction of policy decisions. But—and this is an important qualification—city elections in recent years are considered important by only 20 percent to 25 percent of the public, the politically informed and attentive public. The anomaly of Ann Arbor (which we shall discuss in a later section in greater detail) is that despite sharp party competition, only a minority of adults participate in electoral decisions. As in most American cities turnout in elections for mayor and council is low, but that does not minimize the significance of the vote. Elections do make a difference. The leadership and policy consequences can be considerable, as our subsequent analysis will explore.

There are several dimensions, then, on which cities differ in the way they are governed. Two key ones are, obviously, the dimensions of party conflict and of council centrality (strength of role). As the accompanying diagram suggests (Figure 2.3), Ann Arbor is in a special subset of communities on these two dimensions. It combines high party conflict with a strong city council—which leads to adversarial politics, which is usually programmatic and responsible. Other combinations lead to other types of politics, which may or may not be functional to community development. The danger with low-conflict systems is that the lack of real opposition may lead to irresponsible politics and nonresponsive elites. The danger of systems with weak councils is that they may lead to personalized, executive or boss-centered systems which may or may not be responsive and programmatic. Strong councils force meaningful deliberation over policy (and less manipulation). Party conflict leads to the competition of ideas and alternation in policy emphasis.

Cities differ, thus, in their systems of governance, and one should not assume that a particular system is superior. The Ann Arbor system does seem to be successful, but this has been, and will continue to be, contingent on whether it operates in such a way as to produce leaders who are effective, especially by having parties that are truly competitive and function well. This system can fail if the parties fail to perform or if elites operate outside the constraints of the model. Further, the secondary components of the system may enhance or weaken elites' capabilities to perform. Ward politics, interest group pressure, and citizen electoral apathy are aspects of politics that must be monitored. If these tendencies become extreme, able leadership may decline to compete, pluralistic forces may limit elite capacity to act, or the product of the policy process may be more manipulative than representative of, and responsive to, public needs. The Ann Arbor system, with its emphasis on party conflict and the centralization of decision making in city council, has its own special character. Ann Arbor citizens do not live in the political environment of a stagnant nonpartisan consensus, nor under the control of a political boss or power elite. And the city has prospered! The ramifications of that story are worthwhile to examine.

The Rules of the Political Game in Ann Arbor

Undergirding the operation of the Ann Arbor system of governance are certain norms, or rules of the political game, expectations about how politics is to be conducted. The norms that we describe here apply primarily to the sector of the public which is concerned about local politics, involved in it, and knowledgeable about it—the politically attentive public. For 75 percent of the adult public, the basic norm, so far as local politics is concerned, is a composite of indifference, complacency, nonparticipation, ignorance, and nonvoting. But for the 25 percent who are attentive to local politics, there is an understanding about specific rules of the political game.

These norms were not always evident thirty to forty years ago. They constitute part of Ann Arbor's contemporary political culture. These norms have been learned by those involved in politics, from precinct leaders to candidates for mayor. What are these norms?

1. They include a belief in partisan elections and in party conflict,, with all the implications of that. It is expected that party leaders and organizations will disagree on issues and fight passionately in council and in campaigns for their positions, as party members. To some extent, people even enjoy the party battle.
2. It is expected that those who are elected believe in something, have a program, but also think in terms of feasibility, and are practical men and women.
3. While a majority believe in party government (the majority shall prevail), they expect a lively concern for minority views and interests (*which* minorities, of course, may well be argued!).
4. And over time it is expected that parties probably will alternate in power, that new leaders with new ideas and skills will replace old leaders (with old ideas and skills).
5. While citizens accept a certain amount of elite conflict, they also expect elite civility—a certain degree of congeniality, honorableness, fairness, and above all, honesty in leaders' relations to each other.
6. Ann Arbor leaders take great pains to see that the public has an opportunity to be heard. At council meetings time is set aside for this; in campaigns, candidates do a great deal of personalized contact and canvassing; neighborhood meetings and other groups expect leaders to listen and speak to them. It is a fairly populist system.
7. The Ann Arbor public is relatively proud of its city and expects leaders to continue to work rationally to provide services as well as leaders committed to development and growth—but not too much development and growth, and along rather carefully circumscribed lines.

Above all, Ann Arbor's citizens expect programs that evolve only after careful consultation with the relevant interests. It is a common phenomenon to see in Ann Arbor, as was the case in 1987, 250 community leaders meet to discuss policies to deal with such problems as "river development," a "lively downtown," an "ecologically aware community," a "drug-free Ann Arbor," affordable housing, racial harmony, and other tricky issues. This is not a sleepy town. It is on the move. The recent characterization of Ann Arbor by a national columnist (quoting *The Economist* magazine) as a center of technological development illustrates this point:

> The fastest growing high tech corridor in the U.S. today is no longer Silicon Valley south of San Francisco nor Route 128 around Boston, but a 40-mile strip of Michigan stretching west from Detroit to the leafy campus town of Ann Arbor . . . The State's Industrial Technology Institute at Ann Arbor is a main reason why Automation Alley is where it is.[11]

Ann Arbor, then, has a political culture which is a mix of many norms and practices supporting a system of governance, the focus of which is party conflict in the city council. It is a system in which elites are linked to the public through party organizations, ward politics, interest groups, and election campaigns. The media in all this play a sometimes helpful communicative role, reporting the actions of the various actors in this system, confirming (sometimes questioning) the norms, but over time socializing people to an understanding and acceptance of the "Ann Arbor system." This system was created by able community leaders, endorsed by the public, and transmitted in subtle ways to all participants and citizens. By and large, most Ann Arbor citizens have come to accept a political system in which partisan competition is the centerpiece. Long exposure to this system has led to its legitimacy here. To what extent is this so?

Acceptance of the Concept of Party Government

Not everyone accepts this partisan concept of city government, in which the basic policies are decided in the explicit context of partisan elections and party warfare. Among cities over 2,500 in population the concept of partisan elections is rejected by 70 percent of the cities (by 74 percent of those cities in Ann Arbor's population range).[12] In the early part of this century, the movement for reform of municipal government, which included an attack on the role of political parties, led to the adoption of a reform model for cities that provided for small city councils, elected at large, on nonpartisan ballots, and with a council-manager system of political control. When Ann Arbor finally reformed its government on April 9, 1956, the new charter incorporated only one of these elements of the reform model: the council-manager (we call it administrator) concept of government. Partisan elections remained as they were in the old system. Ann Arbor, therefore, has committed itself explicitly to a partisan system. Other cities have either tried to suppress parties completely or have taken them off the ballot, although parties may still operate behind the scenes in many of these cities. In the 1960's a study of eighty-two nonpartisan cities in the San Francisco Bay area revealed that in two-thirds of the larger cities (over 10,000 in population), there was evidence of party activity even though it was a nonpartisan system. A type of "latent partisanship" was found in many cities.[13]

So Ann Arbor is in the minority with its partisan electoral system. And the majority of Ann Arbor's citizens accept this system. Yet, even in Ann Arbor a sizable minority disapprove of the concept of party conflict. In three studies done recently (1980, 1981, and 1984), from 40 percent to 50 percent of the adult public in Ann Arbor favors nonpartisan elections. Yet, one must hasten to add, for those citizens who are knowledgeable and active in local politics, there is very strong commitment to partisan elections. (See table 2.3.) The Republican and Democratic activists support the partisan concept at the 80 percent level. Even for the sample of community leaders of groups other than parties, 55 percent of whom were strong party identifiers, the idea of partisanism was supported by a majority. There is a climate of support, then, in Ann Arbor for partisan elections, particularly among those who take an interest in local politics and vote in local elections.

Trust in Government in Ann Arbor

One further point must be emphasized for the Ann Arbor public—the level of public confidence and trust in the local government is high, higher than confidence in the national government. In the 1980 and 1984

TABLE 2.3 The Extent of Commitment to Partisan Elections in Ann Arbor (for Various Sectors of the Adult Population)

	Favor Partisan System (%)	Favor Nonpartisan System (%)	*N*
Nonvoters	53	47	128
Voters	64	36	92
Active party leaders (1982)	80	20	80
Republicans	72	28	36
Democrats	87	13	44
Community leaders (1983)	54	46	101
Total adult sample (1984)	60	40	220

Source: Surveys conducted by the author in the years indicated.

Note: Three separate studies, as indicated, were the basis for these findings. Those responding "Don't Know," who constituted about 6 percent of the adult sample (but were rarely found among the leaders) were excluded from these calculations.

The question was: "In local government some cities have nonpartisan elections (parties do not appear on the ballot) and others like Ann Arbor have partisan elections (parties select candidates and the names appear on the ballot). Which would you prefer?"

studies, we found a remarkably high public confidence based on two types of tests: (1) trust in what the government does, particularly in its concern for all the people, and (2) a feeling that the ordinary citizen has a say in local government (is taken into consideration by local government decision makers). Table 2.4 presents the basic data to illustrate this. In two different studies, we have demonstrated the difference in the public's support for government, locally and nationally. There is a 15 to 20 percentage point greater confidence in government generally in Ann Arbor, and a 15 to 20 percentage point greater confidence in local government than is true of the national public.[14] There is much less alienation from government in Ann Arbor than is normally found in national studies. In Ann Arbor 70 percent of the adults trust their local government; almost 90 percent feel they have some say, some input. To cap it all off, these same studies revealed a relatively high degree of support for political parties. The following statement was put to samples of the U.S. and Ann Arbor publics (in 1980 and 1984, respectively): "Parties are only interested in peoples' votes but not in their opinions." Only 39 percent of the American public disagreed; 61 percent of the Ann Arbor public disagreed. Obviously there is relatively high political satisfaction.

It is hard to gauge the overall level of satisfaction of the Ann Arbor public with the job the city government is doing. This varies over time and is contingent on what problems are evaluated. In 1981 and 1984, only 30 percent were negative, that is, felt that on the most important

TABLE 2.4. Public Confidence in Government in Ann Arbor vs. Nation (in percentages)

	Ann Arbor Public		National Public,
	1980	1984	1980
Trust in Government			
"Trust in the government in Washington to do what is right just about always, or most of the time"	50.0	54.0	29.0
"Trust in local government to do what is right just about always, or most of the time"	71.0	70.5	55.0
Sense of Political Efficacy			
Feel that "people like me" have a say in "what the government does" (general sense of efficacy)	76.0	77.0	60.0
Feel that "people like me" have a say "about what the local government does" (sense of efficacy about citizen say for local government)	87.0	89.0	67.0

Sources: National data: The University of Michigan Center for Political Studies National Election Survey, 1980; local data: Cross-sectional studies of the Ann Arbor public in 1980 and 1984.

problems, which varied for individuals, the city was doing a poor or very poor job. In 1984 the most salient concerns were safety, street maintenance, and economic development. In a 1990 study by the *Ann Arbor News* (based on interviews with 386 Ann Arbor residents), the most salient problems were streets, parking, and traffic flow. On those three problems, an average of 50 percent of the sample felt the city's performance was "poor" or "awful."[15] Thus there is, considerable disapproval of the city's record on certain problems. There was high approval, however, in 1990 of the police and fire departments and the schools—over 70 percent rated them "good" or "excellent." The analysis of the 1984 survey revealed that certain types of citizens were most critical, table 2.5 indicates. Those who are more involved with Ann Arbor partisan politics are clearly more satisfied than the least knowledgeable and least active. Yet, there is a sizable minority of critics even among those engaged in city political affairs.

The Functions of Parties in Local Government

The arguments for parties at the local level can be summarized rather easily. First local problems and issues *are* as debatable in partisan terms as are national or state problems. There *are* different partisan approaches to the allocation of resources for roads, housing, parking meters, police departments, human services, even sewers. Indeed, having party groups articulate these needs, take positions on them, and debate them may lead to more responsibility in government than through a nonpartisan system. Second, party conflict can lead to significant social

TABLE 2.5. Evaluation of the City Government's Job, 1984 (in percentages)

Characteristics of Respondents	Approve	Disapprove	Don't know
April Voters	67	28	5
April Nonvoters	40	39	21
Knowledge of Local Government			
High	69	25	7
Low	48	34	17
Party Affiliation			
Republicans	62	26	12
Democrats	61	30	9
Independents	50	38	12

Source: Survey of Ann Arbor public conducted by author in 1984.

and economic changes (as we shall see when we examine the Ann Arbor record), but it can also lead to consensus, to cooperation. Third, partisanship can lead to more citizen involvement in politics and, hence, improve the quality of the democratic life in a city. A 1975 special study of over eight-hundred cities of population 25,000 and above revealed that voting participation was on the average 10 percent higher in cities with partisan elections, particularly for cities like Ann Arbor which hold separate city elections in April.[16] Finally, political competition through parties forces local leaders to be responsive to the public, aware of citizen needs, and motivated to act to meet those needs. In short, partisan elections impose a discipline on political elites which is quite different than is true for communities with nonpartisan elections.

Party government at the local level can be effective, leading to innovative policy and creative development. That is, if the parties are truly competitive, because then the two parties will (1) debate the alternatives openly, (2) replace each other in control of the government periodically, and (3) when out of power, monitor each other's performance closely. The requisites for sound partisanship emphasize a party system and a type of conflict which is not petty, nor ritualistic, nor characterized primarily by personal rivalry. It assumes that people disagree on value priorities and policy preferences and that the party combat and debate will be responsible and will clarify alternatives and lead to solutions. In the long run, this type of partisan conflict is healthy and integrative. Those who are skeptical of partisan local government forget that in European systems, city councils are very partisan, often with four or five parties represented. Their local governments perform as well as, if not better than, those in the United States.

Conclusion

We have attempted here to describe the institutional and political cultural context within which development has occurred in Ann Arbor since 1945. Institutions are critical for development. As explained in our theoretical statement in the preface, institutions are one major complex of factors conditioning the political and social and economic life of a community. Institutions, resources, leadership, and public support patterns all interact to produce the type of development that actually takes place.

Ann Arbor has over time developed its own political culture, that is, a set of widely shared views—shared by leaders *and* the public—about the scope and direction of public policy as well as the proper behavior of leadership and of public institutions. A political culture has many aspects, but "institutions and processes are at the heart" of culture and politics.[17] Ann Arbor's institutions are of a particular type, and function on the basis of certain key operational norms, particularly council centrality and competitive party politics.

As we explore these institutions further and the way they are linked to development, we will emphasize, first, the type of political leadership that has emerged over time in Ann Arbor in this institutional context and the nature of the decisions on public policy that this leadership has made. The beliefs and behavior of our city political leaders constitute one major focus here. A second emphasis is the two-party system. We are particularly interested in how well organized it is—how cohesive and combative these organizations are, their programmatic and ideological positions, and how these are presented and incorporated in policy. Above all, we will examine how relevant party competition is and how consequential party turnover has been for policy control and innovation. A third emphasis will be on the role of interest groups, their involvement with city government and their interrelationship with the party organizations and their leadership. Finally, we will analyze in some detail the nature of public participation in Ann Arbor's system.

Cities differ in many ways and in many aspects of their politics. The political management of some cities is woefully inefficient; in others, very skilled. City councils in some cities are hopelessly divisive or, in contrast, inert. Party organizational activity in city campaigns may be nonexistent, clandestine, or slack in some cities; in others, competitive, vibrant, and electorally relevant. Some cities have able interest-group leadership concerned about politics and effectively involved; in others, there may be stagnant negativism or, in contrast, segmented rivalries which stymie positive action. Some cities have attentive publics which are alert and articulate, in contact with political leaders; others have publics largely withdrawn into soporific apathy. We think we can demonstrate which of these characterizations are valid for Ann Arbor. Recognizing economic constraints and economic opportunities as not unimportant, our motivating hunch is that probing the type of leadership and the vitality of the partisan character of a community (and its interest groups) is a key to understanding why a city prospers or declines. For Ann Arbor, a community which has prospered, that is in our analysis the heart of the inquiry.

CHAPTER 3

The Postwar Reconstruction of Ann Arbor's Party System

Before World War II, the Republicans and Democrats contested fairly closely, but in the 1930's the Republicans were usually in the majority. A Democratic mayor, Edward W. Staebler, did serve four years, retiring in 1931, then the Republicans won thirteen consecutive mayoral elections spanning twenty-six years. They were often opposed by able Democrats for mayor and council, and the Democrats were a strong opposition party up to 1938, usually winning three out of seven council seats and an average of 44 percent of the vote. By 1938, however, the Republicans became dominant. In the next ten years they won over 80 percent of the council seats with 68 percent of the vote. The total vote and the Democratic vote dwindled during the war, particularly from 1942 on, and politics seemed adjourned until the late 1940's.

The city was a thriving community after the war, increasing in population from less than 40,000 in 1940 to almost 50,000 by 1950. Important city leaders ran for office for both parties, debating the issues associated with city growth. From 1946 to 1956, the Democrats ran eight university professors for council as well as many community leaders with no university affiliation—a leadership which was "professorial" as well as "professional" and "business." The Republicans also included professors and even a university administrator, as well as many business leaders, executives of fairly large firms as well as secondary entrepreneurs. In short, both parties fielded candidates who were of diverse backgrounds. The Republicans had a 22 to 8 comparative advantage among the business-managerial candidates during this period (including attorneys), the Democrats a 12 to 4 advantage among the candidates with a lower professional or small-business status. Both parties had many candidates from the university side. Despite certain common recruitment patterns, the two parties did in a sense represent different social interests. The bottom line, however, was that in this postwar period up to 1957 the Republicans swept the elections for the mayoral and council positions 89 percent to 11 percent.

The issue controversies in this period, at low ebb in the forties, became more confrontational in the fifties. The push for charter revision divided the parties as well as produced some disagreement within both parties. There was also argument over how the city should grow, how it should meet its health needs, and how to deal with its traffic problems as the city became larger. Its outgrown sewer and water treatment systems, its need for parking space, the pressure for more housing and the concomitant pressure to annex more land—all these were on the agenda of party politicians in the fifties. In 1950 the Democratic platform attacked the Republican administration for its "failure to make even the slightest gesture to use federal help to ease the housing shortage in Ann Arbor, while other cities in the state and nation are using it to solve their housing needs."[1] The Democrats began to push for other improvements—bus service on Sundays, and a large outdoor municipally owned swimming pool! The Democrats also began their drive to get the city to do something to deal with problems of racial discrimination. The 1952 platforms of the two parties reveal the issues preoccupying the parties and the different positions they took on these issues (table 3.1).

The Postwar Party Regeneration

The transformation of Ann Arbor's party system after the end of the war was dramatic. At the time of the 1948 election the Democrats received 29 percent of the vote for president, and in the subsequent city election the Democrats received an almost identical 28.9 percent. In 1956 the Democrats secured only 31 percent of the presidential vote, but 53 percent for mayor the next year. In the 1957 election they received 46 percent of the vote for city council. This is a tremendous change in party strength in local elections. The party system that had been one-party dominant, by 1957 was moving to a genuine two-party type. How did this occur?

Theorists of party realignment or, more appropriately, of party system change, characterize this process in different ways. It can be sudden (the result of a "critical election") or gradual. It can be a major change in the character of the system or a moderate shift in the patterns of popular support. It can be seen as a "dealignment" (the withdrawal of support for parties) or a "realignment" (a switch in party allegiances). It can be seen as a mobilization of new voters or the conversion of regular voters. These and other variations identified by scholars reveal party system change to be a complex phenomenon, both as to type and causes.[2] How relevant are such conceptions to party change in Ann Arbor?

What happened in Ann Arbor from 1948 on is in its own way a complex pattern of development. The key question at the outset is whether there was indeed a breakdown in the previous party system and the replacement of the old system with a new one. If one studies the pre- and postwar strength of Ann Arbor's parties it becomes clear that replacement did not occur. Rather, there was a reconstruction of the old prewar two-party system after a steep decline in the vote cast

TABLE 3.1. A Comparison of Early Party Platforms for the City, 1952

	Platform Proposals Presented	
	Democrats	Republicans
Capital Improvements	New city hall, fire station, civic center, additions to municipal garage	New courthouse, highway by-passes, fire protection facilities, additional park lands and recreational facilities
Housing	"A thorough going study of Ann Arbor's present and future housing needs and the mobilization of private and public effort to meet those needs"	A study of "the housing problem" and "the formation of a commission for a long-range study and action program to provide adequate housing for all people"
City Charter	An overhaul of the city charter with special attention on home rule powers	Continuing study of city charter in order to make it at all times an effective instrument of government
Human Relations	A study of areas of racial and religious friction by a "civic committee or commission"; new classification and pay plan for city employees	Better employee relations and higher wage scales for city employees
Other	A study of the city's sources of revenue, particulary to investigate new ones—"the city needs broader powers of taxation" "A unified city-wide recreation program" Expansion of services, especially rubbish and garbage Expanded city planning but opposition to "haphazard annexations" University should bear fair share of cost of municipal services	"Investigation of new sources of revenue for city government operation" "A careful scheduled improvement program which will coordinate city, county, and school system projects . . . through a joint committee" Better relations with townships

Source: Ann Arbor political party documents; *The Ann Arbor News.*

for city council from 1941 to 1948, an unbelievable drop from 5,800 votes to fewer than 2,000. (See table 3.2.) The percent of eligible voters voting dropped to 2.5 percent in 1946. Subsequently the two parties resumed their competition after the hiatus of the war years and by 1949 already were attracting many of their old supporters. Thus, what occurred was a remobilization of partisan backers of the prewar years. The one key difference was that at first the Republicans did this more effectively than the Democrats. It was not really until the late 1950s that the Democrats demonstrated their comeback, securing 46 percent of the mayoral vote in 1955 and 53 percent in 1957. In between, the city had one-party dominant, Republican-controlled, rather consensual politics, although the Democratic opposition was contesting ever more energetically in both mayoral and council elections throughout the fifties.

Party Cycles or Eras in Ann Arbor

Party strength has fluctuated greatly in the past forty years, as the accompanying graph reveals (fig. 3.1). The elections of 1955 and 1957 were a critical step in the development of a truly competitive two-party system. But there have been important deviations since then. While it appears that the Democratic party's growth had a linear and continuous upward character, there actually were large fluctuations. Indeed, instead of linear growth, there appear to be irregular party strength cycles, which cumulatively did lead to an extremely evenly balanced two-party system.

TABLE 3.2. The Redevelopment of Ann Arbor's Two-Party System: Pre- and Post-World War II Voting Trends

Distributed by Party	1935	1941	1943	1945	1947	1949	1951	1953	1955	1957
Mayoral Vote										
Republican	55%	57%	70%	100%	100%	70%	59%	64%	54%	47%
Democratic	45%	43%	30%	0%	0%	30%	41%	36%	46%	53%
Council Vote										
Republican	60%	54%	75%	76%	95%	69%	73%	66%	71%	54%
Democratic	40%	46%	25%	24%	5%	31%	27%	34%	29%	46%
Council Seats Held										
Republican	9	14	12	12	12	11	11	13	13	8
Democratic	6	1	3	3	3	4	4	2	2	3
Total Seats	15	15	15	15	15	15	15	15	15	11

Source: All tables presenting the results of city elections are based on reports and documents of the Ann Arbor City Clerk's office and the City Election Commission.

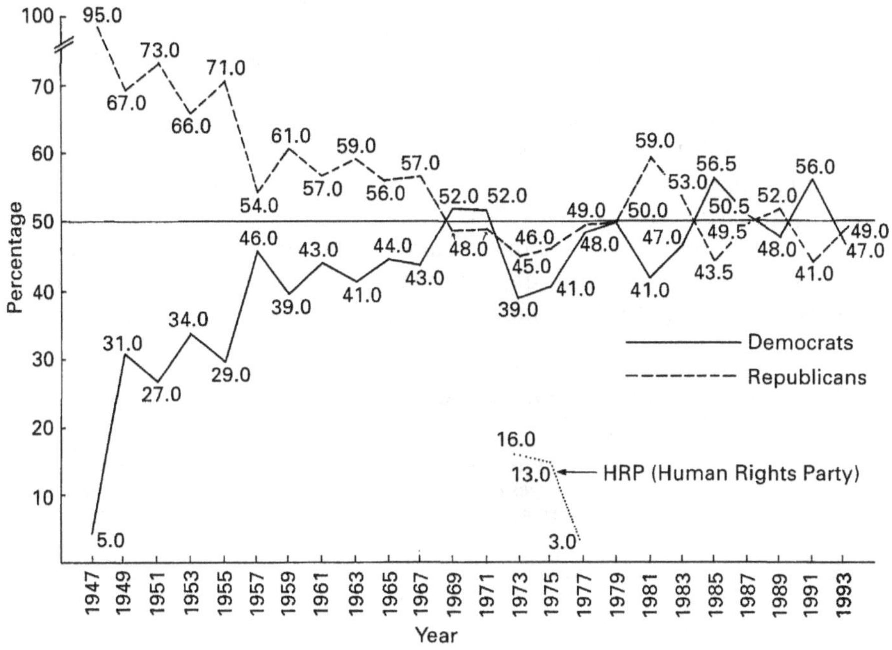

Fig. 3.1. Convergence in party strength, 1947–93. Percentages based on the vote for council in mayoral years. (From election reports of Ann Arbor city clerk.)

Four fairly distinct cycles or eras can be identified. These were:

1. 1947–56: A period of Republican dominance but the beginning of a Democratic comeback.
2. 1957–71: The completion of the rebuilding of the two-party system.
3. 1971–77: With the appearance of the Human Rights Party, a turbulent pluralistic period of three-party politics.
4. 1978–91: The return to very evenly balanced two-party competitive politics.

The evidence in support of the existence of such cycles is found in table 3.3. These data reveal the shifts in party strength in each of these four eras. They mask, however, the ups and downs of the parties with these eras which one could find by scrutiny of specific elections. For example, in the second era or cycle, the Democrats' strength in council elections varied from 49 percent in 1958 to 39 percent in 1959, 53 percent in 1964,

43 percent in 1967, and 52 percent in the victory of 1969. By taking the obverse of these percentages, one can see the fluctuating fortunes of the Republican party. Hence, this was no straight-line consistent pattern of change. Impressive, however, are (1) the movement toward closer competition until in recent years council seats are split on a 51–49 percent ratio by party, and (2) the decisive return to two-party competition after the pluralistic threat of the 1970s.

One is tempted to see these phases in the postwar development as cycles of party competition, or rhythms of ideological change, or upward-moving spirals of cumulative political change. If they are cycles,

TABLE 3.3 Cycles or Eras in Ann Arbor's Postwar Politics, 1947–91

	Party Strength in Council Elections (averages in percentages)			Party Distribution of Council Seats (in percentages)			Shift in percentage of Party Strength in Council Vote during Period		
Periods	Dem.	Rep.	HRP	Dem.	Rep.	HRP	Dem.	Rep.	HRP
1. Early Republican dominance and beginning of Democratic comeback, 1947–56	31	69	—	11	89	—	+41	−41	—
2. Building a two-party system, 1957–71	46	54	—	38	62	—	+6	−6	—
3. Pluralistic three-party politics, 1971–77[a]	42	45	13	38	53	9	−4	+1	+3
4. Established, close two-party politics, 1978–91	49	51	—	51	49	—	+7	−7	—

Note: Dem. = Democratic party; Rep. = Republican party; HRP = Human Rights party
[a]The strength of the Human Rights Party in Period 3 was as follows:

	Vote for Council	Vote for Mayor	Council Seats Won
1972	24.4%	—	2
1973	16.1	16.3	0
1974	18.3	—	1
1975	13.1	10.8	0
1976	3.3	—	0
1977	2.7	1.7	0

they are not precisely regular and periodic, as Arthur Schlesinger refers to them in his book *The Cycles of American History*.[3] Nor are they clear swings of the pendulum from conservatism to liberalism and back again. Perhaps for Ann Arbor politics they are better seen as spirals of increasing party competition (in the sense of the elder Schlesinger), because despite alternation in party control, the closeness of the party competition achieved successively higher levels and with, as we shall see, a cumulative set of consequences for change in policy.

Whatever descriptive language we use, it is quite clear that the party system went through a forty-five year period of different types of change. From one perspective, it changed from one-party dominance to moderate competitiveness to three-party pluralism to very close competitiveness. From another perspective, after a dealignment in the immediate postwar period, that is, a falling off in party support, with a decline in voting turnout, the system then remobilized in the late forties and fifties and was reconstructed. Then, with the development of strong party organizations, the two-party system was reinstitutionalized. During these periods of party development, there may also have been some realignment occurring, or the switching of party allegiances, but in the absence of good survey data it is difficult to determine the magnitude and the episodic character or duration of such switching in party support. By the late eighties and early nineties, the two-party system looks in terms of party-strength distribution like it did in the thirties (55 percent to 45 percent). But this is only a superficial similarity probably. The two parties have formed very well-articulated structures and leadership systems, and they have the tools and personnel for conducting campaigns that now can be more technologically sophisticated. The parties have endured for some time as cohesive precinct organizations with a loyal citizen supporter base. One can only conjecture whether this was true before—probably not.

Party Turnovers

In a two-party system, the defeat of the party in control of the city council is a dramatic event and may lead to innovative decisions. These turnovers are key analytic time periods for a city. Ann Arbor has had nine elections since World War II when power in city hall (the council) changed hands. For example, in recent years control shifted to the Democrats in 1985, to the Republicans in 1988, and back to the Democrats in 1991. Earlier, turnovers occurred in 1969, 1971, 1972, 1973, 1975 and 1976. In addition, there have been five elections that brought a new mayor in, from the opposition party, but with no change in the majority control of city council: 1957, 1959, 1975, 1978, 1987. In forty-five years, this is evidence of considerable capacity for political change—a major power change every 3.2 years (or 5 years, depending how one chooses to calculate it). Clearly Ann Arbor is not living in a system of stagnant consensus.

The data on the characteristics of the turnovers suggest that these are rarely landslides. The shift in the percentage of the party vote is usually in the 5 to 6 percent range—only in 1959 and 1991 did it reach 10 percentage points in turnovers, including mayoral changes. The average winning percentage of the party is only 52 to 53 percent (table 3.4). When a turnover occurs, there is usually only a marginal change in seats. Only in the Democratic victories of 1969 and 1991 did three or more seats change (a sizable change in an eleven person council). The average is just under two seats. One reason for the relatively small shift at the time of the turnover is that the change begins in the preceding election. Hence, there is a buildup which in a sense "anticipates" a turnover. In the years follow-

TABLE 3.4. Party Turnovers in the Postwar Years: Patterns of Electoral Change

	Mayoral Turnovers[a]	Council Turnovers: Real Shift in Party Control[b]
A. Magnitude of Turnover		
Voting		
Average strength of winning party	53.0%	52.2
Average shift in the party vote in the turnover year	+6.7	+1.2
Average change in seats	+2.0	+2.0
B. Anticipation of the Turnover		
Average shift in party vote in the election preceding the turnover year		
Mayoral elections	+1.2	+2.2
Council elections	+3.7	+4.8
C. Duration of the Turnover Party's Strength[c]		
Average strength of the turnover party in the next election	52.8%	47.9%
Average strength in the second succeeding election	50.8%	48.8%

Source: All tables presenting the results of city elections are based on reports and documents of the Ann Arbor City Clerk's office and the City Election Commission.

[a]We use here seven mayoral turnovers, excluding 1973 and 1975 when the vote for the Human Rights Party complicates and distorts calculations. The seven are 1957, 1959, 1969, 1978, 1985, 1987, and 1991.

[b]We use the five "real" council party turnovers—that is, in which there was a shift in control from one major part to the other: 1969, 1971, 1985, 1988, and 1991. The council control changes for 1972–77, are, thus, not included here.

[c]The 1991 turnover calculations can not be included, because we do not have data yet for succeeding elections.

ing the turnover election, the pendulum seems to slowly swing away from the party in power, and the cycle moving to another transformation seems to be in motion. The implications of this are important. In particular, one implication is that if major policy innovation is to be undertaken by the turnover party, the honeymoon period is a short one.

The Conditions Facilitating Party System Redevelopment

Why and how did the rebuilding of Ann Arbor's party system occur, from one-party control to two-party balanced competition? It must first be kept in mind that there was a prewar reservoir of support for the Democratic party that was waiting to be mobilized. One can see this by looking at the party vote in presidential elections from 1932 to 1944. During this period, an average of almost eight thousand votes were cast for Republican presidential candidates and over five thousand for Democratic candidates. This can be considered the potential vote for each party. In city elections, ever-smaller proportions of this vote were mobilized in that period, reaching a low point of 19 percent in the April election of 1945 (table 3.5). But the major point is that in the late forties there were large numbers of potential voters more or less committed to the parties, available for appeals in city elections. The problem was how to bring these potential voters to the April polls.

The process by which this took place had two phases: the regeneration of the public's interest in politics generally and the mobilization of these interested citizens to vote in local elections. Voting turnout in Ann Arbor's presidential elections (one index of the public's interest in politics) reached a low point in the 1948 presidential election—only 49.8 percent of those eligible participated. That turnout increased to 61.6 percent by 1952 and continued at that level in subsequent elections. The turnout at local elections, much lower, tended to follow that trend, but with certain deviations. The comparative data are given in table 3.6. As national election turnout began to return to higher levels in the fifties, local turnout also picked up, reaching a postwar high point in 1957. The turnout differential was still sizable, however. If it were not for the partisan mobilization activities of the parties, which were becoming better organized by the early Fifties, city election turnouts might well have been much lower.

One should note that the Democrats did a much better job of mobilizing their potential vote from 1948 on. Indeed, their mobilization efforts matched or exceeded those of the Republicans in proportionate terms in the late forties and fifties. And in the 1957 election there was a striking asymmetry in these mobilization efforts—77 percent for the Democrats, 41 percent for the Republicans. Finally, the potential vote (measured by presidential elections) began to favor the Democrats. And the Democrats did as well at, if not a better job of, getting out their vote as did the Republicans.

TABLE 3.5. The Mobilization of the Potential Vote in the Postwar Period

Presidential Election Year	Republicans	Democrats
A. Prewar and War Years		
1932	61	67
1936	38	38
1940	36	53
1944	19	19
B. Immediate postwar period		
1948	45	47
1952	36	35
1956	41	77
C. The Sixties: Building of the Two-party System		
1960	46	59
1964	79	45
1968	61	64
D. Recent Years		
1980	49	25
1984	35	34
1988	41	23

Source: County Clerk election records; Ann Arbor City Clerk's Election reports.
Note: Indicates percentage of the party vote cast in presidential elections which was turned out for the following April vote for city council.

TABLE 3.6. Turnout in Presidential and Local Elections for Ann Arbor

	Presidential Election Turnout	City Election Turnout (in April election after the presidential election)
1940	79.8	37.2
1944	67.0	11.9[a]
1948	49.8	21.6
1952	61.6	22.2
1956	59.1	31.4
1960	63.7	31.4

Source: County Clerk election records; Ann Arbor City Clerk's Election reports.
[a]No Democratic candidate for mayor.

While this theory of mobilizing the prewar reservoir of votes appears credible, in addition one must recognize the consequences of the increase in Ann Arbor's population and the growth in the university's enrollment and staff during the postwar period. University enrollment more than doubled from 1945 to 1960. The population increased about 60 percent. An estimated five thousand new eligible voters settled here from 1945 to 1950 and another ten thousand in the following decade. This was a better-educated and more affluent population (median family income doubled 1950 to 1960), which apparently was somewhat more interested in city affairs. Local interest groups were active, such as the League of Women Voters, the chambers of commerce, the labor unions, and the black organizations such as NAACP and Civic Forum. These groups, as well as the leaders of the Democratic party, and some Republicans, were pushing for more change in certain aspects of city development. There was a demand for charter revision, a housing commission, a human relations commission, effective planning and zoning, better parks, and playgrounds, as well as policies aimed at providing other services (such as a city-run garbage collection system, adopted in 1950), and infrastructure development. This new population and these social forces articulating these demands were in a sense the crucible in which the Democratic party was rejuvenated, while the Republican party also continued to grow. In the absence of good survey data, it is difficult to demonstrate that both parties were successfully appealing to the new influx of postwar voters. But by using election data broken down by wards we can establish the point fairly well. We can identify five basic geographical areas in the city and characterize their populations by socioeconomic status and by political tendency, in 1949 and as a result of the annexations that occurred in the fifties. We can then get some idea of the pervasiveness of the Democratic mobilization of voters, new and old (table 3.7).

One can see the increase in total vote in all of these areas, particularly in old Wards 2, 3, and 7. One important observation is that the Democrats were actually participating more in the increase of the vote than were the Republicans—even in the areas traditionally very Republican (and with the most affluent electorate), the so called Burns Park area as it expanded to the east. While by 1957 the Democrats were not yet winning council seats in these traditional Republican areas, they were reaching 38 percent and 45 percent of the vote. In the old northern wards 4 and 5 (now ward 1), the lower-income and black wards, the Democrats were already winning by 1955.

These data strongly suggest that the explanation of the Democratic party's comeback was not only due to the remobilization of the prewar vote, but also was due to the mobilization of new residents in all sections

TABLE 3.7. Vote Increase in Most-Affluent and Least-Affluent Wards for City Elections, 1949–57

	Total Vote		Party Proportion of Total Vote Increase		Democratic % of Total Vote			
	N	% Increase	Rep.	Dem.	1949	1953	1955	1957
Old Wards 4 & 5 (New Ward 1) Lower-income area, residence of Ann Arbor blacks, traditional Democratic wards	678	82%	40%	60%	47%	49%	52%	52%
Old Ward 2 (New Ward 4) Traditional Westside conservative, moderately affluent, Republican ward	1,056	95	41	59	32	31	31	45
Old Ward 6 & 1 (New Ward 2) Well-to-do conservative Eastside Burns Park area, very Republican wards; also includes student residences	459	35	31	69	28	36	35	38
Old Ward 3 (New Ward 5) Northwest area, moderately affluent, transitional from Republican to moderately Democratic; an area of great population explosion	1,810	251	46	54	29	40	47	47
Old Ward 7 (New Ward 3) Southeast area, affluent, strongly Republican ward, but some evidence of Democratic inroads	1,066	59	25	75	28	30	37	45

Note: The vote for coucil is used here for all elections. In 1956 the numbering of wards was changed by the new city charter (as well as reduced from seven to five). The old ward numbers, thus, are for the pre–1957 period, the new ward number (for the same area, expanded by annexations) refers to the 1957 election.

of the city. Those involved in the rebuilding of the Democratic party organization in Ann Arbor from 1949 on can attest to the great efforts exerted by Democratic precinct workers in developing files including the names of all new voters who had moved into their precincts, keeping these records up-to-date, and using them to get out the vote. The Republican organization was also very active, but it was the new mobilization efforts by the Democrats, of both old Democratic supporters and new migrants to the city, that helped primarily to move the city toward a two-party system.

The Role of the *Ann Arbor News*

The news media also may have played a significant role in the postwar revival of the two-party system. At that time, the *Ann Arbor News* was the key source for information about local politics. Its Ann Arbor circulation increased regularly in the postwar period, from approximately 9,000 in 1940 to almost 12,000 by 1950 and to over 22,000 in 1970.[4]

If one assumes that two adults are exposed to each newspaper, by the 1950s 25,000 or more adults could have been readers. The *News* is, and has been, thus, available to a large proportion of the 8,000 to 11,000 Ann Arbor adults who voted in the fifties. A 1981 study revealed that 57 percent of Ann Arbor adults are regular readers, 46 percent claiming to follow the stories on local politics.[5] Among long-time residents (over 10 years), 76 percent are regular readers. Whether these same proportions were true in the 1945–60 period is not known, but probably the levels and differentials in readership were similar.

We know also from recent studies that readership of the *Ann Arbor News* is linked to voting in local elections (table 3.8).[6] Readership in conjunction with other factors—age and residence—appears to have a "moderate causal impact on voting."[7] In the early postwar period, when television was not yet important in local elections, the newspaper constituted a major source for political information and propaganda.

If we keep this in mind then the data we have on the frequency of articles and political advertisements in the *News* over this period is relevant.[8] (See table 3.9 and fig. 3..2) These data reveal that during the 1957 campaign, in the two week period before the April election day, the *News* reached an all-time high in the number of articles on all aspects of the approaching election, a total of fifty-four articles (35 percent of them dealing directly with the parties, the issues, campaign meetings, and related topics). After 1957 there was a sharp decline in such articles—an average of fewer than fifteen articles in each two week period directly focused on the parties. Indeed, never since then has the *News* matched the level of its 1957 coverage.[9] There was a gradual

TABLE 3.8. Percentage Voting in 1981 April Election By Degree to *Ann Arbor News*

	Percentage Voting in 1981 April Election	
	Readers	Nonreaders
Age Groups		
18–24	24	4
25–45	39	16
45+	63	38
Residence Groups		
1–4 years	13	7
5–10 years	39	10
11–20 years	61	27
20+ years	53	25
Total	45%	12%

Source: Survey of Ann Arbor Adults, 1981.

TABLE 3.9. Political Articles and Advertisements in the *Ann Arbor News,* 1947–91

	1947–49	1950–57	1958–68	1969–78	1979–87	1988–91[a]
Ann Arbor News Articles (average number)						
On the parties	5.3	10.8	14.6	12.0	13.0	12.0
Total articles on election	7.7	21.9	20.9	18.5	19.7	24.0
Highest year	1948	1957	1961	1975	1983	1991
(total number of articles)	(13)	(54)	(34)	(29)	(40)	(27)
Political Advertisements (average number)						
By Democrats	1.7	8.9	21.8	52.7	23.4	19.5
By Republicans	3.7	10.3	32.7	83.0	26.2	65.5
Total—all groups	6.0	21.9	56.9	156.5	58.9	91.5
Highest year (total number of ads)						
Democrats	1948	1957	1966	1974	1985	1989
	(3)	(30)	(95)	(86)	(53)	(37)
Republicans	1949	1956	1968	1977	1987	1989
	(9)	(39)	(73)	(118)	(81)	(106)

Source: Ann Arbor News.

Note: Data are based on a count of all articles (by type of article) and advertisements (by group) for the two weeks before the April election in each year, 1947–91.

[a]The data of 1989–91 are for the mayoral elections only.

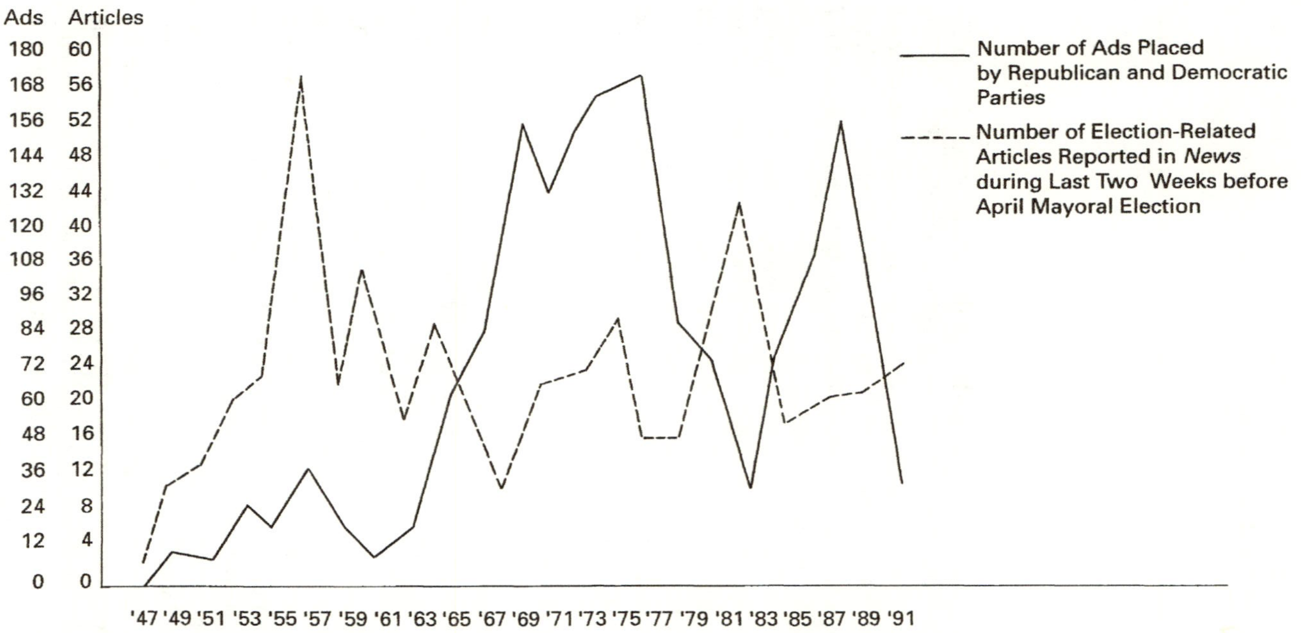

Fig. 3.2. Variations in *Ann Arbor News* coverage of April elections. (From analyses of the *Ann Arbor News*.)

buildup in news coverage leading to the 1957 Democratic mayoral victory. The total number of articles in each mayoral year was:

1947	1
1949	9
1951	12
1953	20
1955	24
1957	54

There was also a gradual increase in the number of ads which the parties placed, rising from none in 1947 to 38 in 1957. Ironically, after 1957 as the *News* cut its coverage in the articles it printed, the advertisements placed by the parties continued at a fairly high level. (See fig. 3.2) These ads reached a high level in the late 1960s and 1970s but have tapered off in most, but not all, recent years.

Clearly both the articles and the advertisements in the *News* during the period of postwar party system reconstruction were increasing. This meant that those attentive to politics were exposed to local politics much more. They had more information about parties, the campaign issues, and the candidates of both parties. This no doubt contributed to the mobilization of old and new voters in this early period.

Party Change and Voter Turnout

There used to be a theory (for some writers there still is) that a larger vote worked to the advantage of the Democratic party. However, the relationship between voter turnout (defined here as the proportion of eligible adults voting) and increased party strength is curious and erratic. Therefore, one must be cautious about interpreting the impact of turnout. To always expect a close relationship to increased Democratic strength is misleading; this certainly has not always been the case in Ann Arbor. Party mobilization efforts are indeed linked to higher turnouts, but it is not the Democrats who benefit exclusively. Three findings emerge from our study for Ann Arbor: (1) increased turnout may benefit one party and not the other; (2) increased turnout may benefit both parties in the same election; and (3) the strength of the Democratic party (and also the Republican) increased in some years when turnout declined. Thus, increased turnout by itself is not the major determinant of increased party strength of either Democrats or Republicans. Rather, it is asymmetric mobilization of voters by the two parties which is crucial.

The analysis of turnout over the years has revealed the following variations in the proportion of eligible voters participating in Ann Arbor's city elections:

1946	2.5% Low point »1
1949	21.6
1957	31.4
1965	37.0
1971	42.9
1973	43.7 High point
1978	33.9
1980	10.7 Low point »2
1983	26.6
1985	22.3
1988	28.6
1991	24.6

It is true that the increase in Democratic strength in the immediate postwar period coincided with increased turnout. But after 1957, this relationship is not at all consistent. Despite the decline in turnout in the seventies, the Democrats won the mayoralty in 1975 and 1977. And in 1985, despite a decline in turnout, the Democrats again won the mayoralty and control of city council.

If one compares the turnout in mayoral elections from 1949 to 1991, we find that in eleven of these twenty-two two-election comparisons, there was a positive relationship between increased turnout (that is, increase in the total vote cast) and increased Democratic actual vote. The correlation was a significant .408. Turnout is therefore not insignificant for Democratic success, but it is not turnout *per se* that is the crucial explanation. After all, the Republican vote increased in all these eleven elections also. Rather, it is the *relative* turnout of the two parties, or to put it differently, the *relative* mobilization success of the two parties in any given election. Further, one must ask what happened when the vote decreased. In eight elections the vote decreased; the Democrats won three of these races despite a decline in the Democratic vote, and the Republicans won the other five. The parties did this by a *relatively* better vote mobilization than the opposition (that is, experiencing a smaller decline). The overall comparisons are found in table 3.10.

Concluding Observations

In trying to understand the redevelopment of Ann Arbor's two-party system in the postwar period and its maintenance as a highly competitive system since that time, the types of candidates who confronted each other in each election and the issues on which these elections were fought are of great importance. The substance and quality, and intensity, of the campaigns contributed to that development. It is impossible here to present that chronology in detail. From our presentation here it should be clear that there were ups and downs in party strength, or, to put it differently, great variations in the voters' response to party candidates and programs. There have been many party battles or partisan rivalries over the years, but throughout these forty-five years, the close competitive character of the system has periodically been renewed.

As one studies these fluctuations or cycles, one notices low points and high points for each party and a gradual building of party strength until a party wins control of the mayor's office and/or of council. In 1949 the Democratic mayoral vote was at a low point, and it gradually increased until it reached 53.1 percent in 1957. In 1961 the Democrats were again at a low point and built up their strength until it reached 51.4 percent in 1969 and 58.6 percent in 1971. From that low point of 41.4 percent for the Republicans, they in turn gradually increased their strength (despite the 1975 and 1977 crises of three-party politics) to a high point of 62.9 percent in the Republican victory of 1981. The Democrats recouped from that low point until in 1985 they won with 53.1 percent. In 1987 the Democrats lost the mayoralty (47 percent of the vote), but by 1991 recouped and won an 8 to 3 majority in the city council and 54 percent of the vote for mayor. But in 1993 this dropped to

TABLE 3.10 Party Mobilization Efforts and Party Success in Relation to Increase and Decrease in the Vote Cast

	Elections When the Total Vote Increased (N = 14)		Elections When the Total Vote Decreased (N = 8)	
	Dem.	Rep.	Dem.	Rep.
Proportion of the Vote Change for Which the Party Was Responsible				
All Elections	53%	47	46	54
When the Democrats won the mayoralty	82	18	22	78
When the Republicans won the mayoralty	29	71	60	40

Source: All tables presenting the results of city elections are based on reports and documents of the Ann Arbor City Clerk's office and the City Election Commission.

41 percent when the Republicans recaptured the mayor's office. Thus, the pendulum swings and the party strength ebbs and flows.

This system appears to be rather volatile. Indeed, if we compute a volatility index—the average shift in the party's percentage of the vote from election to election—for the past forty-five years, we see the extent to which that is true (table 3.11). In presidential elections Ann Arbor has been more volatile than is true for the presidential vote nationally, but the shifts in local elections have not demonstrated as great a volatil-

TABLE 3.11. The Volatility of the Ann Arbor Party System

	Mayoral Elections	Council Elections
Total for 40 Years (1947–87)		
Democrats	6.9%	5.4%
Republicans	5.5	5.5
By Decades		
1947–59		
Democrats	8.7	6.7
Republicans	8.7	6.7
1959–69		
Democrats	3.3	5.2
Republicans	3.3	5.2
1969–79		
Democrats	7.2	4.9
Republicans	2.8	5.3
1979–91		
Democrats	7.8	4.0
Republicans	7.8	4.0
Comparison with National-Level Shifts (1960–80)		

	Average Shifts in the Parties		
	Presidential Vote (National)	Presidential Vote (Ann Arbor)	Mayoral Vote (Ann Arbor)
U.S. Presidential Years			
Democrats	11.7	15.6	6.2
Republicans	10.3	16.0	3.8

Source: All tables presenting the results of city elections are based on reports and documents of the Ann Arbor City Clerk's office and the City Election Commission.

Note: Numbers indicate average shift in the percentage of the vote from one election to the next for each party.

ity. Yet, over the years there have been periods of considerable fluctuation in party fortune. Note the short-term shifts in mayoral elections shown in table 3.12.

There is an average shift of 11.7 percentage points. The potential for great partisan shifts is considerable. Council shifts have usually been smaller, but there have also been sizable shifts in support for council. The events of 1991 certainly underscore the volatility.

This system over the long haul, while volatile, has real continuity. It is a stable equilibrium system, in that it maintains itself as a two-party system despite historical tendencies in other directions. Scholars have characterized America's national party system as in a "state of dynamic equilibrium."[10] Similarly, the swings and fluctuations in party support in Ann Arbor always seem to bring the parties back into a two-party equilibrium. As shown in figure 3.1, after the early period of Republican dominance, rarely does the strength of either party exceed 60 percent (only in 1955, 1965, and 1981). So there is change, but within the constraints of the patterns of party allegiance of the Ann Arbor public, and there is also stability. The only threat to this two-party equilibrium was the three-party politics from 1972 to 1975, a brief interlude from which the two parties quickly recovered.

The evolution of a party system in a community is significant to study: its early development, its patterns of change, its response to apathy and to threats of disruption. Ann Arbor rebuilt its two-party system after World War II and has now functioned as a classic two-party competitive model. This has become a somewhat unique, atypical system for American cities. In the succeeding chapters we shall describe and explain the organizational, leadership, and public foundations of that system today. Then we shall analyze the relevance of such a competitive party system to Ann Arbor's development.

TABLE 3.12. Short Term Fluctuations in the Vote for Mayor

	Democratic Vote %
1957–59	53.1 to 43.1
1967–71	44.5 to 58.6
1971–73	58.6 to 36.6
1973–77	36.6 to 49.2
1979–81	48.3 to 37.1
1989–91	43.6 to 53.7
1991–93	53.7 to 40.8

Source: All tables presenting the results of city elections are based on reports and documents of the Ann Arbor City Clerk's office and the City Election Commission.

CHAPTER 4

The Party Organizations: Links between Citizens and Elites

As we have seen in the preceding chapters, Ann Arbor developed new political institutions in the postwar period: a new set of governing institutions under the 1956 charter and a reconstructed party system during the 1950s and since. The emergence of a truly competitive two-party system that is durable requires strong party organizations. Without an effective organization, a political party can not survive as a significant force. And without strong Republican and Democratic party organizations, the party conflict model of Ann Arbor politics would not work well; indeed, it would atrophy. A great deal of community development in Ann Arbor has been the product of responsible party conflict, and responsible party conflict depends on two well-structured and competitive parties. These organizations, in turn, consist of, and depend on, a set of activists who constitute probably one-half of one percent of the adult population. The beliefs, motivations, and actual political work of these activists are therefore the focus of attention in this chapter. Without able and active activists there can not be effective parties.

Democracies, if properly based on the consent of the governed, require a set of political groups linking the public and its top elites. Such intermediate groups provide a political and social base for leaders as well as a means by which public opinion can be transmitted to leaders and properly reflected in public policy. Political parties have been and still are such key linkage groups in Ann Arbor. Many scholars have argued that American parties are disintegrating, that party organizations, particularly at the local level, are weak and ineffectual. This is highly exaggerated if one looks at the empirical evidence; for Ann Arbor's parties, however, it is clearly and certainly untrue, to anyone who has followed this city's politics.

What are the requisites for effective party organizations in this type of competitive two-party politics? The simple answer is that parties must develop cohesive structures that function competitively. This was the classic formulation of that early theorist of parties, V. O. Key.[1] As structures, party organizations must meet several important tests. Are the activists a competent set of individuals who perform their tasks with a satisfactory level of efficiency? And, although a diverse and relatively inclusive group of persons, are those who work in parties committed to the party and motivated to achieve its goals? Is their morale high—that is, do they feel they have an important role and input into organizational decisions and actions? At least these three structural requisites are critical: competence, commitment, and morale.

In functional terms, the requisites are even more demanding. First, party organizations need to constantly attract people to participate in party politics, to empower them in the political process. Second, they have to also recruit people for political leadership and have some control over the leadership selection process. If the top leadership of a city is not screened by or promoted through the party organizations, this is a sign of the irrelevance of parties. Third, parties must be ideological arenas, where the issues are debated and proposals for problem resolution are advanced. It is hoped that the party organization in the last analysis will have an impact on the policy decisions of the city leadership. Fourth, party organization activists have the job of mobilizing the vote in campaigns, of "getting out the vote," and doing this in campaigns that present the party's program and its candidates effectively in combat with the opposition party. Finally, the party organization must perform the function, in all of these ways, of representing and channeling the public opinion and interests of all major sectors of the community. Parties should convert social preferences into political action.

The argument in this chapter is that Ann Arbor's parties have become truly competitive and durable structures because they do a relatively satisfactory job of meeting these requisites—not perfectly, by any means, and in some years much better than in others, but well enough to maintain the two-party system.

There are many tests of the performance of party organizations. One may be inclined to use a simple test such as the mobilization of a high turnout of voters in April elections. If that were the test, the party organizations would not seem very impressive since normally only 20 percent to 25 percent of the eligible voters vote in Ann Arbor's April elections. Ann Arbor suffers, as do all American cities, from the disinterest, complacency, and disaffection of the public for voting. Rather, the test for parties is meeting a broader and more complex set of expected roles. They must compete efficiently and programmatically, with able leadership, for the electoral market that in reality exists, for those voters who *are* mobilizable.

One of the real tests is the capacity of the parties to maintain large and loyal partisan support groups who regularly vote for their party. In the past twenty Ann Arbor local elections, the two parties have done this very competitively. The Democrats and Republicans have nearly split the two-party mayoral vote, 48.3 percent to 51.7 percent, and the vote for council, 49.3 percent to 50.7 percent. That is indeed close competition. It is one major evidence of the durability and viability of the two party organizations. The evidence in support of this argument is based on three surveys conducted in 1980, 1982, and 1986, in which we interviewed a large sample of Democratic and Republican party leaders at the precinct and city level. In all, 189 such organization activists were interviewed. The 1986 study will be primarily used. It included precinct workers as well as prominent city leaders, including candidates for mayor and city council.[2]

The Role of the Party Organizations in Recruiting Top Leadership

In the early postwar period, up to the late 1950s, the party organizations had a limited role in selecting candidates. Indeed, the large majority of candidates had little experience in party work and were essentially self-starters, particularly the Democratic candidates. With the development of coherent organizations in the fifties, that began to change. Prominent candidates in both parties were more frequently asked by the parties to run. Candidates came up through the organization as precinct leaders, campaign workers, ward chairs, and officers on the city party committee. Republican mayors such as Gerald Jernigan (party chair in 1982), Louis Belcher (party chair 1970), and James Stephenson (active for twenty years in the party organization) are particularly good examples. Democratic mayors Elizabeth Brater, Albert Wheeler, Edward Pierce, and Samuel Eldersveld worked long and hard within the organization, as did many other candidates.

A thorough investigation was made of all candidates for mayor and council from 1946 to the present. On the basis of available evidence, it is clear that the party organization has became increasingly important as a training ground as well as launching pad for candidates for local office. The data are summarized in table 4.1.

Candidates are more likely today than ever to come up through the party organization. In the most recent period from 1981 on, two-thirds of the Democratic and the Republican candidates had party experience, many at the level of the city party organization as well as in precinct and campaign work.

Of even greater significance is the relevance of party organization experience to winning the mayoralty or a seat on the council. A summary of all data for the postwar period suggests the change that occurred. Before 1976 19 percent of all candidates who won had party experience, compared to 17 percent of those who lost. After 1976, the percentages with party experience were 67 percent for those who won, compared to 41 percent of those who lost.

Earlier there were candidates who won without party experience (80 percent), that is, self-starters who were not exposed very much to politics through parties. Today there are still persons who run without such experience, but the probability of winning is much lower. The party organizations clearly have become more important as channels or arenas for selecting the city's leaders and mobilizing support for them to win.

How Inclusive and Representative of Social Sectors Are the Party Organizations?

Ann Arbor's parties face the same problems and dilemmas in attracting people into their organizations as elsewhere, but despite much apathy and many constraints they have done quite well. The basic dilemma is whether to claim to be completely open to all persons or in fact to discourage from becoming activists certain types of persons who might be less loyal and effective. In reality parties usually do both. In addition, persons with certain social backgrounds will not be attracted because they do not have the time or inclination to be active. As a result, a social bias is found when one looks at the social background of organization activists, as the 1986 study found (table 4.2). The imbalances in relation to the Ann Arbor population are obvious: this is a white, well-educated, bourgeois elite, which does not match certain characteristics of Ann Arbor's population very well.

Nevertheless these are diversified sets of activists (table 4.3). They are not dominated by males! Further, many occupations are represented

TABLE 4.1. Increase in Party Experience For Candidates, 1946–91

	% of Candidates with Experience in the Party Organization			
	1946–60	1961–70	1971–80	1981–91
Total	10%	22	39	65
Democrats	3	24	40	69
Republicans	20	21	38	62
Total candidates (data available)	106	77	108	93

Source: The *Ann Arbor News* and party records.

(for example, fewer lawyers than one might have expected). In some respects the two parties attract activists with quite different social backgrounds. The Democrats with more Jews and Catholics and those not religiously active; the Republicans with more Protestants and regular church-goers the Democrats more people with professional occupations; the Republicans more from the business community. Between the sexes, Democratic women outnumber men by about a 3-to-2 ratio, while the proportions are reversed among the Republicans. These asymmetries in recruitment are the result of differential organizational appeals as well as the natural processes of self-recruitment into parties. The result is that the parties, despite much social overlap, have some different constituency emphases. They are by no means identical social coalitions. This means also that the social groups in Ann Arbor have alternative opportunities for involvement in local party organizational work.

Ann Arbor's party organizations in some respects have a different social profile than we find in cities like Detroit and Los Angeles where similar studies of activists have been done (table 4.4). Party organizations tend to reflect and adapt to their populations if they are to successfully mobilize the vote. The Detroit population was 63 percent black in 1980; in Los Angeles it was only 17 percent black; in Ann Arbor, 9.5 percent. The party organization activists reflect these population distributions clearly.[3] Similarly the proportions of blue collar workers and union members in the

TABLE 4.2. The Social Bias in the Background of Party Activists

	Republicans	Democrats	Ann Arbor's Population (1980 census)
Education			
% college graduates	83.0%	81.0%	56.0%
Median Family Income[a]			
1980	$35,000	$30,000	$25,202
1986	$44,000	$46,000	—
Age Distribution			
% under 30	32.0%	17.0%	54.0%[b]
% 60+	20.0%	4.0%	5.0%[c]
Race			
% black	3.0%	1.0%	9.3%

Source: The data in this chapter are derived from or based on the studies of the party organization activists conducted by the author and referred to in the text—except where otherwise indicated.

Note: Data for activists are from the 1986 study unless otherwise indicated.

[a]Income calculations are estimates based on responses in interviews with activists in each year.

[b]Represents ages 18–34.

[c]Represents ages 55–64.

work force in Detroit and Los Angeles are related to the socioeconomic characteristics of party activists in these cities, in contrast to Ann Arbor. Two key points emerge, therefore, as we study these comparisons: (1) the organization activists reflect (though imperfectly) the changes in the character of the population, and (2) social groups have decidedly different opportunities for involvement in politics by community, dependent on their proportionate strength in the population. Blacks, union members, blue-collar workers, and those with no college education are major components of party organizations in Detroit, but not in Ann Arbor. Communities have their own organizational culture, and activists are linked to their particular culture in their community.

Ann Arbor's party activists are closely integrated with the Ann Arbor community. They have lived in their neighborhoods a long time (over 40 percent more than ten years), a high percentage (60 percent) are married with families, and 80 percent belong to at least one community group

TABLE 4.3. Social Diversity and Opportunity within the Party Organizations, 1986

	% of Each Party Group	
	Republicans	Democrats
Gender		
Women	42	62
Men	58	38
Occupations		
Lawyers	7	6
Teachers	7	10
Other Professionals	30	55
Business-Managerial	10	2
Sales/Clerical/Service	23	18
Students/Homemakers/Retired/ Blue-collar Workers	23	10
Total with professional jobs	44	71
Religious Affiliation		
Protestant	76	42
Catholic	16	8
Jewish	0	23
No religion	0	19
Religious Activity		
Attend religious services "usually"	68	29
Nationality Origins		
Northern Europe	79	60
South and Eastern Europe	15	15

Source: The author's survey of party activists.

(45 percent to two or more such groups). Above all, over 50 percent of these activists have worked in their parties for more than ten years. Most of these activists, then, know the city, its politics, and its political culture.

In terms of the party conflict model of Ann Arbor politics, these findings are very relevant. They reveal the two parties with activists who are well-educated and diverse occupationally and in the representation of age groups, genders, and religious affiliation. They are well integrated in the community. They are by no means a socially representative elite. But neither do these activists constitute a homogeneous, narrow social force. The activists of the two parties are too pluralized and diverse for that, and they clearly appeal to and find support from different social groups. This asymmetry bolsters the operation of the two-party system in Ann Arbor.

Political Backgrounds

Party organizations need workers who are trained and fit, then properly motivated and deployed. The level of competence and experience is

TABLE 4.4. A Comparison of Ann Arbor Party Activists with Those in Two Other Cities, 1980

	Ann Arbor		Detroit		Los Angeles	
% of each party group	Dem.	Rep.	Dem.	Rep.	Dem.	Rep.
Race						
Black	1	3	59	35	10	2
Union Status						
Members	26	18	60	32	47	15
Nonmembers	74	82	40	68	53	85
Education						
Graduate or professional education	65	43	36	37	47	48
High school education or less	0	0	20	14	6	5
Religion						
Protestant	42	76	44	41	40	65
Jewish	23	4	4	5	19	7
Blue-collar workers	0	10	26	16	22	19
Gender						
Women	47	46	42	38	37	37
Men	53	54	58	62	63	63

Sources: The Detroit and Los Angeles data came from studies completed in 1980, and reported in S. Eldersveld, *Political Parties in American Society* (New York: Basic Books, 1982), pp. 171–74. The Los Angeles study was done by Dwaine Marvick at UCLA, the Detroit study by the author. The Ann Arbor data used here are from the 1980 study, for purposes of comparison with the other two cities. They differ somewhat, but not significantly, from the 1986 findings.

critical for party success. The studies of the activists indicate that Ann Arbor does have such party structures. Each party appears to have a revolving elite, consisting of new activists, those active for a short period, and those with long careers in party campaigns. Many of them were socialized to politics in their youths, entered party work purposively, find it interesting and self-satisfying, and "have been around" in the local parties either intermittently or continuously for many years.

Some of the evidence that this is so is found in table 4.5. The activists are exposed to politics while growing up. In their families politics was discussed a great deal—47 percent said "very much," compared to 27 percent for the Ann Arbor public generally. Their parents were active in community and party affairs. They have held a great variety of

TABLE 4.5. The Political Backgrounds and Experience of the Party Activists

	Democrats	Republicans
Parental Involvement (at least one parent active)		
in community affairs	65%	50
in party affairs	40	32
Discussion of Politics in the Home While Growing Up		
% "very much"	59	36
Years Active in the Party		
over 20 years	12	14
10–20 years	36	43
5–10 years	32	13
less than 5 years	20	29
Types of Party Positions Held		
Precinct Leader	77	75
Convention Delegate	69	58
County Committee	35	33
District Level Official	23	17
National Convention Delegate	4	6
Contacts with Party Leaders (% who see them at least monthly)		
County or district leaders	66	59
State party leaders	17	17
Time Commitment to Party Work: Hours per week spent on campaign		
Over 20	19%	16
11–20	8	8
Up to 10	65	71
No hours or "little time"	8	5

Note: Figures based on 1986 data.

party positions at the precinct, city, county, and district level, so their perspectives are not too narrowly parochial. They are an interactive elite, seeing party leaders at the levels above them very frequently. Above all, they commit much time to party politics, especially in campaigns. Over 25 percent spend more than ten hours a week; few give no time to party work.

The image that emerges from these data is of two hard-working cadres of activists, many well-trained, committed to and giving many hours of their time as volunteers (they are unpaid), and with fairly wide-ranging and cosmopolitan party contacts. There is a periodic invigoration of new talent and energy to complement the experience of the stalwarts.

The interviews with these activists yield other significant findings. When asked whether they would be willing to continue working and taking a more responsible position, over 50 percent say yes. When asked whether they find party work satisfying, 90 percent respond affirmatively. To most, it is a worthwhile activity and they aspire to stay on it. They also want to have a say in their organizations. While generally of the opinion that they are consulted to some extent (69 percent of the Republicans and 90 percent of the Democrats), almost 60 percent in both parties want more say. This is evidence, again, of rather high morale, basic interest in the organization, and commitment. These are, after all, strong partisans (over 90 percent are "very strong" or "fairly strong" in their party loyalty), and they insist on a decisional role in their parties.

Finally, the surveys reveal that Ann Arbor party activists have a strong motivational basis for their involvement. But their motives are considerably diverse. Table 4.6 gives some of the most prominent reasons given for *becoming active.*

TABLE 4.6. Motivations of Activists for Becoming Involved

% Saying Item is "very important"	Democrats	Republicans
To influence the policies of government	69%	66
To fulfill my sense of community obligation	50	57
Strong attachment to my political party	39	31
Enjoyment of the fun and excitement of campaign	31	24
Enjoyment of friendship and social contacts with party workers	27	20
A personal friendship for a candidate	27	15
I am trying to build a personal career in politics	15	12

Source: The data in this chapter are derived from or based on the studies of party organization activists conducted by the author and referred to in the text—except where otherwise indicated.

Ideological, philosophical, and social incentives predominate in the explanations for becoming active. There is very little of material incentives here as a reason for engaging in party organization work. When asked, "What are your *current* satisfactions?" we find that there is a shift while they are in party work toward solidarity satisfactions (social contacts, friendships, campaign fun, and the like). In the 1986 study, 80 percent of the activists said their primary motivation for *joining* was ideological or philosophical; when asked their primary motivation *currently*, only 47 percent still said it was ideological or philosophical. This does not mean that ideology is unimportant, as our analysis in the next section reveals. The party organization thus means different things to people. For some it is a significant policy relevant group, for others a social group, for others a group to advance more instrumental personal goals.

There is a considerable sense of dynamism when one looks at the motivations, career paths, aspirations, morale, and experience patterns of the activists. These Ann Arbor party structures appear to be diversified, fairly competent, high-spirited collections of activists. They have evolved over time their own organizational esprit, ethos, and culture. They appear to have the potential to be very efficient structures. Whether they are will be discussed subsequently.

The Role of Ideology: Activists and Voters

If anything, political ideology and issues on public policy have become more important for party activists. In 1986 almost half of the activists said their motivation was primarily ideological. Previously this was true of no more than one-fourth. Party conflict has probably become more confrontational in issue terms—for activists and for the top elites. This can be demonstrated by a comparison of the first study (1980) with the third study (1986). In 1980 71 percent of the Democratic activists said they were "liberals," but 88 percent did so in 1986. On the other hand, 43 percent of the Republicans were self declared "conservatives" in 1980 but that increased to 60 percent in 1986.

Ann Arbor's parties have always been ideologically distinctive, but this has become increasingly so in the 1980s. There is a 17 percent increase in liberalism for the Democrats and a 17 percent increase in conservatism among Republicans a 64-point ideological gap has become an 83-point gap!

The positions of the activists on specific issues tend to document this basic asymmetry in ideological position (table 4.7). On most of these issues, the Democrats were so liberal in the early survey that very little change occurred. The Republicans did become more conservative, particularly on nuclear disarmament, defense spending, and helping the poor. On only two issues did they become more liberal: pollution and helping third-world countries. Yet their average liberalism on these eight issues is only 24 percent compared to over 80 percent for Democratic activists. On the question in 1986 of working toward the adoption of a workable gun-control ordinance locally, 38 percent of the Republicans approved and said we should "do more" while 85 percent of Democrats approved. There is internal disagreement and hidden conflict in both parties on some of these issues. But on balance, it is clear there are two sets of party cadres which are basically different in ideology and which are associated with different policy choices at the governmental decision-making level.

Ideology is important to these activists, but they are also pragmatists—their responses to particular statements demonstrate that. For example, from 70 percent to 80 percent of the Democratic and Republican activists disagree with the statements "Parties should not take controversial stands on issues" and "Parties should play down hot issues in campaigns if they will hurt the chances of winning." But they are also supporters of volunteerism, opening up participation, and decentralizing control of their organizations. And they do not believe in excluding people or running them out of the party just because they may disagree on specific issues or candidates. Their responses to two other statements bear this out (table 4.8).

Thus these are not ideologically rigid structures. Dissent is certainly

TABLE 4.7. Specific Issue Positions among Ann Arbor Party Activists

% Taking the "Liberal" Position of Wanting the Government to Do More	1982		1986	
	Dem.	Rep.	Dem.	Rep.
Nuclear disarmament	97%	82	92	27
Cut defense spending	94	63	88	17
Expand opportunities for the poor	97	54	92	28
Desegregate housing and schools	69	19	69	6
Stop air and water pollution	94	50	92	60
Require energy-saving practices	71	30	68	19
Help third-world countries	57	4	69	24
"Reduce" America's military strength[a]	83	14	81	11
Average "liberalism"	82.8	39.5	81.4	24.0

Source: The author's studies of party organization leaders in the years indicated.
[a]Percentage who want the government to do "less" on "increasing" America's military strength.

tolerated. The party belongs to its activists, whoever they are. At the same time, the party is serious ideological business.

The Link between Activists and Loyal Supporters

The link between the activists and the regular supporters of the party in the public is a close one ideologically. The 1984 study permitted a study of the congruence of the party elites and their mass supporters. The "loyal supporters" are defined as those who identified with either the Democratic or Republican parties and voted regularly for that party in city elections. A comparison then becomes possible between these two strata for each party: the organization activists and the loyal supporters (table 4.9).

One should note that the loyal supporters are distinctive from the rest of our public. Table 4.9 gives some illustrations. The loyalists clearly have a fairly high level of political interest. Using a question asking respondents to state how they would label themselves ideologically (liberal, moderate, or conservative), the juxtaposition of activists and supporters can be demonstrated. The match is very close. Practically no Democrats call themselves conservatives (no activists, and only 6 percent of the supporters), and practically no Republicans call them liberals (5 percent of the activists, 4 percent of the supporters). The contrasts with the distributions for the Ann Arbor public are obvious, as is the distance between the parties: on the liberal side, an 83-point difference between the activists and a 58-point difference for the loyal supporters. The Democratic activists are more liberal than their followers; the Republican activists are more conservative than their followers.

The congruence of activists and followers is also demonstrable for the two particular issues on which data were available in both studies. The almost identical Democratic percentages for activists and support-

TABLE 4.8. Responses by Party Activists

	Percent agree	
	Democrats	Republicans
"If you disagree with a major stand of your party you should stop working for it"	19%	14
"A good party worker must support any candidate nominated by the party, even if he or she basically disagrees with the candidate"	16	34

ers is truly striking. The Republicans are also relatively congruent, although on both defense spending and providing economic help for the poor and minorities, the Republican supporters reveal more liberalism than their activists.

The implication of this analysis is that activists are strongly committed to general ideological positions as well as clearly taking sides on specific issues. In both respects, they appear to be responsive to and representative of the positions of their loyal supporters in the public.

TABLE 4.9. Elite-Mass Relationships: A Comparison of the Ideology of Party Activists in the Organization and Loyal Supporters in the Public

	Democrats		Republicans		
	Activists (1986)	Loyal Supporters (1984)	Activists (1986)	Loyal Supporters (1984)	Ann Arbor Public (1984)
Ideological Self-Classification					
Liberal	88%	62	5	4	36
Moderate	12	32	35	44	44
Conservative	0	6	60	52	20
Illustrative Issues					
Defense Spending % expressing preference for cuts	88	88	17	32	82
Economic Assistance for the Poor and Minorities % favoring more government help	92	96	28	48	59
N	39	47	29	27	220

Sources: Two studies are used as a basis for these data: the 1984 sample of the Ann Arbor public and the 1986 study of Republican and Democratic party activists. This time lag of two years should be kept in mind.

TABLE 4.10. The Distinctive Involvement of Loyal Party Supporters

	Loyal Democrats	Loyal Republicans	Rest of the Public (sample)
Voted in Most Elections	53%	63	10
Knowledgeable About City Government	87	84	52
Contributed Money to the Parties	58	68	28
Support Partisan Elections	71	68	54

Source: Author's 1984 survey of Ann Arbor adults.

Activism and Its Impact

This is really the critical issue: What does the organization do and with what functional consequences? If the party organizations are to survive and be the effective political base for the top leaders as well as the effective link with the public, their actions need to be especially, though not exclusively, relevant for vote mobilization. Many of these activists are experienced, committed, and competent. They report that they put in long hours during campaigns. What do they do and how effectively do they do it?

There is a great variety of tasks performed by the activists in both April and November campaigns (table 4.11). If one examines the data carefully one notices certain patterns:

1. The two parties are relatively combative, with the Democrats revealing slightly more effort than the Republicans (except for canvassing in November).
2. There is almost as much campaign effort in the April as in the November elections. The greatest differential may be getting out the vote on the day of election, higher in November for both parties.
3. Canvassing by telephone is engaged in by more activists in both April and November than is house-to-house canvassing. But both parties use both techniques.
4. There is considerable "slack" in both parties. Neither of them are operating anywhere near their peak capabilities.

TABLE 4.11. A Comparison of Campaign Activity Before the April and Fall Elections, 1986

% of Party Activists Engaging in Each Activity	Democrats		Republicans	
	April	November	April	November
Registration	30%	44	8	5
Fund-raising	44	59	30	38
Getting out the vote on election day	55	74	46	57
Canvassing, house to house	33	30	27	43
Canvassing, by phone	52	37	46	49
Distributing literature	70	74	49	65
Average[a]	47	53	34	42
Performed 2 of 3 critical tasks[b]	59	67	40	51

Source: The author's 1986 study of party organization leaders.
[a]Figures rounded to nearest whole number.
[b]Critical tasks are registration, convassing, and getting out the vote.

The three critical tasks of registering voters, canvassing them, and on election day bringing them to the polls are not performed by more than 25 percent of the activists. If we measure their task performance in terms of the execution of two of these three critical tasks, 40 percent of the Democrats failed in the April election and 60 percent of the Republicans did. Neither party fully exploits its potential organizational power, in April or in November.

Both groups of party leaders agree on what are the best techniques in Ann Arbor for persuading voters. Face-to-face canvassing at voters' homes, however, is considered very effective—by 89 percent of the Democrats and 64 percent of the Republicans. Their evaluations of other techniques are shown in table 4.12. Personal contact efforts seem to be important, but the use of other approaches is still considered effective. The increased role of the media is recognized by the activists in both parties as a new development in politics in recent years (by 73 percent of the Democrats and 95 percent of the Republicans), but they do not feel it has harmed the party organization very much (less than 10 percent feel it has weakened the parties). Rather, they think the parties are utilizing the new technology of media specialists to promote their candidates. While most activists see the local parties as "about the same" as ten years ago, our data suggest there may be somewhat less emphasis now on certain activities (such as voter registration). But one must remember that the parties never have operated at peak efficiency.

The question of the impact of party organizational activity on the vote is a key one, but poses considerable difficulty. Does the organization actually get out the vote? After all, that is a major test of the party's effectiveness. There has been much research on this question, most of it concluding that the organization can play a role in mobilizing the vote, but this varies by type of election, other stimuli to which people are

TABLE 4.12. Evaluation of Campaign Techniques by Activists

	% Saying Technique is Effective	
	Democrats	Republicans
Mailing Literature	57%	64
Media Ads (in newspapers, radio broadcasts, TV)	43	67
Telephone Canvassing	46	33
Billboards and Posters	20	20
Appeals at Group Meetings	34	39

Source: The author's 1986 study of party organization leaders.

exposed, and the strength of the rival organizations.[4] In such research, it is difficult to control for all influences on the voters, influences pressing them to vote or to stay home. However, although a difficult question, there are three key questions that can be answered with the Ann Arbor data. First, to what extent does the Ann Arbor public report that they were contacted by the parties during the campaign? The evidence for this in the 1984 study is impressive. Almost 50 percent reported that a party organization worker had contacted them in the fall campaign. This is very high and probably a bit exaggerated. Normally in national surveys, we find from 25 percent to 30 percent of the adult sample reporting such contact. What is interesting is that 24 percent claimed that both parties had canvassed them, suggesting the extent of overlap in party work, and the somewhat non-selective way in which parties do their canvassing. Sixteen percent said they were canvassed by Democrats only and 7 percent by Republicans only. Further, only 10 percent of the respondents objected to these canvassing efforts, and the remainder were split (44 percent positive, 44 percent neutral).

Second, does there seem to be an association between canvassing efforts and the vote for the parties? Again, the answer is affirmative. The data in table 4.13 are very suggestive: Obviously one must be very cautious in relying on these data, primarily because contact by itself was not the only distinguishing mark of the first group, nor was lack of contact the only distinguishing mark of the second group. Voting behavior is a multicausal phenomenon, so these results can be only suggestive, not definitive.

It must be recalled that in 1984 Mondale won in Ann Arbor by eight thousand votes over Reagan, and Carl Levin won overwhelmingly, with 65 percent of the vote over Jack Lousma. The 1984 election produced a higher turnout of eligible voters in Ann Arbor than nationally—60 per-

TABLE 4.13. Voting Behavior in Ann Arbor in the 1984 Presidential Election, by Party Contact

	Democratic Identifiers	Republican Identifiers
Among those contacted by the parties		
Voted for Mondale	90%	5
Voted for Reagan	4	90
Among those Not Contacted by the Parties		
Voted for Mondale	77	12
Voted for Reagan	9	80
Difference Between Contact and No Contact	13	10

Source: Based on Author's Survey of the Ann Arbor Public in 1984.

cent compared to 53 percent. These contact efforts may have contributed to this higher turnout, and it is possible to see from these data how contacts may have led to a Mondale victory. More people were contacted by Democrats, and Republicans crossed over more than Democrats did.

Third, is nonvoting possibly increased as a result of the lack of party canvassing efforts? Again, the evidence is slightly affirmative. There was 5 percent greater nonvoting reported by those not contacted by the parties. Again, no cause-effect relationship can be clearly demonstrated, and the finding is merely suggestive. A further question is whether contact reduces the defection of party regulars—that is, those who split their ballots, voting for the candidate for president of one party and for the candidate for Congress of the other party. In 1984 it was found that party contact efforts may be relevant. Those engaging in ballot-splitting on the Democratic side (supporting the Republican candidate for Congress) were more likely to do this if not contacted by party workers during the campaign. The Republican congressional candidate won in Ann Arbor that year with 55 percent of the vote, and this desertion of Democrats was largely responsible. No Republican identifiers split their ballots for the Democratic congressional candidate.

An analysis of the April election in 1984 reveals similar patterns of voting behavior related to party organizational contacts. Only 32 percent of the public reported that they were canvassed by the parties, lower than in the fall campaign. The results, based on the responses to the survey, suggest again that contacts are linked to higher voting turnout. Of those citizens not contacted 76 percent said they did not vote, compared to a nonvoting record of 55 percent for those who were contacted. Further, those contacted by Democrats voted for Democrats (33 percent to 5 percent) while those contacted by Republicans voted Republican (38 percent to 0). While clearly the parties were inclined to seek out their own partisans, there was overlap again—half of those canvassed were approached by both parties. In the 1984 city council election, the vote was low (a 16 percent turnout) and the results were close (49.6 percent Democratic, 50.4 percent Republican). It may be that the greater canvassing efforts by the Democrats (at least a two-to-one advantage) saved the Democrats from a much greater defeat during a period when the Republicans were controlling city hall and voter apathy was high.

Overall there is evidence here that organizational activism is important and has effects. Both parties in Ann Arbor are fairly involved in campaigns, and this may be linked to (1) the reinforcement of the vote of their partisans, (2) the reduction of defection and desertion, (3) the increase in participation, and (4) the maintenance of the parties' organizational strength and the morale of the activists.

What is baffling is the low turnouts in April elections. Turnouts of eligible voters in April elections hover around 22 percent to 24 percent: 1987 (22.9 percent), 1988 (28.6 percent), 1989 (20.1 percent), 1990 (27.8 percent), 1991 (24.6 percent). Turnouts in the fall elections are 60 percent or higher. Why cannot this competent set of activists produce higher April turnouts? A variety of explanations are possible. Some Americans rebel at the frequency with which they have to go to the polls, and April seems less relevant to their lives than does November. One also can argue that the candidates are not as attractive in April, nor are the campaigns as stimulating. In April campaigns, the job of motivating voters is more difficult, and Ann Arbor party activists have to confront the same voter apathy trends that pervade all sections of America. Actually, the turnouts in Ann Arbor for national elections are higher than is true generally in the country, and the work of the activists probably keeps voter participation from declining further. Another point to be made is that the organizations clearly are not working at their peak levels of performance. At most, they have a 30 percent efficiency level. By motivating and utilizing their potential activist work force, they may be able to increase turnout another 10 or 20 percent. In 1971–73, the highest turnouts in city elections occurred—over 40 percent of eligible voters. That might well be the goal today for both parties. This problem of voting participation will be discussed in greater detail in a subsequent chapter.

Concluding Observations

The basic thesis in this chapter has been that the party-conflict model requires strong party organizations staffed from the precinct level to the city level with able, motivated, committed cadres of activists integrated with the life of the community and linked to loyal partisan groups in the electorate.

In reviewing the data from the studies done in the 1980s and reflecting on their significance, this thesis was demonstrated to a considerable extent. Certain basic points stand out in the analysis. These organization activists are clearly very bourgeois in socioeconomic status, part of the professional-business structure of the Ann Arbor community. They are well educated, well-off financially, and white. They are integrated with the city and satisfied with life in Ann Arbor.

These leaders are an experienced elite for the most part, veterans of many partisan confrontations. They have not only worked many years in party politics, but have held many party positions, from precinct leader to the state central committee to state and even national convention delegate. They work, they say, rather long hours, many spending over twenty hours a week on the campaign. They are strong and loyal followers of the party, over 50 percent intending to stay on (and perhaps move up). They also demand a say in party affairs.

The motivations for party work are complex and difficult to disentangle. Activists have a strong desire to influence governmental policies, but they also admit that leaving party work would be distressing above all because they would miss their social contacts and the fun of politics. As individuals and as structures, they are a complex blend of idealistic amateurs and pragmatic professionals.

While bourgeois in social backgrounds, ideologically they diverge sharply. The Ann Arbor Democratic and Republican cadres are in ideological terms asymmetric: they are distinctive in their views on policy questions. The Democrats are likely to see themselves as radicals or liberals and the Republicans as moderates and conservatives. More important, their positions on specific issues are often in striking contrast. Nevertheless, there is considerable variation by issue, as well as a certain amount of genuine dissensus within each party organization on certain issues. The Democrats appear to be the more homogeneous group, among its leadership and in terms of the leadership relationships to its followers. Above all, here are two truly contrasting and combative sets of party leaders providing the Ann Arbor public some real policy and participatory choices.

As to their activities in the campaign, their performance is as good as, if not better than, elsewhere probably. The Democrats do at times perform at a higher level than the Republicans, although the competition is very close. But a major mystery emerges: Why cannot such a competent set of activists produce a higher turnout at city elections? We have suggested some reasons why this may be so. Despite considerable party work, the parties just cannot counteract voter apathy in April, apathy greater now than it was in the 1970s. Yet, the parties maintain themselves as strong organizations through the work of their activists and compete fairly evenly. That is the crux of the matter. While the apathetics stay home, the party organizations maintain close competitive relationships with their loyal partisans and the attentive public. For the effective survival of the party system in Ann Arbor, those functional relationships have been, if anything, strengthened. This strong linkage of the organization to loyal support groups has been critical. Despite voter apathy, then, the party organizations have fulfilled rather well the requisites for a vital party system.

CHAPTER 5

Interest Groups and Party Politics in Ann Arbor: A Social and Political Symbiosis?

Scholars of American state and national politics have in recent years expressed much interest, if not concern, over the proliferation of interest groups and their influence. Indeed, it is alleged this has led to the decline of parties. This used to be the case also for city politics. Scholars saw either certain interest groups dominating city government or a diversity of specialized interest groups seeking control over decisions in particular policy areas.[1] The former analysis led to the power elite model of local government, and the latter approach produced the pluralist model, which caught on with American political scientists. The theory emerged that in U.S. cities, interest groups played major roles in the representation of citizen demands, in the selection of leaders, and in policy formulation. Parties were considered only as one actor among many, if important at all.

More recently, recognized scholars are more inclined to see the group infrastructure of most cities as very weak. Peterson writes, "Local politics is groupless politics," citing other scholars with the same basic observation.[2] In Ann Arbor, politics is certainly not groupless. Rather, the important question is: What is the relation between the many interest groups and their leaders to parties and, hence, to city hall? Under a system of partisan government, where do the city's interest groups fit in? Are they dominant, weak, or nonexistent? And for those that do take a major interest in city policy concerns, how do they interact with the parties—are they supportive, collaborative, or hostile?

Ann Arbor has had a long tradition of lively interest groups, general or special, city wide or neighborhood. Interest groups have been part of the political conflict environment often in the period following World War II. The chamber of commerce has had from time to time a considerable influence on city council, particularly on economic and land-utilization decisions. One example in the 1980s was the establishment of the Downtown Development Authority D.D.A. The Realtors also have played a role in planning decisions. The League of Women Voters is an example of another group that has fought for certain specific actions, one very significant one being the charter revision adopted in 1956. Neighborhood groups have been visible in supporting or attacking proposed council action on shopping centers, rezoning efforts, the location of public housing sites, and the like. Even the University of Michigan has been an interest group, working with the city as well as pressuring the city on a variety of planning and service decisions. Other specialized interest groups (such as the Homeless Action Group recently) have also been involved in specific policy areas,

Many political battles in Ann Arbor have featured aroused and voluble interest groups. These confrontational episodes, however, are sporadic. They occur over particular questions, reach a crescendo of involvement, then subside. There are those who are critical of these groups and their actions, as Mayor Robert Harris was in his speech to council in 1973 at the close of his term of office. He felt that neighborhood groups in particular represented "parochial interests" versus the general interest and "already (have) too much power." On the positive side, however, interest groups contribute to the public debate, can intensify it considerably, and can influence the agendas and actions of city council. Whether they should is another matter.

The major objective in this chapter is to analyze how and to what extent interest groups are involved in city politics and, above all, what their relationship to the political parties is. There is no question they have influence. The more basic question is how they fit into the party conflict model of governance in Ann Arbor.

In the 1984 study of the Ann Arbor public, 39 percent of the respondents said they were active in at least one group, a rather high proportion-but this includes a great diversity of groups, ranging from the chamber of commerce, to the Square Dance Club. The proportion who belonged to political interest groups relevant for *city* politics was 20 percent.[3] This 20 percent, which constitutes the relevant public base for the discussion here, was distributed as follows by the type of political interest group: business (11 percent), labor (4 percent), civic (33 percent), women's (19 percent), fraternal and veterans' (6 percent), environmental (18 percent), and residual groups including pacifists, racial or ethnic groups, senior citizens associations, and others (9 percent). These data reflect the existence of a considerable interest by Ann Arbor citizens in a diverse set of political groups, some explicitly focused on city government problems, others more generally and occasionally aroused by political questions. These data validate the decisions made in the study of interest group leaders later.

The Study of Interest-Group Leaders

In the 1983 study of Ann Arbor's political interest groups, the emphasis was to do a study of leaders, not of the organizations in great detail. The primary aim was to discover what types of persons provided leadership for these groups, and particularly what their views were about partisan politics in Ann Arbor. The number of groups who may at some time take an interest in public questions is large, probably several hundred (no one census is available). The final selection of groups was purposefully done, selected from a large potential list. This was based on what experience had suggested were those groups probably most likely and most frequently to be concerned with city policy issues. The final list included the following:

Chamber of Commerce
Junior Chamber of Commerce (Jaycees)
Board of Realtors
League of Women Voters (LWV)
National Association for the Advancement of Colored People (NAACP)
Ann Arbor Community Center
Veterans of Foreign Wars (VFW)
Washtenaw Bar Association
Washtenaw County Medical Society
Physicians for Social Responsibility
American Friends Service Committee
Inter Faith Council for Peace
United Auto Workers (UAW) Locals 782, 898, 1776 and Court Employees Association
American Federation of State, County and Municipal Employees (AFSCME) Local 2733
American Federation of Labor-Congress of Industrial Organizations (AFL-CIO) Local 434
Huron Valley Labor Council
Women's Peace Camp
Michigan Daily
Ann Arbor News
Ann Arbor Cablevision
WPAG
WAAM
University of Michigan

This list does not include any specific neighborhood groups, and a systematic study of neighborhood groups or their leaders was not done; resources limited what was possible. While spreading the net wide, we did impose certain limits. The focus was on Ann Arbor politics, not on school board politics, nor on groups oriented to county or township politics. Certain groups were excluded also, such as church and sports groups, whose interest can be political but usually is not, at least not primarily. Nevertheless, while not inclusive, this set of groups probably provided good coverage and representation of the major relevant interests. There were one or two group refusals, such as the American Legion, and the hunch that all these groups were interested in city problems was not borne out, as the interviews indicated. But that was one of the purposes of the research—to discover the extent of group interest in local politics.

Two approaches were used in selecting the persons to be interviewed. Included were those in the top positions in each organization—chairs, vice chairs, other officers. This positional elite was the leadership base with whom interviews were conducted. Then a sample of board members was drawn for the large organizations. For the lawyers, for example, two lists were developed, from which samples were drawn: a "politically active" list, arrived at by the advice of experts knowledgeable about Ann Arbor lawyers, and a "random" list, a set of lawyers picked at random from the complete list of all lawyers.

After a great deal of work, interviews were completed with 107 of these leaders of community interest groups. The respondents were generally very cooperative, although there were some refusals. Interviews were completed with over 70 percent of those contacted. Among the respondents were 15 chairs, 16 other officers, 25 board members, 15 who held other positions in their organizations, plus several former officers. Thus, while the number of respondents seems small, it should be remembered that interviews were done with most of the top officers and board members who were in directive roles in their organizations. These included the top leaders of the three business groups (Chamber, Jaycees, and Realtors); key labor leaders, several of the LWV leaders involved in city political affairs; the officers of the NAACP; four top reporters and editors for the *News*; three editors at the *Daily*; top managers for Cablevision, WPAG, and WAAM; top physicians; and many prominent lawyers who had been or were currently active in politics. The very top University of Michigan leaders were somewhat reluctant, but nine officials provided interviews, persons who were close to the top and highly knowledgeable about the university's relations with the city.

On the basis of this evidence, there is considerable confidence that the study included interviews with persons who can be said to represent fairly well the political interest group infrastructure of Ann Arbor. Of the 107 leaders interviewed, 83 turned out to be the core group who obviously held key interest group positions or were active in city relevant policy/ political affairs. Most of the respondents had been active in their groups for many years—60 percent for over five years 44 percent over ten years. Many had been on their boards or held executive positions for half of that time. When asked the hours per week they devoted to their organizations, 33 percent said "full time." And 72 percent agreed that their work was indeed "political." Some were reluctant to admit this and made convincing arguments that they were not very "political." By type of interest group here is the distribution of respondents:

Business	23
Labor	10
Law	18
Physicians	6
Media	20
LWV	7
Vets	3
Pacifists	7
Blacks	4
University	9

Those considered least involved in city affairs were the VFW, the pacifists, some of the Jaycees (who insisted on their minimal interest in city government), and most of the physicians. Others, often despite their arguments to the contrary, were included in our core group of 83.

The Thesis

This study of interest groups in Ann Arbor is a limited one. It did not focus on the origins and history of these groups, nor their organization and membership, nor their resources, nor their day-to-day operations. Instead, the study concentrated on the leadership of these groups, particularly their political backgrounds, attitudes, approaches to city politics, evaluations of city government performance, contacts with the parties, and assessments of the functioning of the parties in Ann Arbor's political life. There were three possible theoretical positions concerning the relationships of the interest group leaders to parties which could be explored:

1. *Interest-group leaders could view the parties with hostility*. They could be critical of the leadership of parties, be unwilling to work with and through parties, and hold a strong preference for a nonpartisan system.
2. *Interest-group leaders could take a neutral, arms-length, stance vis-à-vis the parties*. They could consider them tolerable, but not particularly effective. These leaders could see themselves as separate from, not working through, the parties, but minimally accepting of them.
3. *Interest-group leaders could demonstrate strong support for the Ann Arbor party system*. This would include positively evaluating the roles of parties, finding it quite possible to work through parties—indeed, contributing activity and financial support to the parties and socializing frequently with party leaders.

While exploring all three theories, the thesis advanced and argued for here is the third theoretical position. It comes closest to reality, although for some groups the second theoretical position has some validity. In effect, the contention is that interest groups and parties work side by side as two key institutional components of the system. There are supportive, truly interactive relationships between the leaders of the two sets of groups, although party leaders may become exasperated at certain times with interest group leaders, and vice versa. The ties of the leaders of parties and interest groups to each other are often close—professional ties and organizational ties—so close that in institutional terms, it may appear to be a symbiotic relationship for the leaders of some groups. It is clearly often a cooperative relationship. Yet, because the leaders of these groups are ideologically very different, there is conflict, with each other and with the parties, and hence, the need for resolution, which in the last analysis is a party function. After the decision is made, however, the ideological conflict subsides. Rarely do the leaders of these groups (or the party leaders) attack the Ann Arbor system—the party government model. Rather, while they may criticize a particular decision, they do not usually demand a change in the system. They appear to have been socialized to the acceptance of the Ann Arbor system, with the conviction that all things considered, it works quite well. Ann Arbor's party government model has considerable legitimacy with interest group leaders.

What strikes one in reading the 107 interviews with these Ann Arbor leaders is that few of them claimed a great deal of political influence for their groups. They did not express any feeling of "dominance" in Ann Arbor politics. Aside from one chamber of commerce board member who claimed that "the power center in Ann Arbor has been the business community," the interviewer was more likely to get comments such as the following from this person's fellowmembers and others: "The chamber is apolitical"; "business is not influential"; "business-people are the worst people in the world to get involved in the political process"; "business has influence but we aren't a controlling group." It is not that the chamber's goals are not political—members frankly admitted to being the "watchdog and advocate for business" at city hall and elsewhere. Rather, they said they are concerned with "any community problem related to business growth and the business climate." They didn't claim great success for their strategies, nor control over City Hall.

The university leaders, in contrast, claimed they "should be (and are) nonpolitical," and that "we have no contacts with political parties," but only "deal with our professional counterparts at city hall," which is disarmingly ambiguous and does not describe well what contacts university personnel do have and for what purposes. University leaders admitted close attention to city hall actions and frequent discussion with the mayor and councillors but they insisted on partisan neutrality.

Labor leaders claimed they are an important force in political life. They mobilize voters at election time, and may as individuals work in campaigns, but they did not claim that this gives them any explicit leverage at city hall.

Groups like the League of Women Voters formally disavow partisan positions and influence or attempts to exert such influence. "We have to be nonpartisan" is their slogan, although they admitted their members are often very partisan. The media wish to appear very neutral politically also, and none of the respondents from radio, cable, or the *Ann Arbor News* reported any experience in political parties or other groups. The *Daily* was more ready to make such an admission of party politics experience.

The Realtors, like those in the chamber, openly admitted to political goals. Their representatives said they did contact city council leaders directly, with some effect. But when pressed as to the extent of influence, there was the reply that "we are effective, but less so in Ann Arbor than elsewhere." Another set of leaders who asserted that they are not heard enough are the blacks, who said that working through the parties is more effective than working as an interest group, but that blacks as a group are not very influential. The most negative group in terms of attitude to parties was the pacifists, most of whom said that "neither party really addresses peace and justice issues."

The lawyers are a mixed set of respondents. Some argued that they are much less effective today than they used to be. Others saw lawyers as very influential, because they still run for office and/or work in the party organizations.

There are considerable variations, then, in the perceptions these leaders have of the importance of their groups in the Ann Arbor polity. For some leaders this leads to criticism of parties and a desire for another type of system. For the majority, however, there is basically fairly strong support for the current party governance model. This is probably linked to their positive evaluations of life in Ann Arbor. Almost all of them praise this community. It is to them "a nice town," "exciting intellectually," "a very stimulating place to live," and, above all, "a city that functions well."

Empirical Findings

Social Backgrounds

In terms of social backgrounds, interest-group leaders are a mirror image of the party organization leaders described earlier (table 5.1). They are well educated (53 percent with graduate education), hold professional and business-managerial occupations, are longtime residents, are more often Protestant (51 percent) than Catholic (16 percent), and are typically white, married, middle aged, and male (75 percent)—bourgeois elite, much like the party organization leaders. Interest-group leaders are more likely to have lived in Ann Arbor longer and are led more often by men, but otherwise, in terms of social class, the party and interest-group leaders seem interchangeable.

Interelite comparisons for Ann Arbor are in fact striking. It is as if the educated, professional-managerial, middle-aged, Protestant elite class is fractionally divided into those who lead interest groups and those who lead parties. If a third comparison is added, with those who are candidates for city office (to be analyzed in detail in a succeeding chapter), a remarkable coincidence of social backgrounds is discovered. The interelite comparison is given in table 5.2. This is very suggestive—three sets of political elites in close social symbiosis.

Political Backgrounds and Involvement

While fairly homogeneous in social backgrounds, these interest-group leaders are very divided in party identification (table 5.3). As is true for the Ann Arbor public, they tend to support the Democrats more than the Republicans—50 percent to 30 percent, roughly. Fewer than 20 percent prefer to consider themselves independents. Those uncommitted to parties are found primarily among the pacifists, the media leaders, and the League of Women Voters.

The party-identification contrasts of the interest groups are sharp. Labor is 90 percent Democratic (black 100 percent), while the Chamber of Commerce and Realtors are 80 percent Republican. Yet one must be

TABLE 5.1. The Similarity of Social Backgrounds: Interest-Group Leaders and Party Leaders

	Interest Groups (1983)	Party Organizations (1982)		
		Dem.	Rep.	Total
Occupational Status				
Professions	51%	72%	27%	52%
Business-Managerial	26	9	23	15
Other White-Collar	8	4	7	6
Blue-Collar	7	0	10	5
Students, Homemakers, Retired	9	15	33	23
Educational Level				
Less than a College Degree	22	8	31	19
College Degree	26	12	28	18
Graduate/Professional Education	53	80[a]	41	63
Length of Residence in Ann Arbor:				
10 years or longer	71	36	52	43
5–9 years	11	33	28	31
Age Distribution				
Under 30	10	14	11	12
31–59	81	83	75	79
60 and Over	9	3	14	9
Religion				
Protestant	51	31	71	50
Catholic	16	14	21	17
Jewish	8	23	4	14
No religion	16	23	4	14
Other	9	9	0	5
Church Attendance				
Attend "usually"	34	29	68	42
Race				
Black	8	3	0	2
Marital status				
Married	73	69	76	72
Gender				
Women	25	47	46	47

Note: We have used the 1982 study of Ann Arbor parties because it is in closer proximity to the the 1983 interest-group study. The 1986 party study reveals the same basic patterns. Some sections total 101 percent due to rounding.

[a]The Democrats' proportion of 80 percent graduate education in 1982 was high. In 1980 it was 65 percent; in 1986, 56 percent.

TABLE 5.2. The Social Background of Ann Arbor's Interest-Group and Party Leaders

	Interest-Group Leaders (1983)	Party Organization Leaders (1982)	Candidates for Ann Arbor City Government Office (1976–86)
Occupation			
Professional	51%	52	54
Business-managerial	26	15	18
Education			
Graduate/professional	53	63	52
Religion			
Protestant	51	50	38[a]
Catholic	16	17	13
Jewish	8	14	19
Race			
Black	8	2	10
Gender			
Women	25	47	33
Men	75	53	67

Source: Author's surveys of three types of leaders in the years indicated.
[a]These data on religion of candidates are based on a partial analysis (1980–86); complete religious data on candidates are not easily available.

TABLE 5.3. Party Identification of Interest-Group Leaders

	Total Group (*N* = 104)	Core Group (*N* = 83)	Lawyers (*N* = 18)
Strong Democrat	38%	39	28
Weak Democrat	12	14	28
Independent	19	13	6
Weak Republican	12	14	22
Strong Republican	19	20	17

	Other Groups							
	Business	Labor	Media	U of M	LWV	JC's	Blacks	Pacifists
Strong Democrat	13%	90	20	44	57	25	100	43
Weak Democrat	0	0	30	0	14	12		14
Independent	7	0	30	11	29	12		43
Weak Republican	27	10	5	22	0	12		
Strong Republican	53	0	15	22	0	38		

Source: Survey of Ann Arbor's interest groups conducted by author in 1983.

careful not to assume that these are support groups for the parties, even labor and business, though in their political loyalties and connections one can see where their preferences may lie. They maintain their separate interest-group identities. Note also that there is considerable party identification dissensus within certain groups. Only 50 percent of the media is pro-Democratic. The Jaycees are 50 percent Republican and 37 percent Democratic. The University of Michigan's leaders in the sample reflect a perfect balance—44 percent Democratic, 44 percent Republican, 11 percent independent.

The more important question is whether interest-group leaders are and have been active within the political parties in the city, or whether they ignore party involvement. The evidence reveals that the majority have had party and campaign experience. The basic breakdown by types of experience is given jin table 5.4. This set of interest-group leaders has obviously had close links with partisan politics—with both parties. Of the actives, 67 percent were involved with the Democrats, 33 percent with the Republicans. Business leaders (two-thirds of whom had some such experience) split 7–1 for the Republicans; labor leaders (90 percent of whom were involved) split 7–1 for the Democrats. Their work for the parties was varied: organizational, fund-raising, campaign management, and such.

To push this linkage analysis a little further, it is interesting again to compare interest-group and party organization leaders. Here we find evidence of a kind of reciprocal group involvement: interest group leaders are active in parties (66 percent); and party leaders are (and have been) active in interest groups (55 percent). Both sets of leaders have multiple group involvement. In addition, candidates for mayor and city council are active in politically relevant interest groups (67 percent). By confining the analysis of these three sets of political elites to only those group memberships that are politically relevant one can see the considerable mutuality of organizational involvement. While some elites do indeed tend to specialize in parties or in interest groups, the majority are

TABLE 5.4. Types of Political Activities of Interest-Group Leaders

	Total Group	Core Group	Lawyers
Worked in Campaigns	41%	43	50
Held Position in Party or Organization	23	28	44
Have Ever Run for Public Office	24	25	22
Have Held Local Appointive Office	18	33	28
Total with Some Type of Party or Campaign Involvement	62	66	78

Source: Survey of Ann Arbor's interest groups conducted by author in 1983.

joiners, and joiners of groups involved with political questions. While there appears to be an armslength posture between interest groups and the parties, there are in fact multiple interactions. This suggests again not only a social, but also a political, symbiosis in interelite networks.

Ideology

Just as with party loyalties, interest-group leaders reveal considerable dissensus in their ideological positions (table 5.5). Here again they mirror the ideological divisions between and within the party organizations. There are few straight, avowed, conservatives (12 percent of the total) and they are found, as expected, in the business groups. Only 9 percent of the business leaders call themselves liberal, while 67 percent of the civic group leaders do and 45 percent of the lawyers do. Overall, this is a

TABLE 5.5. Ideology and Issue Positions of Interest-Group Leaders

Basic Ideology (Self-Classification)	Interest-Group Leaders: Core Group	Interest-Group Leaders: Total Group	1982 Party Leaders: Dem.	1982 Party Leaders: Rep.
Liberal	34%	41	83	11
Moderate	50	42	17	61
Conservative	11	12	0	29
Other, unclear	5	5	0	0

Ideology for Specific Groups	Business	Labor	Law	Media	Civic	Univ.
Liberal	9%	20	45	30	67	33
Moderate	52	60	50	55	14	56
Conservative	35	10	5	5	5	11
Other, unclear	5	10	0	10	14	0

Ideology by Party Identification of Interest-Group Leaders	Democrats: Very Strong	Democrats: Strong	Democrats: Weak	Independents	Republicans: Very Strong + Strong	Republicans: Weak
Liberal	80%	64	29	45	0	0
Moderate	13	36	59	35	58	69
Conservative	0	0	6	5	42	31
Other, unclear	7	0	6	15	0	0

Source: Survey of Ann Arbor's interest groups conducted by author in 1983.
Note: Some columns total 101 percent due to rounding.

liberal—moderate set of elites, even among the strong Republicans. But, one should emphasize, it is not overwhelmingly liberal—only 41 percent so classify themselves (only 34 percent of the core group).

Therefore, the fit or matchup between interest-group leaders and party leaders is far from perfect. The Republican party leaders are somewhat more conservative than this set of interest-group leaders, 29 percent compared to 11 percent. The Democratic party leaders are *much* more liberal than these leaders, 83 percent compared to 34 percent. This indicates that there may be difficulties for some interest-group leaders to work with party leaders, and vice versa. There are few battles between the Democratic leaders and the chamber of commerce, but one can see why there might very well be. Similarly, civic leaders and Republicans might not get along together well ideologically. Again, note how nicely positioned the University of Michigan leaders are in terms of these data—some conservative, a representative group of liberals, but most of them in the moderate middle.

To demonstrate, and dramatize, this point better, one should look at some specific issue positions and note the extremeness of the Democratic and Republican parties vis-à-vis the interestgroup leaders. Five issues that tap ideological orientations were selected, issues on which the respondents reported whether they thought government should do "more," "less," or the "same as now" in these policy areas. For example, should the government do "more to help the poor," "less," or the "same as now?" (The federal government was referred to, but that is not of great consequence, since the aim was to get at the respondent's basic feeling about the role and responsibility of government to take action.) In table 5.6 the comparisons with the party leaders are presented.

The range in extent of liberalism within these groups is great. On "expanding the opportunities for the poor," it is a 55-point difference—the media and business are low, the blacks and LWV are high. On desegregation, the chamber's score is actually zero, while for blacks, as expected, it is very high—a 75-point difference. The balance in favor of social, economic, and international egalitarianism is very low in some interest groups, very high in others. On the other hand, while for the chamber free enterprise scores high, the balance within labor is low, as it is surprisingly in other groups.

The ideological distance between the party leaders and interest-group leaders is dramatically evident in table 5.7, using two of the issues here to demonstrate this contrast. At one extreme is the Democratic party, 92 percent liberal on the issue of helping the poor, and close to the blacks, labor, and the LWV, but far removed from business and law leaders—by 40 percent. At the other extreme is the Republican party,

TABLE 5.6. Interest-Group Leaders' Positions on Specific Liberal-Conservative Issues

"The government should do more (same or less) to":	Business	Labor	LWV[a]	Media	Univ.[b]	Blacks	Pac.[c]	Law	Total Groups
Expand opportunities for the poor	40%	90	86	45	67	100	100	55	65
Desegregate housing & schools	0	40	57	35	33	75	71	44	34
Stop air and water pollution	48	70	71	75	55	100	100	89	70
Help third-world countries	4	0	71	10	33	50	0	44	21
Encourage free enterprise	65	30	43	30	11	50	14	0	32
Average Liberalism (Based on first four items)	23	50	71	41	47	81	68	56	48

Source: Survey of Ann Arbor's interest groups conducted by author in 1983.

Note: A "percentage difference" calculation is used—that is, the percentage saying "less" is subtracted from the percentage saying "more"; the balance is the percentage of liberalism used for each group.

[a]LWV = League of Women Voters

[b]Univ. = University of Michigan

[c]Pac. = Pacifists

TABLE 5.7. A Comparison of Party and Interest-Group Leaders on Certain Issues

	"Liberals"								"Conservatives"
"The government should do more (same, less) to":	Democratic Party Leaders	Blacks	LWV[a]	Labor	Law	Univ.	Media	Business	Republican Party Leaders
Expand opportunities for poor (% "more")	92%	100	86	90	55	67	45	40	22
Desegregate housing and schools (% "more")	65	75	57	40	44	33	35	0	−30
Ideology, self-classification (% "liberal")	83	75	57	10	40	23	25	−26	−18

Source: Based on 1983 interest group survey and 1982 survey of party leaders.

Note: A "percentage difference" calculation is used here—that is, the percentage saying "less" is subtracted from the percentage saying "more"; the balance is the percentage used for each group. Similarly, on the ideology measure the % conservative is subtracted from the % liberal to get the % liberal score. On the issues there was an intermediate category "same"; for ideology there was an intermediate category "moderate." 1986 data were used for party leaders since the 1982 study did not use comparable questions. Minus (−) means the group is in balance more conservative than liberal.

[a] LWV = League of Women Voters

only 22 percent liberal on this issue. Closest to it are the business leaders, who are much more liberal than the party—52 percent compared to 22 percent. Clearly neither party is in the center where coalition theory might argue they should be but out on the flanks, at the extreme ends of the continuum. Such data reveal that the conflicts between the parties in ideological terms is more extreme than for interest groups. It also suggests who interest group leaders must see as their ideological friends. The consistent middle groups on most of these issues are the lawyers, the University, and the media. The latter's moderate-to-conservative stance on all but the pollution issue documents the media's basic ideological stance on political issues locally . .

Interest-Group Leaders' Views of the City and of Parties

These leaders, long residents in the city, are very satisfied with Ann Arbor as a place to live—84 percent say so. That does not mean they rate all city services a plus. Here are the proportions not satisfied with specific services:

street maintenance	—55%
public housing	—42%
industrial and business development	—33%
social welfare services	—29%

On parks and recreation, safety (fire and police), and trash and garbage collection, less than ten percent were critical. It should be noted that this was in 1983 and is no measure of the exact level of satisfaction today, though these findings probably are still relatively true.

There was high group consensus on most of these evaluations. On parks and recreation, there were almost unanimous positive feelings from all groups, while on street maintenance and public housing the reverse was true. On their evaluations of the progress toward new business and industrial development, there was some disagreement—40 percent of the business leaders were dissatisfied, as were 39 percent of the lawyers, but only 16 percent of the LWV, the blacks particularly had negative evaluations of business development.

These questions were used as an introduction to probing the views of these leaders about parties and the job they have been doing at City Hall in dealing with these problems. Here evidence was found of some ambivalence and negativism toward the parties. When asked how effective the parties have been in problem solving, the responses were:

very effective	—39%
somewhat effective	—19%
not effective	—42%

On balance, a majority were at least somewhat positive, but it was not an overwhelming endorsement.

Using other questions to determine their attitudes toward partisanism and the parties, these leaders appear on balance to be supportive. But some responses were critical. Thus, 65 percent preferred the present two-party system to any other, but a sizeable minority preferred more than only two parties. Overall, 52 percent believed in a partisan system (46 percent preferred to have nonpartisan elections). When asked what they would recommend if someone in the Ann Arbor public wanted to take a greater part in community affairs, that is, whether the person should "work through the political parties and their organizations or through other types of groups, or through both," they responded:

only parties	—15%
only interest groups	—19%
both	—66%

That perhaps is one fairly reliable measure of the respect interest-group leaders have for the parties. Many comments in the interviews underscore this mentality. Some specifically mentioned the effectiveness of parties in picking able candidates, in providing visibility of these candidates, and in giving the public information about them. When asked specifically how well the parties performed particular functions, it was found that over 60 percent said parties did an important job—in selecting leaders, for providing "an opportunity for protest," in helping "maintain freedom of expression," and the like. Only on the question of the "adoption of good laws" was there a 50–50 split as to whether this function was carried out effectively by Ann Arbor parties. Hence, again, there was some evidence of marginal support. One can interpret these results rather positively, supportive of parties, however, because these were interest-group leaders responding, and one might well have expected much more negative evaluations of the parties from them.

While on these questions these leaders overall tended to be supportive of parties there were variations by specific groups (table 5.8). At the time this study was done in 1983, the Republicans controlled city council. They had just won the mayor's position in a close race, 52 percent to 48 percent, and held a narrow 6-to-5 majority on council. It is interesting, then, to see the strong support by business leaders for the

TABLE 5.8. Variations in Interest-Group Attitudes Toward Parties

Specific Attitudinal Orientation	Business	Media	Labor	Univ.	LWV[a]	Blacks	Lawyers	All Groups
Prefer partisan system	50%	42	40	44	50	75	72	53
Prefer two-party system	78	65	50	89	43	100	72	65
Evaluation of effectiveness of Ann Arbor parties in dealing with most important problems								
effective	62	45	30	33	43	0	35	39
uncertain	5	10	0	56	43	50	12	19
not effective	33	45	70	11	14	50	53	42
"Political parties are important in our political system because they are capable of representing more than one interest at a time and formulating reasonable compromises on political issues."								
% agree	70	70	70	50	100	75	78	70
% neutral	22	10	10	25	0	25	6	15
% disagree	8	20	20	25	0	0	16	15
"Parties do more to confuse the issues than to provide a clear choice on issues."								
% disagree	43	60	50	38	43	100	61	53
% neutral	30	15	10	12	43	0	22	21
% agree	27	25	40	50	14	0	17	26

Source: Survey of Ann Arbor's interest groups conducted by author in 1983.

Note: The last two items were agree-disagree items. The respondents were given a statement as indicated, and asked to determine on a seven-point scale to what degree they agreed or disagreed. Point 4 on the scale was neutral. We have combined here the percentages scoring 1 to 3 and 5 to 7.

[a]LWV = League of Women Voters

party system—62 percent felt the parties were doing an effective job—while only 30 percent of labor leaders felt that way, and none of the black leaders were positive. The media, LWV, university officials were split, and the lawyers were slightly more negative than positive. On all measures, in the last analysis, the parties are negatively evaluated by only a minority of interest-group leaders, although the minority was as much as 40 percent on some questions.

To further test interest-group feelings about parties, the study administered six short agree-disagree statements to the respondents. They were the same ones used in the public surveys in 1981 and 1984. Two of these are reported in table 5.8 and reveal a fairly strong affect for parties in all groups on one item, and mixed results on the other, keeping in mind that there has been a consistent, long standing tendency in the United States to support candidates over parties. For example, note the responses to this simple statement: "The best rule in voting is to pick a candidate regardless of party label." In a national survey of adults in 1980, 73 percent agreed with this. In Ann Arbor in 1983, 75 percent agreed. Among interest-group leaders, 67 percent agreed. But when one uses other statements to tap feelings in parties, one gets different patterns of response. The one most relevant for interest groups perhaps is the fourth item in table 5.8: "Political parties are important in our political system *because they are capable of representing more than one interest* at a time and *formulating reasonable compromises* on political issues (emphasis added)"

What does one find in Ann Arbor on this? Seventy percent of interest-group leaders agree with that statement, and in 1984, 68 percent of the public agreed. Similarly, on another test concerning the issues role of parties (fifth item in table 5.8) 56 percent of adults surveyed in 1980 agreed, but only 34 percent of the Ann Arbor public agreed, and 26 percent of interest-group leaders agreed. The distinctive role of Ann Arbor parties is reflected in these findings. Community leaders and the public appear to be much more accepting of parties in Ann Arbor.

Conclusion

Ann Arbor's interest groups are sometimes very assertive, often very dormant. The limited study of them analyzed here provides some special insights. Their leaders are very alert to political issues. They are a well-educated, experienced group of men and women who have been active politically in the past and had considerable exposure to partisan politics. They, together with the party leaders, constitute a significant set of intermediate structures through which citizens can work if they wish to have some influence on city affairs.

The emphasis here has been on the close linkages and reciprocal relationships of interest-group leaders and party leaders. There is a striking similarity in the social profiles of interest-group and party leaders. There is also an organizational exchange relationship—interest group leaders work in politics, party leaders are active in interest-groups. The ideological splits among interest-group leaders match the ideological split between the parties, although the latter is more polarized.

Additionally, interest-group leaders are inclined to be more supportive of parties than hostile toward or critical of them. On balance, they support partisan elections, feel parties are necessary, and believe parties perform important functions. Some groups believe parties do an effective job in working on, and resolving, at least some of the important problems facing the community. But there are dissidents from that view, as well as some ambivalence, and the potential for conflict with parties is present.

Interest groups and parties in Ann Arbor seem on the basis of these data to be important cogs in our political system. They seem to work well, mutually supportive, even collaborative, but still independent actors in the Ann Arbor system of party governance.

CHAPTER 6

The Political Involvement of the Ann Arbor Public

In understanding a city's political system, it is necessary to have an empirically based image of what the political orientations of the public are. Political parties confront each other before the public; leaders are selected by and responsible to that public; the policies adopted by city government are evaluated by the public. Hence, the extent of the public's interest and participation in politics, its partisan preferences, and the public's ideological moods constitute the context within which the party battle is waged. Basic questions are: How large is the politically attentive public? How active is it, at election time and between elections? To what extent is it mobilizable by the parties? What is the public's level of conservatism or liberalism? What is its level of interest in or alienation from parties? Who, in the last analysis, are the sectors of the population, the core public groups, who undergird the functioning of the partisan system of government in Ann Arbor? If the public is at all involved, what types of citizens are, because of their attention to politics, at the heart of the system? Those questions are the focus of attention.

The Levels of Public Interest and Involvement in City Politics

A first, quick look at the participation data leads one to think the Ann Arbor public is rather attentive to politics, indeed quite active (table 6.1). Over 50 percent report that they read the *Ann Arbor News* regularly and over 40 percent usually follow local and national TV newscasts. A fairly high percentage (over 40 percent) seem to be very knowledgeable about political matters, national and local. In fact, compared to national survey results, the Ann Arbor public seems quite involved. Now, there may be some overreporting in these figures and some differences due to the fact that the survey questions asked may not be identical. Yet, the Ann Arbor public does seem to be in some respects a rather politically active community.

The paradox, however, is that voting turnout for the Ann Arbor public, particularly for those calling themselves Democrats, is low in

April elections. Compared to November voting turnout, the public is quite apathetic about city elections. For example, in 1988, 61 percent of the Ann Arbor public voted in the Presidential election (53,309 voters) but only 22 percent in the 1987 April election (19,407 voters). The contrast between November and April elections is extreme. At least 30,000 eligible citizens vote in presidential elections, then stay home for local elections. (The result is the same if one takes the April election *after* the November election.) There is a fairly good participation rate in November—60 percent or better. But in recent years, April turnouts have been 16 percent (1984), 22 percent (1985), 20 percent (1986), 22 percent (1987), 28 percent (1988), 19 percent (1989), 24 percent (1991). Either the public is exaggerating its involvement in activities other than voting, or much of this participation energy and enthusiasm is dissipated

TABLE 6.1. Levels of Public Interest and Involvement in Politics

	1980–81	1984
Exposure to Mass Media		
Follows national news on TV broadcast frequently	50%	41
Follows local news on TV frequently	48	41
Reads *Ann Arbor News*	57	63
Reads stories on local politics in the newspaper	46	[a]
Level of Knowledge about Politics		
Overall index—Based on knowledge of candidate names and party affiliation for office of Senate, House, and city mayor and council		
high (5 or more of 7 items)	52	45
medium	22	26
low (0, 1, or 2 items)	26	29
Accurate information on the city council majority	61	41
Accurate information on the identity and party affiliation of the mayor	62	40
Political Activities Engaged In		
Contribute money to parties	42	36
Contribute money to candidates	39	35
Held coffee hours for candidates	16	13
Attended coffee hours	41	37
Attended political rallies or meetings	52	61
Did house-to-house canvassing in campaigns	20	23
Did telephone canvassing	19	19
Wrote or spoke to a local official about a political matter	60	59
Held a party position	24	12
Attended city council or school board meeting	26	[a]
Belonged to a political or civic group in community	30	36

Source: Based on surveys of adults conducted in Ann Arbor by the author in the years indicated.
[a]No data for this item available in this year.

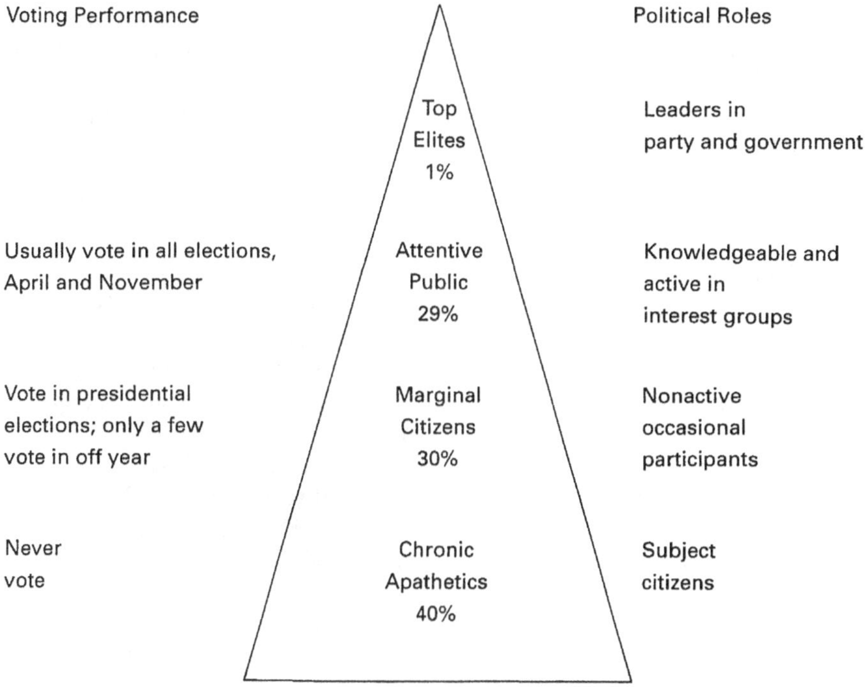

Fig. 6.1. The political stratification pyramid of the Ann Arbor public. (Based on a survey of the Ann Arbor public conducted by the author in 1984.)

quickly. For a variety of reasons, interest in politics does not translate into a desire to have a say in the selection of city leaders. The factors related to voting and nonvoting will be analyzed in a subsequent section.

A careful analysis of survey data for the Ann Arbor public suggests the political stratification picture presented in figure 6.1. About 30 percent of the Ann Arbor public really pays attention to local political affairs, of which 1 percent are the top party leaders and organization activists. Another 30 percent are marginal citizens, about one-third of whom may be fairly well informed about city political matters. They may attend an occasional party rally or coffee hour, and few may give some money, but this middle third rarely votes in city elections. Their record in recent off-year November elections also was poor. The bottom group of chronic apathetics constitute 40 percent of the public—uninformed, inactive, and regular nonvoters in all elections.

The difficulties the parties face are obvious. When 50 percent or more of the public knows little about city government and does not even read the *Ann Arbor News*, to get these people to the polls is difficult. The communication job of the parties is a great one. Many people in the attentive public are active, but they do not seem to be able to educate people outside their groups about city politics nor to bring them to the polls in April.

Historical Patterns of Voting and Nonvoting

There have been great fluctuations in voting turnout in April elections in Ann Arbor. This adds to the electoral paradox. After World War II, turnout was at an abysmal low (only 2.5 percent of the eligible voters participated).[1] This gradually increased as the city and the party system developed, reaching a high in the early 1970s (over 40 percent turnout). Since then it has been irregular, plummeting to under 11 percent in 1980 and stabilizing at 20 percent to 25 percent since (table 6.2 and fig. 6.2). In November, 1993, however, the turnout fell to 13 percent. While the potential vote "market" has tripled (over 50,000 more eligible voters), the actual vote, with the exception of the special years of three-party conflict in the seventies, has remained relatively low. The irony is that the high percentages in the early 1970s (42.9 percent in 1971, 40.5 percent in 1972, 43.7 percent in 1973) occurred despite (or because of) the lowering of the voting age in 1972.

An argument is made sometimes that the registration requirement is responsible for low turnouts. Actually, in Ann Arbor there is no evidence to support this. Using city clerk records, this could be examined over time.[2] Two trends emerge from the data: (1) a persistent increase in the number and percentage of eligible adults who register, and (2) fewer registered voters participating in April elections (and presidential elections) over the years. Table 6.3 gives the over-time data. The decline in turnout cannot be blamed on the difficulties of registration really, just as it is not the result of giving the franchise to 18-year-olds. It is a phenomenon occurring for all types of elections despite increased registration.

Two features of these historical patterns need recognition. The turnout at local elections does not correspond to national trends (fig. 6.3). The April vote does not decline or rise with the vote in preceding presidential elections. There seem to be local forces and conditions at work in April, clearly independent of the factors operative in national elections. Second, the drop off in the vote in April elections is clear and consistent—a differential of great magnitude. From 30,000 to 40,000 presidential voters fail to vote in April. The average differential in turnout since 1948 has been 32.6 percentage points.

One other interesting, though expected, feature of these historical

TABLE 6.2. Overview of the Voting Population and Turnout in April Elections, 1946–91

	1946	1950	1960	1970	1972[b]	1980	1989	1991
Ann Arbor Population[a]	40,522	48,251	67,340	99,797	101,431	107.969	108,000	109,252
Population of Voting Age	24,429	29,491	39,296	60,916	74,122	87,372	85,000	87,500
Turnout (% of voting-age population voting)	2.5%	18.6%	25.6%	32.1%	40.5%	10.6%	19.8%	23.6%
Actual Total Vote in the April Election (for city council)	627	5,385	10,194	19,592	30,035	9,301	16,798[c]	20,686[c]

[a]Based on census figures and intercensal estimates as well as Ann Arbor city clerk's voting reports. See notes 1 and 2 for an explanation of the calculations.

[b]26th Amendment to the U.S. Constitution became effective January 1, 1972, giving 18-year-olds the right to vote.

[c]Since the first ward was uncontested for the council seat, we used the mayoralty vote here.

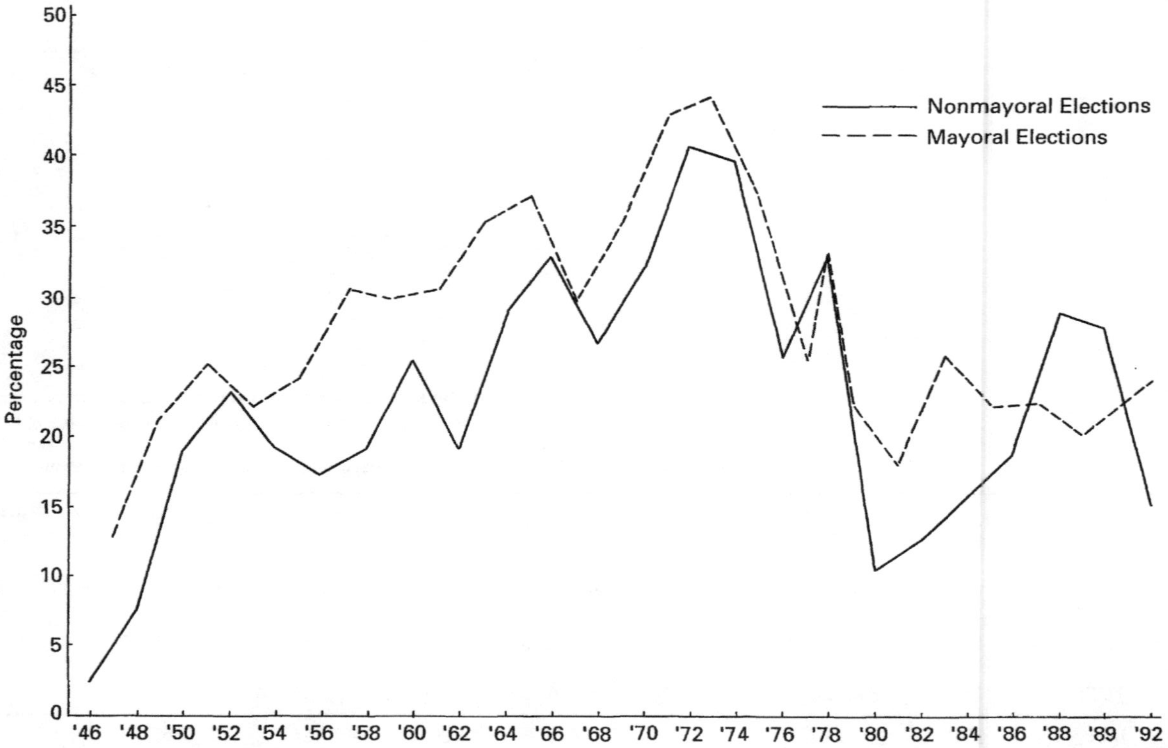

Fig. 6.2. Turnout in Ann Arbor elections: 1946–92. (From election reports of Ann Arbor city clerk.)

trends is the correlation of the party vote increase with the increase in the total vote. The interesting question is: When the total vote increased, which party was responsible for that increase or benefitted from it? The answer varies over the years, fluctuating apparently in terms of the party's dominance in mobilizing votes in the community. Consider the simple figures for mayoral elections in table 6.4. In the 1973–77 period, there was a decrease in the total vote *and* in the vote of both major parties. The Human Rights party's appearance on the scene and its subsequent decline, plus the disarray in the two major parties, was responsible for this. Otherwise, as the above findings indicate, there was a clear association of party vote mobilization and increased turnout.

The bottom line in all this is that after peaking in the early 1970s, voting in April elections has been generally in a state of decline ever since, with a slight upward turn from 1980 on. The differentials in the relation of the Ann Arbor April vote and the vote in national elections have always been considerable, but the gap is greater in the past decade. It is as if voter apathy is institutionalized today. Nonvoting is a recurrent habit, and new cues and stimuli seem to have no effect. This applies to city elections as well as to referenda. Only one-fourth or fewer of the eligible voters have participated recently on crucial referenda, such as street repair, establishment of affordable housing, expansion of city hall, and similar proposals. Tax and bond proposals do no better basically than other proposals. Occasionally, in earlier years, an issue generated a slightly higher vote, as the campus "liquor dry line" issue of 1964 did (34.6 percent turnout) or the parklands acquisition issue in 1971 (42.3 percent). The key issue changing the voting system (preferential voting) brought out 42.8 percent in November 1974, but its repeal in 1976 saw only 26.6 percent turn out. By and large over the years, with few exceptions, 60 to 80 percent of the Ann Arbor electorate is not interested in these important referenda, just as they are disinterested in who runs city hall. (See Appendix for specific results of referenda.)

TABLE 6.3. The Vote Cast by the Registered Electorate in Ann Arbor

	1957	1960	1972	1980	1984	1988
% of Eligible Voters Who Registered	60%	71	78	89	91	87
% of the Registered Who Voted in						
April	51	35	52	12	18	32
November	97[a]	86	73	70	66	70

Source: Reports of the Ann Arbor City Clerk's Office.
[a]Figure is for 1956.

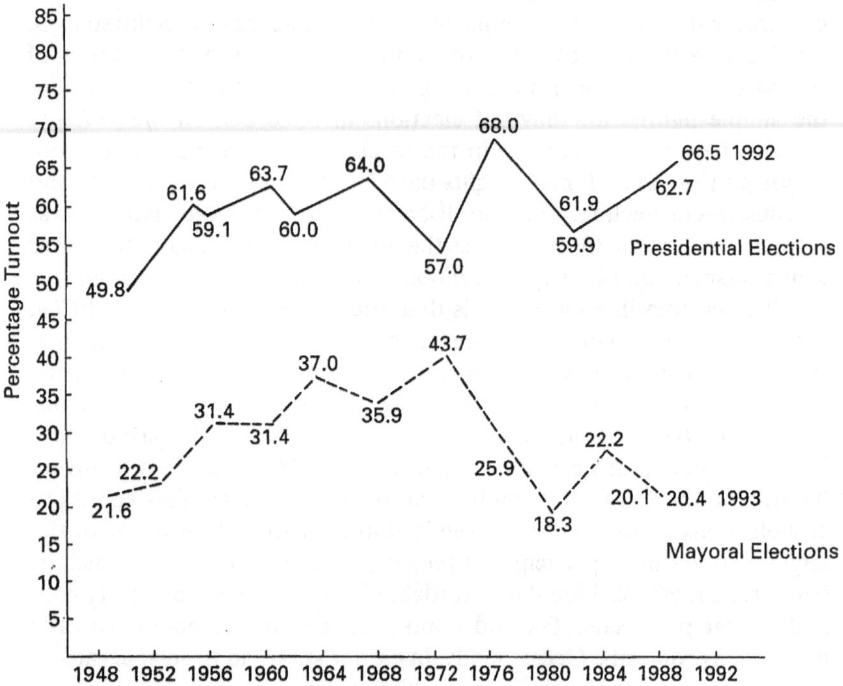

Fig. 6.3. Comparison of the presidential and mayoral election turnouts for Ann Arbor. Mayoral elections occur in odd years. This graph uses the mayoral election in the year following the presidential election.

Explanations of Nonvoting and Voting

Many theories have been advanced to explain voting and nonvoting. The major interest is what factors are relevant particularly to local elections, that is, relevant to April elections in Ann Arbor.[3]

There appear to be three classes of factors that help explain voter turnout in Ann Arbor. First is a set of basic variables called community integration, including length of residence, home ownership, marital status, readership of the *Ann Arbor News*, and discussion of politics with local friends. These variables are generally focused on social integration. Second is a set of variables dealing with attitudes toward government and politics in Ann Arbor: feelings of trust in local government, feelings of personal efficacy about being involved in local affairs, evaluations of local government performance, views of the partisan election system

TABLE 6.4. The Role of the Parties in Increases or Decreases in the Vote

	Increase in Total Vote	Increase or De-crease in Dem. Vote	Increase or De-crease in Rep. Vote	% of Total Vote Increase Attributable to Party in Power's Efforts
Years of Democrats Coming to Power				
1953–57	4,298	+ 3,521	+ 686	78%
1967–71	10,714	+ 8,591	+ 2,123	80%
1981–85	3,154	+ 4,232	+ 1,078	100%
1987–91	1,279	+ 1,902	− 998	100%
Years of Republican Return to Power				
1957–65	7,100	+ 1,315	+ 5,876	83%
1971–78	1,399	− 1,778	+ 3,177	100%
1985–87	322	− 930	+ 1,246	100%

Source: Based on City Clerk's Election Reports.

and government in Ann Arbor. A third set of factors is made up of of factors are those concerned with political exposure, including level of knowledge about local politics, exposure to the party organization and its campaign efforts, and the extent of activity in politics. These can be called the party exposure variables.

Community Integration

The extent of the individual's attachment to and involvement with his or her community is a recognized concept that has political relevance, particularly when one is studying politics at the local level. Some people have only a transient or superficial connection to their city, a limited sense of interest in it. For others there is a deeper and more meaningful connection. This relationship is determined by many considerations but the four selected here as evidence of a deep and meaningful connection to the city are their length of residence, whether they own or rent a home, the regularity of their reading of a local newspaper, and how frequently they discuss politics with friends and associates in the city. Using these separately and together, we can see their relationship to voting in local elections (table 6.5). The results for 1980 and 1984 are different, because one must remember the turnout in 1980 was an all-time low of under 11 percent of the eligible adults whereas in 1984 it was higher.

Each of these four integration variables seems to be linked. If one has lived in Ann Arbor over ten years and presumably has gotten to know the city well, there seems to be a much greater desire to participate in April's voting decisions—a striking 30-point differential in 1984 compared to those who are recent arrivals. Home ownership, which introduces the financial element in the integration concept, also proved significant. Homeowners in 1984 were more than twice as likely as renters to vote in April, (46 percent to 22 percent). Reading a local paper like the *Ann Arbor News* is one indication that a person may be both interested in and aware of local developments, and this seemed to be the case. Those who were regular readers in 1984 voted much more frequently than did nonreaders (46 percent to 24 percent). Finally, having a network of informal friendships, persons with whom politics is discussed frequently, also seemed relevant to the April vote.

TABLE 6.5. Community Integration Variables and April Turnout

	% Voting in April	
	1980	1984
Home Ownership		
Own	22	46
Rent	11	22
Length of Residence in City		
Over 20 years	29	49
10–20 years	21	49
5–9 years	16	35
Under 5 years	4	19
Readership of *Ann Arbor News*		
Yes	23	46
No	6	24
Discussion of Politics with Friends		
Frequently	30	39
Sometimes	17	29
Rarely	11	27
Never	0	25
Community Integration Index[a]		
High	29	56
Medium	16	27
Low	1	13

Source: Survey of the Ann Arbor public conducted by the author in the years indicated.
Note: For 1980, $N = 276$; for 1984, $N = 213$.
[a]The Index is based on the four items used above in the table. A score was calculated for each respondent, ranging, for example, in 1984 from 0 to 10. The index weighted each of the four components equally, except that long residence in the city (over 20 years) was given an additional weight.

As people develop ties to the community, their involvement may become political as well as social and economic. These data suggest that strongly. The most extreme example of the opposite point, of course, is the voting behavior of students, only 6 percent and 8 percent of whom claim to have voted in 1980 and 1984. For these four factors, the correlations (gammas) in the 1984 study and the vote were:

Ann Arbor News Readership	.50
Home Ownership	.46
Length of Residence	.36
Discussion of Politics with Friends	.29

Thus, all factors were positively associated (and they are also correlated with age of respondent). When one combines them into a community integration index (table 6.6) the cumulative relevance of these forces can be seen. If one has lived in the city long, owns a home, reads the *Ann Arbor News*, and discusses politics frequently there is a much higher probability of voting in April—in 1984, 56 percent of such eligible adults did. If these four conditions are not met, the probability is very low—only 13 percent in 1984 of these adults said they voted.

Let us not forget, however, that even many well-integrated Ann Arborites do not think voting is important (see table 6.2)-45 percent of the most integrated citizens stayed home on April election day in 1984. Other factors thus must be considered.

Political Attitudes and Orientations

The beliefs and attitudes people have about politics, parties, political issues, and leaders have long been considered primary explanations of voting behavior. Some of these attitudinal orientations may have a more persistent linkage to political behavior, particularly to local voting behavior, than do others. For example, Ann Arbor studies show that one's ideology (basic view about the role of government in the society and economy) was differently linked to April voting behavior in 1980 and 1984. In 1980, the liberals voted less than the conservatives did, while in 1984 the opposite was true. The summary of findings in table 6.6 illustrates this point. Another basic orientation scholars of voting behavior rely on is party identification (the strength of attachment to, or independence from the Republican and Democratic parties). Again, one can see variations in the way this factor of party loyalty is related to the April vote. It depends on the particular election. In April 1980 the "strong Republicans" turned out to vote more than in 1984 (37 percent compared to 28 percent). In contrast only 16 percent of the "strong Democrats" voted in April 1980, while 47 percent did so in 1984. It is quite clear that these two elections mobilized, or interested, partisans quite differently. In Ann Arbor's local elections, one does not find as high a correlation between either ideology or party identification and voting as was found in national elections. In 1984 the correlations were .10 for ideology and .22 for party identification—not strong associations, though not insignificant.

While keeping these orientations in mind, there are other attitudes more directly related to Ann Arbor's local politics, which, if explored, may have more utility. Four of these seem to be particularly useful: evaluation of city government performance, attitudes toward parties, level of trust in local government, and sense of political efficacy (feeling that one can be effective locally). Table 6.7 presents these data. The theoretical argument here is that the extent to which a person has positive (or negative) perceptions and cognitions about city government, political parties, and the local political process will affect his or her interest in voting in city elections. Since Ann Arbor has a type of government in which parties play a major role, citizen views about parties may be very important in understanding their behavior. Hence, in 1984 a variety of questions were asked to discover how people felt about the parties and the party system.

The results supported this set of expectations, although not as convincingly on all factors. Positive evaluations of city policy were linked to higher turnout—48 percent voted among those who city government had done a good job, compared to 33 percent of those whose evaluations were poor. Citizens who approved partisan elections and, more important, who had an overall pro-party set of attitudes, were much more likely to vote than those with anti-party attitudes—a 30-point differential. Those who trusted local government were also in 1984 more inclined to be April voters as were those with a higher sense of political efficacy. The attitudes that seemed most related to April voting (in 1984) were: evaluation of city government performance and belief in the functions and roles of parties (correlations were .29 and .34, respectively).

One controversy among scholars is between the negative and posi-

TABLE 6.6. April Voting Behavior (% voting)

Self Classification as:	1980	1984
Liberals	17	38
Moderates	13	36
Conservatives	30	30

tive voting models. In the negative model, it is argued that complacent voters, those happy with the state of public affairs, stay home and do not vote, while those who are unhappy or alienated do the voting. The positive voting model takes the opposite position. Neither model is completely supported by our data. Some of the very anti-party people are voters (13 percent) as well as more of the very pro-party people (43 percent). Those low on trust, and who are critical of the job government is doing, vote as well as those who seem quite content about Ann Arbor politics, although they vote at a lower rate. To test this theory more thoroughly, there was created an alienation index (see appendix), and each respondent was scored on this, using information provided on twelve different questions to classify a person as highly, moderately, or minimally alienated. Those least alienated were found to be much more

TABLE 6.7. Political Attitudes and Orientations Linked to April 1984 Turnout

	% Voting in April	Sample
Evaluation of City Government Performance		
Good Job	48	32
Only Fair	45	85
Poor Job	33	49
Attitudes Toward Political Parties[a]		
Strong Pro-party	43	23
Somewhat Pro-party	38	27
Neutral	43	66
Somewhat Anti-party	26	68
Strong Anti-party	13	21
Level of Trust in Local Government[b]		
High	50	14
Moderate	36	123
Low	31	48
Sense of Efficacy About Involvement in Local Politics		
High (Have Much Say)	36	171
Low (Little or No Say)	29	17
Alienation Index[c]		
High (and Very High)	22	46
Moderate	31	45
Low	38	68
Very Low	40	55

Source: Based on 1984 Survey of the Ann Arbor public conducted by Author.

[a]An index based on eight short agree-disagree statements given to respondents. (See appendix.)

[b]Based on the question: "How much of the time do you think you can trust your local government to do what is right—just about always, most of the time, or only some of the time?"

[c]Alienation index used in 1984 combines responses on all the attitudes into a score for each respondent (maximum score 55). See appendix for a discussion of this.

likely to vote in April (40 percent), compared to those most alienated (22 percent). However, when only those index items related to Ann Arbor politics were used (such as trust in Ann Arbor's government and whether the Ann Arbor government was doing a good, fair, or poor job), there was no significant difference in voting. That is, those alienated voted as frequently (30 percent) as those giving no evidence of alienation. Thus, the Ann Arbor voting electorate is a composite of contented and discontented citizens. Only one-fifth of the adult population is quite alienated generally, and only 15 percent are very alienated against Ann Arbor government. But 22 percent to 30 percent of those people do vote. So, withdrawal from the April voting process is not primarily linked to alienation from Ann Arbor's political system. However, it is clear that a general sense of negativism or cynicism is still related to low turnout and must not be dismissed in the analysis of low turnout.

Political Exposure and Party Mobilization

A final set of factors that explain voting and nonvoting in April elections in Ann Arbor includes the political exposure variables. These are essentially measures of the extent to which the individual has been contacted by the parties, been active in campaigns, and acquired correct knowledge about Ann Arbor's government. Together, they indicate whether a citizen is in the mainstream of political life in Ann Arbor, primarily as a result of party mobilization efforts, or is on the periphery of political life. Put another way, the question is: Can parties integrate people into the political life of a community and make it more likely that they will vote?

The data from the Ann Arbor studies (table 6.8) strongly support this theory. Those contacted by the parties were much more likely to vote in 1984 (45 percent to 24 percent). Those active in campaigns were proportionately more likely to vote, depending on the level of their activism. And those who (partially as a result of such activity and contact) were knowledgeable about local government had the highest percent of turnout (57 percent for those most informed compared to 8 percent for those totally uninformed). Clearly these types of exposures are critical for getting out the April vote. (The correlations were .53 for knowledge level, .51 for party contact.) Of the April voters in 1984, 64 percent said they had been contacted by the parties (at least 30 percent by both parties). Cumulatively these three factors were linked to high turnout, as the Political Exposure Index revealed. Of those (18 percent) who were very highly exposed as measured by these three variables, 85 percent voted!

The more significant observation perhaps is that less than one-fifth of the Ann Arbor citizens were very highly exposed to politics. Further, as exposure lessens, voting turnout drops dramatically. Party contact by itself is important, but not enough. After all, 55 percent of those canvassed by the parties stayed home in 1984. To maximize turnout, therefore, other factors and conditions have to be present, reinforcing each other and conducing to a vote decision.

University Students: How Involved in City Politics?

There was a time when university students played a decisive role in Ann Arbor politics. In 1972, the 26th Amendment gave 18-year-olds the right to vote. Reports in Ann Arbor claimed that 18,000 students registered

TABLE 6.8. Political Exposure and Mobilization as Related to the April 1984 Turnout

	% Voting in April	Sample *N*	Sample %
Knowledge Index of Local Government and Politics[a]			
Very High	57%	68	31%
High	39	32	15
Medium	34	57	26
Low	13	48	22
No Knowledge	8	13	6
Ever Contacted by the Parties?			
Yes	45	97	52
No	24	88	48
Activities Participated in During the Campaign (based on 10 possible)[b]			
Seven or more	81	31	15
Five or six	45	38	18
Three or four	25	62	29
Two or less	18	82	38
Political Exposure Index (1984)[c]			
Very High	85	39	18
High	33	51	24
Low	24	58	27
Very Low	12	65	31

Source: Based on 1984 Survey of Ann Arbor public conducted by Author.

[a]The knowledge index was based on a series of questions as to respondent's information about the majority on city council and the mayor's name and party.

[b]The list of 10 activities included: following the campaign in the media; giving money to the parties or candidates; holding or going to a coffee hour, rallies or other meetings; canvassing at people's homes or by phone; writing letters to officials; or holding party position.

[c]The Political Exposure Index included all three of the types of exposure.

for the presidential election that year. Over 41,000 votes were cast in Ann Arbor for president in 1972, compared to 33,000 four years earlier.

In city elections, the students were even more visible. The Human Rights Party (*HRP*) was organized and ran candidates for the positions of mayor and council from 1972 to 1977, winning two council seats in 1972 and one in 1974. To document the student vote influx beginning with the April elections of 1972, the data in table 6.9 may be convincing. From 1970 to 1972, there was a 53 percent increase in the total April vote, of which 70 percent was for the new HRP, and 62 percent of this new HRP vote was cast in the student wards 1 and 2. (Ward 3 is not included although it also had student residents.) The student vote obviously became a significant factor in Ann Arbor politics. Two students were elected to council, splitting the council three ways.

Students seemed to lose interest after 1975, and the HRP presented no candidates after 1977. Many students are still registered to vote in Ann Arbor (at least 40 percent said they were registered when interviewed in a survey in 1981). Over 70 percent claimed to have voted in the 1984 presidential election and 38 percent in the 1986 congressional election. The Michigan Daily reported (November 10, 1988) that from 46 percent to 52 percent of registered students in two residence halls turned out for the 1988 fall election, and a fairly large proportion (25 percent) claimed in 1985 that they have been involved in off—campus activity working for political parties and other political groups. Yet their interest in and knowledge about Ann Arbor city political affairs has been very low in the past decade. In two studies conducted in 1980 and 1985, the research found lower levels of interest, compared to the Ann Arbor public (table 6.10). Clearly a small minority of students reveal any significant involvement in city politics. They just do not seem to be integrated well into the community—only 8 percent are well integrated compared to 46 percent of the public generally. Yet, if an issue appears on the ballot in which they can get interested, they will vote. The Miller

TABLE 6.9. Voting Turnout of Students in the Seventies

Election Year	Citywide Total Vote	Total Vote Student Wards		Total Citywide HRP[a] Votes
		Ward 1	Ward 2	
1970	19,592	3,186	2,535	0
1972	30,035	6,348	5,453	7,334
1974	30,619	5,938	4,420	5,597

Source: Election Reports of the City Clerk's office.
[a]*HRP* = Human Rights Party

study revealed that in the November 1980 election, most students (70 percent) approved lowering the drinking age and our survey revealed that over 70 percent voted on that referendum. Although voting report figures in surveys are inflated, there is evidence that students will under certain circumstances get to the polls.

The 1985 and 1987 studies of College of Literature, Science and the Arts seniors at the university revealed that students are more liberal than conservative. But they are close in the proportions who declared themselves Democrats or Republicans. In a 1987 study of seniors of the College of Literature, Science and the Arts 39 percent said they were liberal, and 20 percent conservative, yet the difference in party identification was negligible—34 percent Democratic, and 29 percent Republican. This may suggest that students might be fertile ground for both the city parties to cultivate. Yet the basic lack of interest of students in city government, barring the appearance of some dramatic issue, restricts their involvement. Their interest in party politics generally (not locally) is relatively high. The studies reveal that their support for political parties is actually higher than that of the general public (only 19 percent are really antiparty compared to 25 percent of the Ann Arbor public). Their sense of political efficacy and trust is higher than for nonstudents. Until University of Michigan students are inclined to effectuate these ideologi-

TABLE 6.10. Level of Student Knowledge about City Politics and Voting in City Election in the 1980s

	U of M Students	Ann Arbor Public
% who read the *Ann Arbor News* regularly	10%[a]	63[b]
Knowledge of city politics (party in control of council, name or party of the mayor)	11[c]	41[d]
Voted in April elections[e]		
April 1980	6	10 (21)
April 1984	8	16 (33)

Source: Based on Surveys Conducted by the Author in 1980 and 1985.

[a]Figure is for 1985.

[b]Figure is for 1984.

[c]Figure is for 1981.

[d]Figure is for 1984.

[e]The figures given for the public (not in parentheses) are based on calculations of the eligible number of voters; the student figures are based on their responses to our interviews. Since there is always overreporting of the vote, these are somewhat misleading comparisons. Actually, 33 percent of the public said they voted in 1984, but in terms of the actual calculations, only half of these remembered correctly. If we apply that to the student interview responses, it is very probable that only 3 to 4 percent of the students actually voted in either of these elections.

cal and partisan orientations at the local level, the local party elites may continue to ignore them or do poorly in getting their support in April elections. But for particular campaigns, it might be worthwhile to selectively mobilize them.

Theoretical Implications

An analysis with considerable explanatory power emerges from this review of the findings. These three clusters of factors—community integration, political attitudes, and party exposure—are important and also are together closely linked to voting. It is interesting to look at their combined effect and the implications for how voting turnout can be improved in city elections. Figure 6.4 demonstrates the combined effect of community integration and political exposure in relation to voting in 1984. Clearly community integration and political exposure together can be associated with very high turnout: a contrast of 85 percent if high on both to 12 percent if low on both. Three phenomena can lead to higher participation: (1) If people have not yet become integrated socially in Ann Arbor but are already exposed a great deal to politics—turnout increases drastically (from 12 percent to 45 percent). (2) If they are low in political exposure but become highly integrated, they can jump from 12 percent to 36 percent in turnout, but if they are low in both and become more integrated at the same time they are very much more exposed to politics, they will register a sensational development in electoral involvement (from 12 percent to 85 percent); (3) Satisfaction with city governmental policy is also important but probably of less signifi-

		Community Integration	
		High	Low
Political Exposure	High	85%	45%
	Low	36%	12%

Fig. 6.4. The combined effects on the vote of community integration and political exposure by the percentage voting in April 1984 in each quadrant.

cance than the integration and mobilization variables. Those who have very negative views of city government tend to stay home, particularly if they are not yet politically or socially involved (only 11 percent vote), but if those with negative views become homeowners, live here longer, and are contacted by the parties, and become more active and knowledgeable, the data suggest that they, too, can approach the 80 percent level of voting participation.

Support for the system and knowledge about the system tend to be linked to voting turnout, although there are skeptical and alienated people who do vote. Those ignorant about local politics rarely vote; but almost 50 percent of the knowledgeable vote. Acceptance of the party system and positive feelings about Ann Arbor parties seem to be also linked to voting—a critical finding in this research.

A Special Problem: Knowledge and Nonvoting

One of the most troubling questions about low voter turnout is that people who are knowledgeable about city political matters often do not vote in local elections. To investigate this, a series of factual questions was put to the respondents about city government and national government. The resultant finding was fairly high levels of factual knowledge: 48 percent knew who their congressperson was, 41 percent were quite familiar with their U.S. Senators, 60 percent knew the name or party of the mayor (40 percent knew both), and 47 percent knew which party controlled city council. Thus, almost 50 percent of the sample was quite informed about certain basic facts of local politics. But among these "knowledgeables" only 52 percent vote in April. What explanations are there for this?

A simple analysis of these knowledgeables using the explanatory factors of this chapter sheds some light on why this situation may exist. First, integration variables help only slightly. They reveal that 66 percent of the nonvoting knowledgeables have lived in Ann Arbor over ten years, and 70 percent are homeowners. (Among voting knowledgeables, 80 percent have lived in Ann Arbor over ten years, and 80 percent are homeowners.) Next, when the variable of political contact was used, a surprising finding emerged, one contrary to expectations. The nonvoters were more likely to have been contacted by the parties than were the voters. Sixty-two percent of nonvoters, compared to 53 percent of voters, reported being contacted. Possibly there was a "boomerang effect" from party canvassing.

A third approach is to try to explain the nonvoting of knowledgeables by their beliefs and attitudes. Here two basic attitudes appear to be relevant. What emerged as partially useful was a person's *strength* and *consistency* of commitment to political parties. This can be demonstrated in two ways. The question about strength of party identification was used ("With what political party do you affiliate and how strongly"), and eight short-answer statements were put to each respondent, asking them to indicate whether they agreed or disagreed with each statement about the importance of parties and how strongly. On the basis of these two approaches, attitude toward parties emerged as significantly linked to voting (table 6.11). There is a strong suggestion here that it is lack of belief plus weak party loyalty that combine to induce the political inertia, indifference, and laxity of many political knowledgeables in Ann Arbor. That is not the whole story, but seems to be a significant part of the story of voter apathy. The images of politics people have, the strength of their conviction, and the intensity of political beliefs seem to be linked to their voting behavior.

Conclusions

Some scholars of American cities are alarmed about the vote in city elections. One has argued that the "levels of voting participation are so low as to question seriously the validity of representative elections."[4] This may be an extreme position, but certainly one should reflect on how one could improve the public's participation in local government. In some respects, Ann Arbor appears to be a rather elitist type of democracy.

One may well ask, then, how to increase voting participation in Ann Arbor's city elections. Little can be done to improve the objective

TABLE 6.11 The Role of Attitudes Toward Parties in Explaining the Voting Behavior of Knowledgeables

	Knowledgeables	
	Voters	Nonvoters
Party Identification		
Strong	52%	39
Weak or Independents	48	61
Belief in Parties (index of 8 items)		
High support	61	50
Medium support	24	19
Low support	15	31
Percentage Difference High compared to Low	+46	+19

Source: Author's Survey of Ann Arbor adults in 1984.

community integration status of citizens, since home ownership probably is not going to increase, and residential status is not something one can do much about. But it might be worthwhile to work to improve the average citizen's subjective feelings about the city, its policies, and its parties. If citizens can be made more knowledgeable about local politics the vote may increase. Higher levels of political knowledge and more positive feeling about the party system have great relevance for voting. Finally, more and better contacts with the parties—more party effort and party contacts (and/or efforts by other political groups) that communicate more positive messages about the city—are needed if citizens are to be brought to the polls.

For many people, city elections seem meaningless, unimportant, and irrelevant for their lives. Some are merely complacent, assuming city government will run well even if they do not vote. This has to be changed for voting to be increased. This is difficult to do because of the preoccupation of citizens with their own personal goals and self-interests. The urban environment, even in Ann Arbor, may not be conducive to a sense of commitment and political involvement. People do not see the city as a "community of citizens" in Aristotelian terms, nor do they see the necessity of "the election of officers [of the city] by all out of all." Yet, in the past Ann Arbor has seen between 40 and 50 percent voting in April. Perhaps it can happen again-o*nly* if many citizens are re-socialized so that they become interested, knowledgeable, and responsible about being members of the community. There are a variety of agents for change: the press, the parties, other political groups, the family, the schools. It is difficult to change the way people live in Ann Arbor. Perhaps it is possible to change the way people think about politics in Ann Arbor, by making politics more interesting to them, worthwhile for them, and important for their lives-important enough so that they will change one aspect of their behavior: to go regularly to the polls in April to vote in city elections.

CHAPTER 7

Paths to Political Involvement: How Ann Arbor Citizens Learn to Become Active

We have discussed in the preceding chapters key factors which seem to be linked to participation in politics in Ann Arbor. Quite a few people, though a minority of the public, are part of the active political stratum in Ann Arbor. They tend to be well integrated into the community, have positive attitudes toward local politics and the parties, and are often exposed to the media and to party contacts. These facts are important to know. But we can still ask—how does it happen that these people are involved? By what process were they involved in politics in the city?

The Importance of Political Socialization

While social background and attitudes and exposure to politics are interesting explanations, the nagging question still must be raised—why? Why these people, with these characteristics? Why are some young people, some low-income citizens, some persons with limited education active, and others not? Why are some well-educated and affluent people active, and others not? A beginning can be made by looking at political socialization processes at work in this community, that is, the ways in which individuals learn about politics and become interested in having a role in the political system. To answer this "why" question, one can look at various time points in a person's life, beginning with influences in the home while the person was growing up.[1]

Respondents were asked about their early exposure to politics, in the family and in school. A high proportion had come from families in which politics had been discussed while they were growing up: 31 percent said there had been much discussion about political matters, 52 percent some discussion, and only 17 percent no discussion of politics at all. In addition, 88 percent said they had had courses in high school that exposed them to American government and party politics. When asked to evaluate their feelings toward political parties as a result of their high school experiences, only about 10 percent said they had negative reactions, while the remainder had positive or neutral feelings, so that for most citizens their youth was generally one leading either to positive orientations toward party politics or ambivalent attitudes. They were certainly not negative then. Respondents were asked, "By the time you were age 17 would you say that your feelings toward the parties were . . . positive, negative, or neutral?" Of all respondents, 98 percent felt they were able to give a useful response to this question. Only 12 percent said they had negative feelings toward parties, while 40 percent were positive and 48 percent neutral. This is an important finding in itself. Before becoming adults, before going to college, before taking up their careers, few Ann Arbor citizens said they were negative in their feelings about parties. Then later in their adult years, it appears they had other experiences. They were exposed to other stimuli, and (as we shall see later) many lost their positive feeling toward party politics. Less than half decided to participate actively.

Yet these early years had an impact on the political behavior of many. The relevance of discussion of politics in the home is strongly suggested in these data. There is a consistent decline in political involvement associated with the amount of frequency of political discussion in the home. And those who at age 17 were positive in their feelings about parties were much more likely later in life to be active in party and campaign work.

As for the impact of the government or civics courses (or variations of these) on the individual's readiness to become active in politics, it is not clear whether these courses *by themselves* made a difference. There is no strong evidence that those who had such high school courses were more predisposed to be participants, and only slight evidence that those who took college courses in political science (or courses related to government and politics) were the citizens more likely to be active in politics. What is more significant is that whereas 40 percent were positive (and 12 percent were negative) toward parties at age 17 (as they recalled their attitudes), when asked to explain their evaluation of parties as a result of their college experiences, only one-third had positive orientations. The majority said the impact of college was neutral or nonexistent.

People are exposed to many stimuli in their lives which can influence their perceptions and feelings about politics and, hence, determine whether they are willing to participate. The early family stimulus is one of these, as are the high school experience, college contacts, and peer-group influences, especially close friendships in the postcollege period. The questions probed carefully to discover the relevance of these stimuli for exploring political activity. The data strongly suggest that there are at least four different paths leading to participation. These are presented in the diagram of fig. 7.1. From this, one can observe certain basic socialization patterns:

1. People can become active in politics without early family socialization—up to 20 percent do (paths C and D).
2. Political involvement is most likely to be linked to early socialization (paths A and B).
3. Early family socialization does not guarantee later involvement politically. Note the 20 percent (path E) who never became active *despite* early family socialization.
4. For some individuals, family influence is most likely to play a role if reinforced by other stimuli (path B).

It is a combination of socialization agents, therefore, which work together. Family influence plus friendship (for some, school also) are positively associated with political participation as adults.

Respondents were asked to provide information about the politics of their three closest friends: their party identification, whether they discussed politics with such friends (and how frequently), and what the attitudes of their friends were toward political parties (if they knew). These data are very revealing. If such information is combined with the reports the respondents provided about their discussion of politics in the family, a clear validation emerges concerning the relevance of these conditions for explaining the level of political participation in Ann Arbor (table 7.1). Where there was much discussion of politics in the home plus friendships that were positive in their orientation toward parties and party politics, the average participation score was 4.60. Any deviation from that ideal set of conditions is associated with lower average scores. For this least socialized group (individuals who were not subjected to any early family socialization nor had friends who were positive in their feelings about politics), the average score was 1.40. Among this latter group, there appear to be certain individuals who become somewhat (minimally) active, clearly because of other stimuli—party contacts, the media, coworkers, or involvement through other community groups or influences.

Few citizens are stimulated by the ideal conditions used in table 7.1. Only about 10 percent were (and are) maximally and positively influenced politically by family *and* friends to participate. Another 28 percent closely approximate this ideal model. Absence of strong and positive peer influence, despite early family socialization, clearly leads to less priority for political action. About 40 percent of the Ann Arbor public came from social environments not positively and strongly ori-

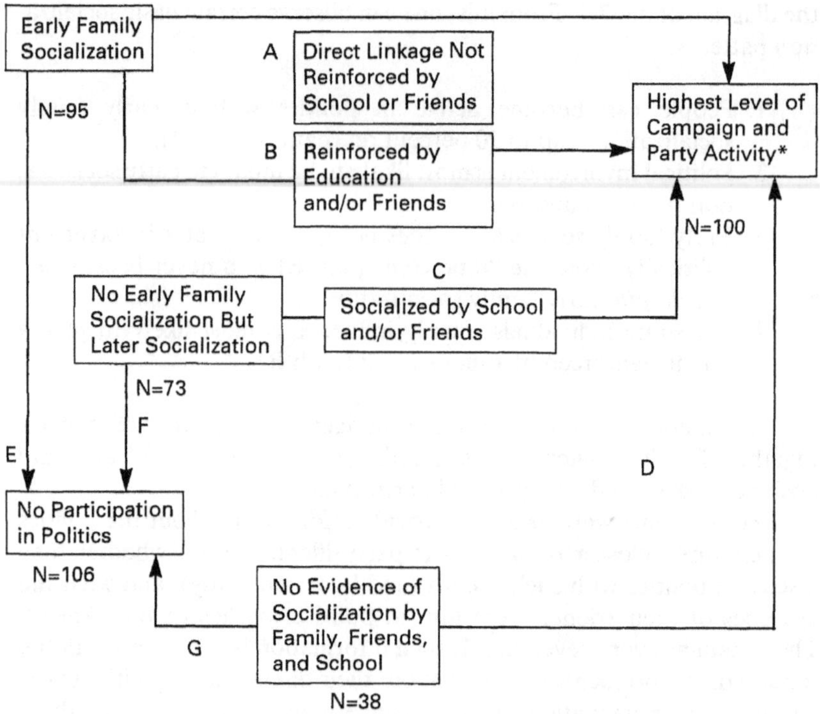

Patterns	Sample Frequencies	Percentage of Group Active
A	15.5%	57%
B	11.7	61
C	17.5	49
D	3.8	21
E	18.9	—
F	18.0	—
G	14.6	—
	100.0%	
	N = 206	49

Fig. 7.1. Basic socialization paths to political participation for the Ann Arbor public. This analysis was based on the 1984 study of the Ann Arbor public with an effective *N* for all variables of 206 individuals. Highest level of campaign and party activity means engaged in three or more activities out of nine possible activities.

ented toward political participation. An additional 15 percent do not have much peer-group support to be participative, although the early family exposure was political.

Party Loyalty and Contact as Linked to Political Participation

It is natural to expect that citizens who are strongly identified with a political party and have been contacted by party workers would be more likely to become active in campaigns. In fact, the argument could be conceived as almost a tautology: the strong "party man" or "party woman" *is* the party participator. To a certain extent, that is so. For example, if one distinguishes by strength of party identification, a consistent difference is found between the strong partisans, weak partisans, and independents in political involvement (table 7.2). As previous studies have noted, independents are just not as active as are the loyal (or weak) party supporters, but the differences are much less than one might have suspected. In Ann Arbor, many of the independents do engage in politics in some way, which is not that much below the proportion of strong partisans.

As for the role of party contact, one must also be cautious, for several reasons. First, a large proportion of the Ann Arbor public reports that they have been contacted by the parties, 47 percent (of which over half say they were contacted by both parties.). This is very high, much higher than the 25 percent in the national sample (1980) who said they had been contacted by the parties. Second, with such a high percentage being contacted, there is a strong probability that there may be a considerable overlap between those who are active and those who are

TABLE 7.1. The Linkage of Family and Friends Political Influence on Political Participation

	Family Socialization		
	Much Discussion of Politics	Some Discussion of Politics	No Discussion of Politics
Friends' attitudes toward parties positive	4.60 (9.4%)	3.93 (28.3%)	2.66 (5.7%)
Friends' attitudes toward parties mixed, neutral, or unknown	2.00 (15.1%)	1.59 (22.6%)	1.40 (18.9%)

Source: Survey of the Ann Arbor public conducted by the author in 1984.

Note: Entries are the average participation scores for respondents in each of these categories. The score is a simple allocation of one point for participation in each of seven possible party and campaign activities. Maximum score possible = 7. Frequencies are given in parentheses.

contacted, that is, one might argue that the party may seek out people who are already active; it does not necessarily induce inactive people to become active. To prove a causal relationship between party contact and political participation is difficult. The data do reveal the following relationship. Thus, of those contacted by a party—34 percent had a high participation and 22 percent low. Of those not contacted only 11 percent were high on participation and 54 percent were low. The correlation (Tau-B) is .4545—a healthy indication of some kind of relationship, but what its meaning is must be clarified.

A third point to keep in mind here is that not all people felt happy or positive about these contacts they had had. When pressed for their evaluations, those who had been contacted responded as follows: 23 percent positive, 12 percent negative, 40 percent neutral, 25 percent mixed. Hence there was no overwhelmingly enthusiastic feeling about those contacts. However, if a respondent reacted positively to such party contacts, there was a considerably higher probability that he or she had been a participant: 67 percent of those reacting favorably to party contacts scored high on our participation index and only 6 percent scored low. Table 7.3 summarizes the possible relevance of party contacts for citizen's involvement in party and campaign work. These findings do not solve the problem of causality. They merely suggest an association—one condition by which party contact may be more effective. Not all people contacted are happy about the experience; not all people contacted participated. But, it appears that if parties can do their work effectively, they not only can mobilize certain types of voters to vote, but they can also get them to work in campaigns. Party contact, if done well, combines with party loyalty to interest people in active party involvement.

Combining this information as to the role of the local party in conjunction with our earlier knowledge of the role of the family, the school, and the friends, the analysis suggests that the party can be a reinforcement agent or force in people's lives. Rarely, however, does

TABLE 7.2. The Relationship of Party Identification to Behavioral Involvement with Parties and in Campaigns

	Strong Identifiers	Weak Identifiers	Independents Leaning to a Party	Independents
Level of Political Activity				
High (3 or more acts)	39%	32	21	20
Medium (1 or 2 acts)	29	39	36	35
Low (no activity)	33	29	43	45

Source: Survey of the Ann Arbor public conducted by the author in 1984.

TABLE 7.3. Average Number of Participatory Acts Engaged In

Respondent's Evaluation of Contacts	Party Contact Occurred	No Party Contact
Positive	3.8	
Neutral	2.25	1.4
Negative	2.6	

Source: Survey of the Ann Arbor public conducted by the author in 1984.

party by itself in the absence of other reinforcement conditions lead people into political participation.

Specifically the data reveal that (1) early family socialization *by itself* seems to still be relevant for about 15 percent of our sample; (2) the party joins with other forces (such as school influences and friendships) to reinforce early socialization in about 40 percent of the sample and thus helps to lead people to participate; (3) despite positive contacts, certain persons do not become interested in political activity—almost 25 percent of our total sample (one-third of whom evaluated the contact favorably).

The basic socialization paths presented in figure 7.1 thus hold very well, supplemented with the knowledge that party organization contact, if viewed positively by the citizen, can be an additional agent impelling people into political work. Party contact can, however, have a negative impact or be responded to with indifference. In such a context, it is not a reinforcer, and it usually cannot bring people to political life who have not been previously influenced to do so. In the Ann Arbor sample, there were only six cases of persons who had not been exposed to early family socialization, and who had not been positively influenced by school *or* friendships, who were motivated to political activity by party organization contact alone!

The Role of Socialization in Developing Pro-Party Attitudes

Why should the Ann Arbor public, on balance, be more supportive of parties than negative? Eight agree-disagree items were used to test our respondents' attitudes to parties. Among them were the following:

	percent with a pro-party response
1. "The truth is we probably don't need parties in America any more"	70

2. "It is better to be a firm party supporter than to be a political independent"	23
3. "The parties do more to confuse the issues than to provide a clear choice on issues"	67
4. "You can't tell much about a candidate on the basis of party labels any more"	53

Using such responses, we constructed an index of party support for each person, using the direction of the response and the strength of belief (strong or weak disagreement or agreement). On the basis of these data, it is possible to characterize the Ann Arbor public as almost twice as much proparty as antiparty. The overall proportions are 45 percent proparty, 24 percent antiparty, 31 percent neutral.

The importance of political experience and socialization for such pro-party orientations is strongly suggested by these data (table 7.4). One must be wary of cause-and-effect conclusions, because it is possible that proparty people consciously seek out certain social and political contexts. There may be a configuration of influences operative here. Any type of socialization to politics through family, school, or peer groups and friendships seems to be rewarding, but family socialization reinforced by contacts and experiences in school and with friends has the greatest payoff. For some individuals, the influence of parents can lead to positive attitudes toward parties. But it is more likely that positive (proparty) adult socialization is necessary to develop attitudinal support for the party system. This finding is borne out by the analysis of party identification. We find that in Ann Arbor, those who were socialized to politics early, then positively reinforced in school and/or by friends, had the strongest party identification—44 percent, compared to only 13 percent for whom there is no evidence of such socialization.

Concluding Note

A large—unusually large—number of people enjoy being active in politics in Ann Arbor, and in a variety of ways: contacting leaders, contributing money, signing petitions, attending political meetings, and working for parties and other groups. This seems to be the result of the emphasis on politics in their earlier family lives, reinforced primarily by contacts with friends, school influence, work in community, and party associations. Party identification is still strong and is somewhat of a factor, although those calling themselves independents are also relatively active.

Party contacts play a supportive role in persuading people to be active, linked to their socialization agents. For the really active person in

TABLE 7.4. The Links between Political Socialization and Support for Political Parties

	Early Family Socialization[a]			No Early Socialization; Later Socialization at School and/or by Friends	No Evidence of Political Socialization by Family, School, or Friends
	Total Group	If Reinforced[b]	If Not Reinforced		
Index of Party Support[c]					
Pro-parties	45%	60	22	52	29
Neutral	27	21	38	36	34
Anti-parties	15	9	24	8	18
Very Anti-parties	13	10	16	4	18

Source: Data based on the 1984 interview study of Ann Arbor public; $N = 206$: 95 with early family socialization, 73 with only later socialization, and 38 with no evidence of socialization.

[a]Includes discussion of politics "very much" and/or parental political activity.

[b]Reinforcement is based on evidence of respondent's positive influence from high school or college courses or experiences, or from exposure to "three best friends" whose attitudes toward parties were reported to be positive.

[c]See text and appendix for description of the index. Scale of *1 to 7* used, with numbers 5–7 proparties, 4 neutral, 3 antiparties, and 1–2 very antiparties.

Ann Arbor, one sees a complex network of social and political influences, associations, and contacts over the life path from adolescent to adult, influences that arouse political interest and effectively sustain it. This political socialization process also is primarily responsible for the relatively small proportion of adults who are consistently opposed to parties. The political environment of Ann Arbor apparently conduces to strong support for parties and the party culture.

CHAPTER 8

The Top Political Elite: Its Changing Social and Political Character

Who runs for office and who runs the city? In the final analysis, this is the big question. It is followed by other questions: Who do those in power represent? How do they perceive the problems of the city? How do they maintain contact with the public? What are their values? What policies do they adopt? In the succeeding three chapters, we will discuss these questions, focusing on the characteristics of the top elites, their beliefs, and their policy actions. In this chapter we concentrate on the background characteristics of the candidates for mayor and council, and the winners. The time period is roughly the past forty-five years.

How elitist is local government in a democracy such as ours? That is a question in a larger perspective which has preoccupied scholars for many years. It is a complex question. It includes not only a concern about social and political backgrounds of leaders, but also their attitudes, values, and patterns of interaction, and whether their behavior is responsive to citizen needs and demands. In the focus on access to leadership positions in this chapter, we will return to that question, as well as a second intriguing query: Have elites in Ann Arbor been changing in this postwar period, and, if so, in what direction? Do we find a genuine "circulation of elites," as the earlier scholars called the phenomenon of elite change over time, or is the change pro forma and not significant? A study of social backgrounds and political experience can provide an introduction to that analysis, to be continued in succeeding chapters.

The term *top political elite* as used here refers to the sitting members of the city council,—that is, the winners—but also those candidates for office who participate in the struggle for political leadership in the community. Thus, there are two components: the governing elite, and the larger group of contestants for office. Analysis of both groups provides insights about the qualifications considered necessary for surviving the first process of getting into the pool of aspirants and the qualifications necessary to survive the final screening process at election time. The credentials may well vary, over time the latter process will influence the former process. The two together constitute a very important section of the "active political stratum."[1]

There are three basic types of changes to focus on. The first concerns the characteristics and credentials candidates for office have and which presumably are considered necessary for success in Ann Arbor. What age level, what religious persuasion, what race, what sex are the candidates? How much education do they have? How much party experience? How much experience in other community groups, and in which groups? Candidates and their backers assume that certain credentials are important, and in a sense voters confirm this. Yet, credentials change over time, as the community changes—new groups, new problems, new demands on leaders at city hall.

A second interest is the social representativeness (or unrepresentativeness) of elected officials. Which social sectors offer candidates or have them accepted, and which ones do not have representatives or are denied? How do the social characteristics of the contenders for power compare with the Ann Arbor adult population's social profiles? Is there as much social bias among the top elites today as there was forty years ago?

Third, there is the question of whether the Democratic and Republican parties differ as to the characteristics of their candidates and winners. Are they recruiting or attracting different types of persons to run, or are they appealing to basically the same social groups? How is this changing over the years as the nature of party conflict changes in Ann Arbor? Are the parties, in short, competitive (or asymmetric) in their candidacies, or homogeneous, selecting persons from essentially the same social pools of available personnel? As a special, intriguing case, what happened when a third party, the Human Rights Party (HRP), joined the scene, from 1972 to 1977? The party conflict model provides hunches as to what we should find in answer to these questions.

The emergence of leaders in a community is not a chance phenomenon. Some may sometimes think so, and ask, why is So-and-so running? Under the direct primary system, there is much opportunity for mavericks and self-starters. But the study of political recruitment strategy suggests that the appearance of new candidates on the scene is the product of nonrandom forces. It is a more regularized process than it appears. In the early stages of this process, the individual usually has had considerable experience interacting with others in the city, particularly having held roles in the group life of the community. During this time he or she has revealed certain characteristics leading to positive or negative evaluations as to eligibility for public office. Those positively evaluated become, in a loose sense, part of an available pool of potentials. Subsequently, they may make the self-conscious, independent decision to run, or they may have to be persuaded, even dragooned! Thus, there is a period of apprenticeship, a period of screening and evaluation, during which the potential candidate is "cleared" and would-be opponents dissuaded, and finally informal endorsement by the party, often clandestine sometimes overt.

The Ann Arbor Political Context

In all of this, one must remember the special Ann Arbor political system in which candidates have to operate. First, of course, it is a partisan system. Candidates run as Democrats or Republicans (except in that brief interlude that also included Human Rights party). Second, it is a system in which council candidates run from one of the five wards, while the mayor runs every two years citywide. Ward and neighborhood may become very involved. Third, it is, in theory at least, a direct primary system. That is, candidates file with city clerk, and may face an intraparty contest in a February primary if there is more than one candidate in their party running for the ward seat or for the party candidacy for mayor. This system permits selfstarters to run, individuals without (or who have not sought) strong party organization support.

A serious primary battle may signify real factionalism within the local party. In fact, however, from 1946 to the present, for only 13 percent of the positions has a primary contest occurred in Ann Arbor. If one looks at the votes cast for the contenders in these primaries, one observes that in only 10 percent of these primaries have there been close battles (where the margin of victory was 10 percentage points or less). Normally, primary contests are not very frequent or significant. Either the party grooms individuals and then persuades them to run ("promotes," or conscripts, them), or the person who announces as candidate is acceptable to a large majority of party followers. In less than 5 percent of all years has this not been the case. Thus, it is partisan forces and the partisan process that heavily influences the decision of individuals to run for office.

In the analysis of the social and political backgrounds of candidates for mayor and council presented here the time period is 1946 to 1991. The total number of positions filled was 277. There were 556 candidates (524 for the two main parties), but only 353 different persons (since many persons ran more than once). Of these 277 positions over these forty-five years, the victories by party were: Republicans 184, Democrats 90, Human Rights 3. Fairly complete data were collected for these candidates on certain (but not all) characteristics. Even where the data are not perfectly complete, information was adequate for close to 90 percent of the persons running for these offices. This permits a careful analysis over four postwar decades.

Turnover of Candidates and Winners

One test of the elitist nature of a system is the frequency of turnover. What do we find for Ann Arbor? There are a few perennials (a candidate four or more times), but on the whole and for a variety of reasons, people do not pursue for long their local political careers. Some find holding two jobs too demanding and exhausting. Many tire of office after two terms or feel they have fulfilled their obligation by then. Some are defeated early. Still others move out of Ann Arbor. But 25 percent do run a second time and a few even more frequently. The data on candidate frequency for mayor and council for the period, by party, are: only 5 or 6 percent run four times or more, 8 to 9 percent three times, and, on the other hand, a large percentage ran only once—50 percent of Republicans and 69 percent of Democrats. Thus, 85 percent or more in both parties ran no more than twice.

Those who win, in comparison to candidates, are inclined to run more frequently. Only 28 percent of the winners ran once, 45 percent ran twice, and 27 percent ran three or more times. Many winners obviously have a desire to stay in power, but losers are easily discouraged. Yet, not all winners in Ann Arbor run a second time—about one fourth voluntarily quit after a first term.

Incumbents are highly favored for local offices, although not as much as in races for higher governmental positions (over 96 percent of incumbents won in the 1990 congressional races). In Ann Arbor in the early years, the Democratic incumbents for mayor and council did much more poorly than did the Republicans, but this has changed in recent years. Up to 1976, 42 percent of the Democratic incumbents lost (compared to 16 pecent of the Republicans). But since 1976 only 17 percent of Democratic incumbents lost (compared to 27 percent of Republicans). These data strongly attest to the rise in the strength of the Democratic party in the past decade. Their incumbents in recent years are actually less vulnerable to defeat now than are Republican incumbents. Yet, in the past fifteen years, over 20 percent in both parties are defeated. That attests to the highly competitive nature of the partisan conflict here, the alteration in power, and the volatility of our system.

This volatility is reflected in the turnover among the eleven members of the city council. Two-thirds of city elections since 1956 have produced three or more new faces on city council (almost 50 percent produced four or more new faces). This has not been quite as true since 1976. In no more than 50 percent of the elections since then have three or four new persons been elected. Yet, this suggests a fairly considerable change in the personnel of the council. Another way to look at it is to determine for what percentage of city councils in a two-election sequence one finds a majority (six out of eleven) who were new (during that period). The answer is 66 percent since 1957, though the figure is less in the last ten years: 50 percent. Nevertheless, the change in personnel at the city leadership level is considerable. The circulation of elites—the regular replacement of leadership at the top of the system—is fairly rapid. Every four years brings in a new set of leaders. For example, there were only two holdovers from 1987 in the 1991 council, and only two from 1986 in the 1990 council. Clearly the "turnover" of the personnel of the council is regular and periodically sweeping.

Social Credentials of Council Members: Ann Arbor Compared to Other Cities

A comparison can be made between Ann Arbor leaders and the elites in twenty other U.S. cities, which were a random sample of cities in the same population stratum, interviewed in 1984–85. Data are also available from a comparable set of cities in two European countries, Sweden and the Netherlands, which are part of this ongoing comparative research.

The social backgrounds of members of the city council in Ann Arbor are somewhat distinctive compared to these cities (table 8.1). Ann Arbor's political elite is much younger (45 percent are under age forty, compared to 22 percent for other U.S. cities), more representative of women, better educated (58 percent with graduate-school training compared to 45 percent for other U.S. cities), and more who hold major professional or managerial occupations than in other cities. Other "university cities" may, of course, have elites similar to those in Ann Arbor. The contrast with the two European countries is in some respects even more striking. In both countries there are proportionately fewer women. In Sweden councillors are much older (only 5 percent below age forty), and the educational level of the local European political elite is less advanced than in the U.S. The Swedish leaders, particularly, are less educated. In Sweden, 60 percent have completed less than what we call the college degree level, compared to 17 percent at that level in Ann Arbor. Actually, by using the most recent Ann Arbor data, the contrasts are even more striking—in the 1990–91 Ann Arbor city councils, close to 60 percent were under age forty, and 41 percent were women. Thus, Ann Arbor's council members are very different demographically. The system seems more open to women, but also quite limited in representation in other respects. It is a bourgeois elite of well-educated professionals and business leaders, and it is primarily white—only one black person (reelected regularly since 1982) has sat on the city council in the past decade.

Even for Ann Arbor's well-educated population, this is an elite or socially biased group of councillors. For example, according to the 1980 census, 56 percent of the Ann Arbor population age twenty-five or older were college graduates, and 42 percent of those employed worked in a professional or managerial occupation, such as lawyers, doctors, teachers, social workers and directors of business firms. The elite-mass discrepancy on these two comparisons is 83—56 percent and 64—42 percent, respectively. Compared to the U.S. Congress, however, Ann Arbor's system is much more open to women (only 5 to 7 percent of the 535 members of Congress in recent years have been women). The occupational distribution is similar, since Congress includes a high percentage of persons with a professional or business managerial background (for the

TABLE 8.1. Elite Social Backgrounds: A Comparison of Ann Arbor and Other Cities, 1984–85

	Ann Arbor	Other U.S. Cities	Sweden	Netherlands
Age				
Under 40	45%	22	5	24
Gender				
Women	27	20	16	16
Education				
Graduate School	58	45	30	34
Completed College	25	24	11	41
Some College	17	9	32	16
Lower Education	0	22	27	8
Occupational Class				
Professional/Managerial	64	53	40	—[a]
Middle	9	34	46	—[a]
Lower—Working Class	0	7	13	—[a]
Not in Labor Force[b]	27	6	1	—[a]
N	22	128	261	201

Note: The other U.S. cities (20), Swedish communes (15), and Dutch cities (20) were random samples used in another project. They were drawn from the same population stratum as Ann Arbor. The other studies were done also in the middle to late 1980s. These comparisons are for the local elected councillors in all three countries. We use the 1984–85 period for Ann Arbor since our data for other cities were secured for that time period. $N = 22$ Ann Arbor, 128 other U.S. cities, 261 Sweden, 201 Netherlands.

[a]No comparable data for Netherlands.

[b]Includes full-time homemakers, retirees, unemployed, and students.

1985–86 Congress, over 50 percent of the members reported professional occupations and over 20 percent had business backgrounds). As for the representation of blacks, the level of discrimination is almost identical in Washington—5 to 6 percent of the members of Congress are black.

Postwar Trends in the Recruitment of the Top Elite

The social profiles of the top elite in Ann Arbor in recent years are somewhat exceptional. They are quite different than 45 years ago. An analysis of postwar trends demonstrates the gradual process by which this change occurred. The data on candidates for office are presented

TABLE 8.2. Trend Data for Social Backgrounds of Ann Arbor's Top Elites

	1946–55	1956–70	1971–80	1981–91
Women				
% of candidates	7%	12	19	32
% of winners	3	10	15	31
Blacks				
% of candidates	4	6	7	10
% of winners	3	8	11	10
Age: Under 40				
% of candidates	27	47	65	50
% of winners	30	49	75	49
Occupations				
Professional				
% of candidates	33	43	48	39
% of winners	47	50	65	50
Business				
% of candidates	41	26	9	29
% of winners	33	41	25	34
Educational level: Graduate work or graduate degree				
% of candidates	49	63	70	53
% of winners	41	43	75	51
*N*s: Candidates				
Actual total	134	168	108	114
Partial *N*s	42–113	108–150	64–104	59–103
*N*s: Winners				
Actual total	75	84	53	61
Partial *N*s	20–37	41–46	20–22	38–39

Source: Based on the *Ann Arbor News* and political party reports.

Note: The data for women and blacks are based on complete information for all candidates and winners. For the other social characteristics we have less complete data, particularly for the early years. The ranges in the partial *N*s for age, occupation, and education are indicated.

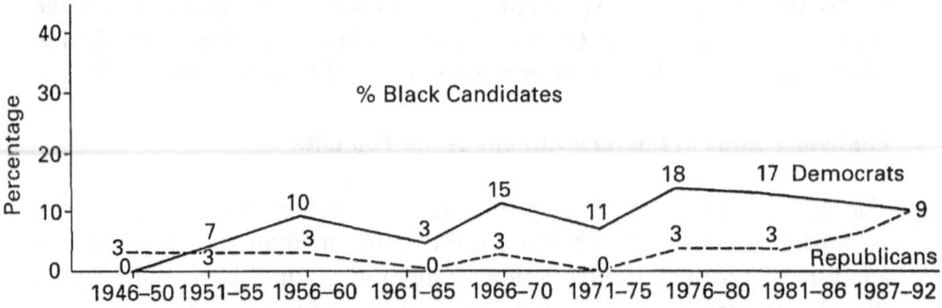

Fig. 8.1. Proportion of black candidates for Ann Arbor mayor and council, 1946–92.

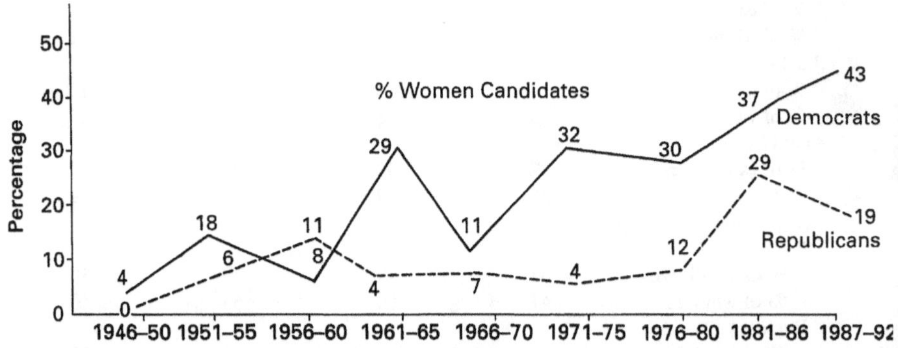

Fig 8.2. Proportion of women candidates for Ann Arbor mayor and council, 1946–92.

first, then the data on the winners (table 8.2; see also the accompanying graphs, figs. 8.1 to 8.5.)

Access to candidacy for office in the early years was primarily the province of white men. Up to 1953 only three white women and two black men ran for council. The proportion of blacks has not increased much over the years, but there has been a dramatic rise in the percentage of women candidates. In the last decade, it increased to almost one-third, and in the last two campaigns to over 40 percent. Ann Arbor has had young candidates for most of the postwar period, but the candidacies flourished particularly in the 1970s after 18-year-olds received the vote and were encouraged also by student involvement in local politics

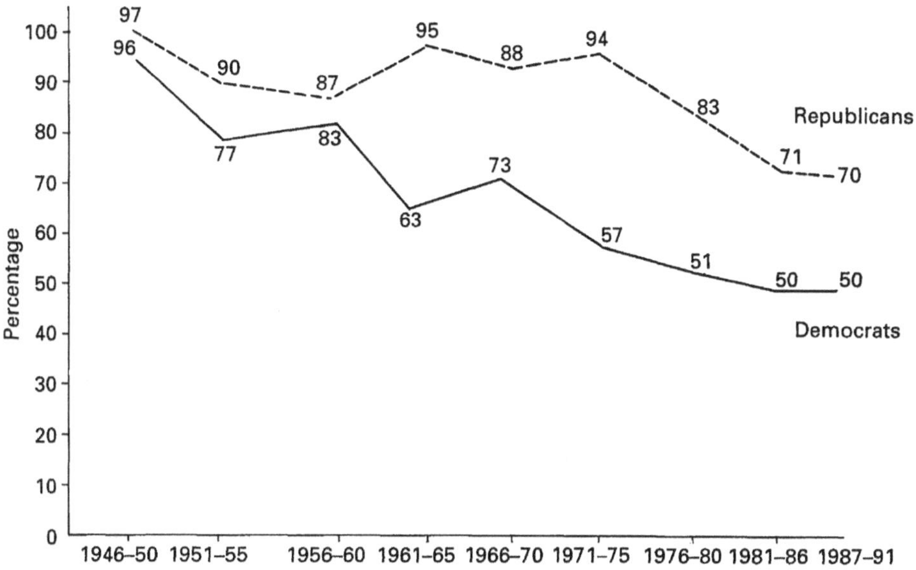

Fig. 8.3. Proportion of white male candidates for Ann Arbor mayor and council, 1946–91.

during the rise of the Human Rights party and its victories in city council races. From 1971 to 1977 60 percent of all candidates were under age thirty-five. This percentage dropped to 40 percent in the following five years and to 30 percent in the later 1980s. Nevertheless, young people under age forty have continued to be attracted to candidacy for city offices.

The other trend that stands out is the rise in the proportion of professionals as candidates for city council. From less than one-fifth right after the war, when persons of business occupational backgrounds were dominant, there has been a considerable surge in interest by those with professional backgrounds. The peak period was the 1970s, but there has been only a slight decline since. At the same time, those with business managerial occupations have constituted a smaller proportion of candidacies. They declined dramatically in the 1970s, but they still represent almost 30 percent of those seeking office. The proportions of those with clerical, secretarial, and lower-level professional occupations have remained a fairly constant proportion of office seekers over the years (almost one-fourth). They increased particularly in the 1970s. Those at the lower level of the occupational scale, lower white-collar and blue-collar, for the most part, have never aspired, or have never

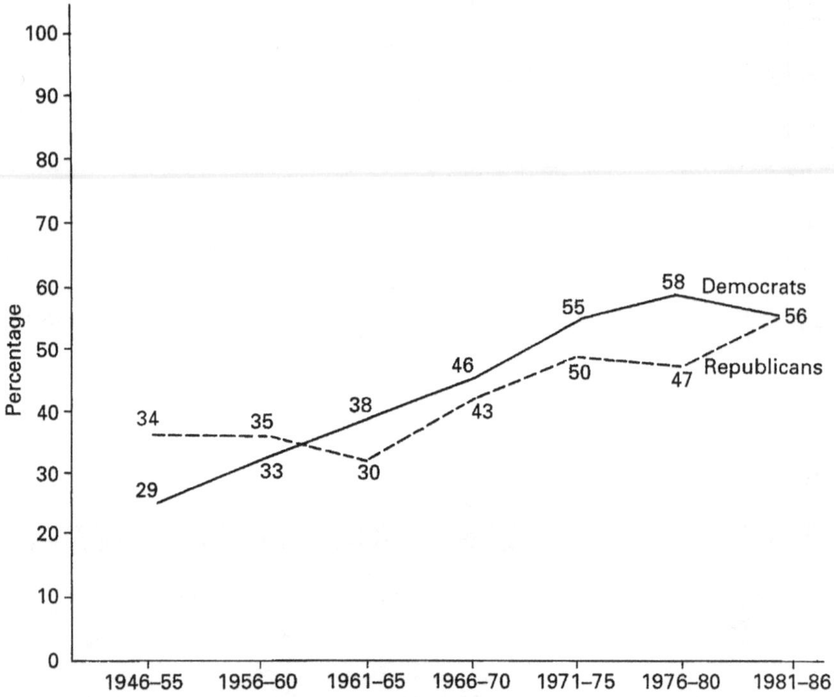

Fig. 8.4. The rise of the professional at city hall, 1946–86. Based on the winners for mayor and council. Each number represents the percentage for each party who had professional occupations.

been attracted, or have never been recruited to candidacy for city offices. They have represented only 2 to 3 percent of all candidacies.

On the basis of candidacies for mayor and council, therefore, whereas forty years ago white men with a business background predominated, today the candidates are more diversified. The greatest change is in their sex, their professional occupations, and their educational level. These have been incremental and not dramatic or revolutionary changes. Yet the social profile of candidates is considerably different today.

Factors Related to the Changes in Elite Social Backgrounds

One of the fascinating and basic questions in elite research is: Why and under what conditions does elite change occur? It is not enough to say that this is the result of elections, which is obviously true. Voters desire

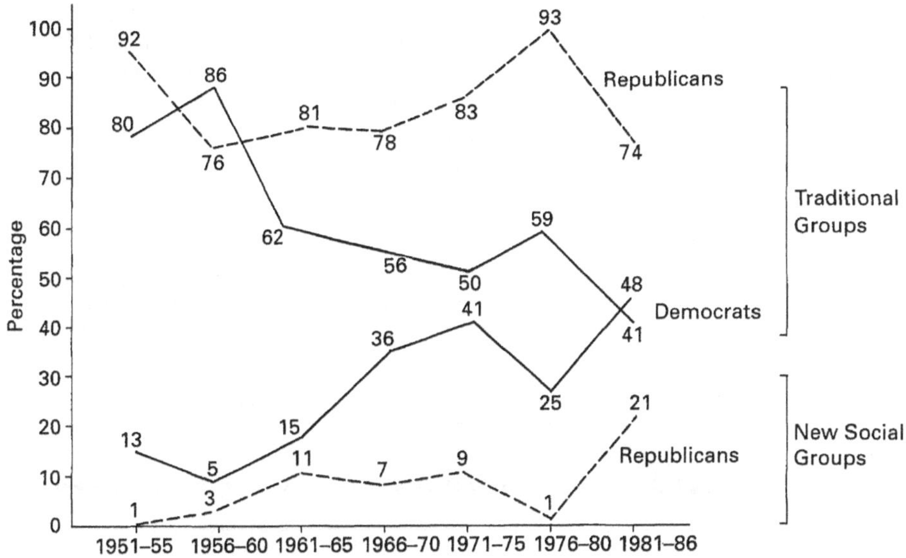

Fig. 8.5. Group memberships of Candidates, 1951–86. Traditional groups included business, professional, veterans, fraternal, charity, older civic, sports, and union groups. Newer groups included feminist, pacifist, environmental, social welfare, arts, racial, and gay rights.

to see different leaders in the mayor's chair and on city council, and each election has specific contextual conditions which help explain that election's result. The concern here is more generic and perspectivist—why, over the forty-five-year period, were there more women, more professionals, more university-educated people,and periodically more young elites? Certain developments occurred incrementally over time to explain this trend.

First is the finding that as candidacies opened up and persons of different social backgrounds were encouraged to seek office, the types of people who won office changed. This is a simple point, and seemingly obvious, but one that has to be made. When the "pool" of candidates became more diverse this was reflected in victories for new types of people. There is a high correspondence between who is in the candidate pool and who the winners are.

This is not a complete answer, however. The key question is: What was responsible for the expansion and diversification of the candidate pool? That leads to the second key explanation. The role and recruitment strategy of the party organizations in Ann Arbor became a decisive determinant. To demonstrate this, data for four time periods are presented, using two measures: (1) the proportion of each party's total number of candidates from a particular social group, and (2) the percentage of all candidates during a time period who were recruited by the Democrats or Republicans (table 8.4). From these data one can see that the early impetus for the recruitment of certain groups, and the sustained interest in

TABLE 8.3. Changes in the Candidate "Pool" as Linked to Candidate Success

	1946–55 Candidates	1946–55 Winners	1981–91 Candidates	1981–91 Winners
Women	7%	3	32	31
Blacks	4	3	10	10
Young (under 40)	27	30	50	49

TABLE 8.4. Differential Party Recruitment of Candidates for City Council By Selected Social Characteristics

	1944–55		1956–70		1971–80		1981–91		Totals	
	Dem.	Rep.	Dem.	Rep.	Dem.	Rep.	Dem.	Rep.	Dem.	Rep.
Social Characteristics (*N* in parentheses)										
Women										
Measure 1	11%	3	18	7	31	8	38	26	22	8
Measure 2	78	22	71	29	80	20	63	37	71	29
	(61)	(74)	(84)	(84)	(55)	(53)	(58)	(56)	(258)	(267)
Blacks										
Measure 1	3	4	10	2	15	2	14	6	9	4
Measure 2	40	60	80	20	89	11	73	27	74	26
	(61)	(74)	(i4)	(84)	(55)	(53)	(58)	(56)	(258)	(267)
Age: Under 40										
Measure 1	42	17	48	46	55	65	64	44	53	43
Measure 2	61	39	49	51	49	51	52	48	54	46
	(23)	(19)	(52)	(49)	(36)	(24)	(46)	(41)	(157)	(133)
Occupation										
Professional										
Measure 1	31	33	55	30	51	44	44	23	46	34
Measure 2	52	48	65	35	61	39	66	34	62	38
	(39)	(30)	(55)	(53)	(37)	(27)	(43)	(44)	(174)	(154)
Business										
Measure 1	23	40	12	42	5	15	7	50	13	36
Measure 2	43	57	21	79	33	67	12	88	25	75
	(39)	(30)	(55)	(53	(37)	(27)	(43)	(44)	(174)	(154)

Source: Based on the *Ann Arbor News* and political party reports.

Note: Measure 1 indicates percentage of each party's candidates to which given characteristics applied. Measure 2 indicates percentage of all candidates bearing the given characteristic recruited by each party.

these groups, was to a great extent the result of Democratic party efforts. Even though the first woman and the first black person elected to city council were Republican, it was the Democratic party that took up the challenge and really was more inclusive of these groups over the years. The Republicans became more competitive concerning women, particularly in the 1980s, but their overall encouragement of such candidates lagged behind the Democrats. The younger age cohort (under forty) was attracted early to Democratic candidacies, but the Republicans soon matched the Democrats. As for occupational groups, it was the professionals who were recruited by the Democrats, especially from 1956 on, while the Republicans were responsible for recruiting those with business backgrounds (although this declined greatly in the seventies). The aggregate data over these forty-five years are thus very revealing (table 8.5). The Democrats contributed much to changing the social profile of the pool of candidates as well as the social profile of the city council. The Republicans responded also but lagged behind the Democrats in the opening of candidacies to women, those under 40, and professionals. In recent years the relevance of this differential party recruitment has been reinforced. Table 8.6 gives the party proportions of the winners of these

TABLE 8.5. Types of Candidates and Winners Recruited by Democrats and Republicans.

	Candidates Recruited by		Winners who were	
	Dem.	Rep.	Dem.	Rep.
Women	71%	29	67	33
Blacks	74	26	95	5
Under 40	54	46	44	56
Professional occupations	62	38	50	50
Business occupations	25	75	12	88

Source: Based on the *Ann Arbor News* and political party reports.

TABLE 8.6. The Proportions of Candidates from Selected Social Categories who were Successful, by Party

	Democrats	Republicans
Women	71%	29
Blacks	100	0
Under 40	53	47
Professional occupations	63	37
Business occupations	25	75

Source: Based on the *Ann Arbor News* and political party reports.

social groups from 1971 to 1991 (that is, the percentage of the candidates of each social group, by party, who won).

The relationship of these changes to increased party competition, particularly the increase in the electoral strength of the Democrats, is suggested strongly by these data. This can be illustrated nicely by looking at the increase in women among candidates and winners as competition increased, (table 8.7). While the Democrats played a major initiating and sustaining competitive role, the entrance of a third party on the scene was a further stimulant to diversity. The Human Rights party contested elections from 1972 to 1977. Its twenty-six candidates were in some respects markedly different: almost all were under age 35, half were students or homemakers and held lower professional and blue-collar occupations; 32 percent were women. The appearance of the HRP was associated with efforts by the two major parties to meet the competition (table 8.8). Democrats responded by recruiting more women and young people to run, and Republicans by selecting younger men. The contrast in the age of candidates was sharp in the prepluralist period. Before 1972, the two major parties had selected only one-fourth of their candidates from the under-35 cohort; from 1972 to 1977, this increased to 55 percent for the Democrats and 58 percent for the Republicans. In the period after 1977, it dropped to one-third. The consequences of having a third party on the scene in terms of types of candidates can be significant. The types of actors contesting in the political arena changed considerably. In addition, there may have been some carryover effect on candidacies of the two main parties in succeeding years.

The impact of party competition on candidate recruitment is thus demonstrable. To this must be added the important role of the party

TABLE 8.7. The Relevance of Party Competition to Changes in the Recruitment of Women

	Average % of Democratic Vote for Council	% of Candidates Who Were Women	% of Winners Who Were Women
Early period of Republican dominance	31%	7	3
Period of increasing Democratic strength (1956–71)	46	11	8
Period of pluralist politics (1972–77)	42	23	21
Recent period of two-party competition (1978–91)	49	32	31

Source: Based on the *Ann Arbor News* and political party reports.

organizations. This has become more relevant as the parties became stronger and as people began to see that experience in the party organization was useful for eventual candidacy for city council. The over-time data based on available biographical data for the candidates reveal striking changes in exposure by candidates to party organizational work. Up to 1960, only 3 percent of Democratic candidates had party experience (20 percent of Republicans). This increased in succeeding years until in the last decade (1981–91) 64 percent of Democratic candidates and 68 percent of Republicans had such experience. The local party organizations clearly have become a channel or training ground for the majority of candidates for city hall positions. This close linkage between city hall politicians and the two party organizations is corroborated by the data we presented in an earlier chapter on the characteristics of the party activists. (See table 8.9.) The top elite is in many respects the mirror

TABLE 8.8. A Comparison of the Human Rights Candidates with the Candidates of the Major Parties, 1972–77

	Human Rights (*N* = 26)	Democrats (*N* = 33)	Republicans (*N* = 32)
Women			
% of All Candidates	32%	33	9
Age			
% Under 35	95	55	58
Occupational Status			
Student, Homemaker	48	25	29
Lower Professional or Blue-Collar	52	30	29
Higher Professional or Business Managerial	0	45	43

Source: Based on the *Ann Arbor News* and political party reports.

TABLE 8.9. Comparison of the proportions of Selected Social Categories in the Party Organizations and in the City Council in the 1980s

	City Council Members (1984–85)	Party Organization Activists (1982 study)
Women	27%	47
Under Age 40	45	46
With Graduate education	58	63
In Professional/Managerial Occupations	64	67
Blacks	9	2

Source: Based on the *Ann Arbor News* and political party reports.

image of the party organizational elite. Its members have career paths that take them through the party, and thus, as expected, they are very representative of the parties. The composite picture of the city council reflects the partisan differences in social status.

One should also note here that the governmental experience of city council candidates also has increased over the years. In the early years, about one-fourth of the candidates (especially Republicans) had had experience on city commissions or council boards or had even worked for state agencies. Today this is true of over 40 percent of Republican and Democratic candidates, attesting to the governmental interest, involvement, and competence of these persons who seek city office.

The role of interest groups as instigators of candidacies should not be overlooked here. Such groups stimulate interest in city politics, are training grounds about city affairs, and seek to influence city policy. In chapter 5, we described a type of symbiosis between interest groups and party organizations—66 percent of interest group leaders were active in parties, and 55 percent of party organization leaders were active in politically relevant interest groups. The data for city council candidates reveals that this is a triangular relationship: 67 percent of those aspiring to city council seats have memberships in political interest groups. Figure 8.6 describes this relationship.

What is particularly relevant and interesting here is the type of groups that candidates belong to today compared to thirty and forty years ago (table 8.10). A distinction can be made between the traditional and established groups on the one hand (civic, business, professional, fraternal, veterans, etc.), and the newer types of special interest groups which have emerged over time (social, ethnic, feminist, environmental, pacifist, and the like) as well as neighborhood groups. There is a considerable change in the type of group memberships of candidates over time. In the early 1946–55 period, candidates were more likely to belong to the established, traditional groups—91 percent did. In recent years we find almost no candidates reporting memberships in fraternal and veterans groups (compared to 24 percent earlier) and 35 percent reporting membership in the newer types of special interest groups and neighborhood groups (compared to 9 percent earlier). The Democrats are particularly affiliated with these newer types of interest groups today (48 percent Democrats, 20 percent Republicans). Two significant aspects of this difference should be emphasized: (1) Democrats have a somewhat different interest-group representative base in the community, and (2) Democrats come into their elite positions as a result of experiences with somewhat different types of groups than do Republi-

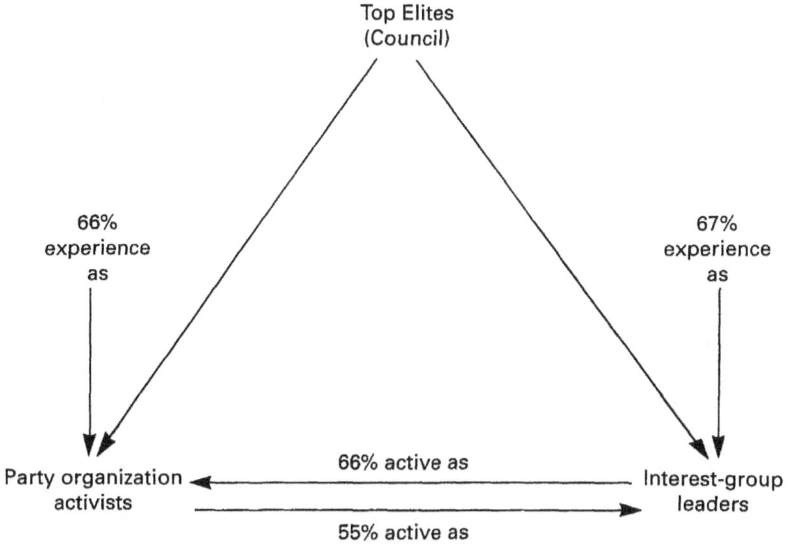

Fig. 8.6. The triangular relationships of city councillors, party activists, and interest group leaders. (Based on surveys of elites, activists, and interest group leaders conducted by the author in 1986, 1982, and 1983.)

cans. The social group ties and constituencies of the two sets of rival candidates overlap but are by no means identical.

Concluding Observations

In reflecting on these data it is clear that the characteristics and backgrounds of those who seek office and who are elected to the top positions in Ann Arbor's government have changed considerably in the past forty-five years. It is also clear that the emergence of a competitive two-party system made a difference. The changes in credentials are apparent. The increase in women among candidates and winners, as well as the decline in the age of candidates, their higher level of education, and the shift in the emphasis on professional occupational backgrounds have taken place rather gradually. In addition, the types of interest groups with which the leaders are affiliated have also changed. This means that the probabilities of victory for persons with particular social and political backgrounds also have changed, in certain respects dramatically. (table 8.11). In the early period, Democratic candidates had limited probabilities, so their candidates suffered. Nevertheless, overall the chances of victory have increased for women, blacks, younger candidates, and pro-

TABLE 8.10. Changes in Political Interest Groups to which Candidates for City Council Reported They Belonged

% of All Groups Reported by Candidates	1946–55	1956–70	1971–86
Established, Traditional Groups (Civic, Business, Professional, Charity, Union)			
Total	50%	42	41
Democrats	43	35	35
Republicans	59	50	51
Older Specialized Groups (Church, School, Sports, Arts, etc.)			
Total	16	22	23
Democrats	23	26	17
Republicans	6	19	28
Fraternal and Veterans Groups			
Total	24	11	1
Democrats	22	9	0
Republicans	26	13	1
Neighborhood Groups			
Total	0	2	9
Democrats	0	1	11
Republicans	0	3	6
Newer Specialized Types of Groups (Race and Ethnicity, Environment, Pacifist, Feminist, Social Welfare, etc.)			
Total	9	23	26
Democrats	10	29	37
Republicans	8	16	14
N Total	108	199	171
Democrats	59	89	102
Republicans	49	110	69

Source: These data come from the biographical files of city council candidates reported by the *Ann Arbor News* and filed in the Ann Arbor Library. The total *N* refers to all groups mentioned by candidates.

TABLE 8.11. Probabilities of Victory for Candidates with Certain Credentials

	1946–55	1981–91
Women	22%	54
Blacks	40	55
Under Age 40	44	51
Professionals	57	66
Business Occupations	62	52
For Democrats	13	53
For Republicans	91	50

Source: Based on the *Ann Arbor News* and political party reports.

fessionals, while declining for those with business occupations. There has been a greater diversification of the candidate pool and of the type of persons on council. Since the expectations of victory have been modified, there has occurred a change in the electoral climate and the political culture. Incrementally electoral politics has become more open.

The reasons for this change have been explored carefully. It is not primarily due to changes in the sociological structure or population of the community. It is true that the expansion of the community and the increased educational level of its population have taken place. But women have always been here and have always been able politically, and there have been approximately the same proportions of able black people and young people. Likewise, there has always been a large number of professionals. It is clearly due to changes in the *political* system and political environment that candidates of these types have run and sometimes won. With the development of the two-party system and closer party competition, more candidacies were opened to sectors of the population who previously were not encouraged or did not find running for office attractive or worthwhile. The differential recruitment orientations of the two parties, with the Democrats appealing to different social groups, provided the impetus for change and helped sustain that change. The role of the Human Rights Party in the 1970s also stimulated new types of candidacies. Finally, the changing character of Ann Arbor's interest-group complex provided support and pressure for new types of candidacies.

What have been the consequences of this change in the social and political backgrounds of Ann Arbor's elites? In some respects the system appears more open, diverse, and representative; in other respects it still reveals social bias and is elitist. The top elite is professional, well-educated, relatively young, and almost completely white, but by no means homogeneous in these terms, and the inclusion of women recently has changed one major characteristic of the council. It is, however, very bourgeois and not closely representative of the public, although the gap has narrowed recently. Table 8.12 compares census data and elite data on education, age, and race. For whatever relevance it may have, these comparisons suggest there is a closer correspondence in recent years between population characteristics and elite backgrounds. Yet, a disproportion in public-elite characteristics clearly exists. Women, although doing better, are still not equally represented among top elites in *both* parties. The younger age group, 18 to 34, has poor representation, accounting for 24 percent of the winners (1979–82) compared to 54 percent of the population (1980). Those with professional-managerial occupations in the top elite made up 64 percent of the council in the early 1980s, compared to 42 percent of the Ann Arbor labor force (1980). Only 3 percent of candidates held blue-collar jobs..

Three other characteristics stand out in the analysis, which some might argue are the saving grace of our system. The Ann Arbor top leadership is competent, integrated in the community, and so competitive that there is relatively high turnover. Their competence is attested to by their educational level and their political experience: two-thirds of those on council have had governmental experience, two-thirds have worked actively in community interest groups, and 40 percent have had some type of governmental experience. The statistics also bear out their integration in the community: 77 percent have lived in Ann Arbor more than ten years, 47 percent more than twenty. The probability of a candidate winning today with less than six years residence is virtually zero; with longer residence but no political or governmental experience, the probability in recent years is 5 percent. Over 80 percent of council members are married and have children. Thus on a variety of measures these leaders are and have been involved in and committed to Ann Arbor and its politics for a long time.

In the larger sense one must see here an elite that is not cohesive socially, and is constantly changing in personnel. The considerable turnover, in the council is comprised of two types: approximately 80 percent do not stay on for more than two terms, and incumbents who seek reelection are fairly frequently defeated—over 20 percent have been in recent years.

Thus, there is a circulation of elites over time, and one that is not just pro forma. The top elite today is different in significant respects compared to forty years ago. Party competition is the crucial factor in such elite change—party competition supported by strong party organizations that seem to be adaptive to the changes taking place in Ann

TABLE 8.12. Comparison of Elite Data and Census Data on the Public for Certain Selected Characteristics

	1960		1980		Elite-Public Difference	
	Elite	Public	Elite	Public	1960	1980
College Graduates	91%	39	91	56	52	35
Age 18–40	25	48	45	59	23	14
White	91	94	91	85	3	6

Source: U.S. Census reports and the data on all members of Council secured from the Ann Arbor News and other reports.

Note: The term *elite* refers to city council membership.

Arbor's society. This has seemed over these years to moderate the effects of the type of "elitism" which might be said to have existed in the past in the Ann Arbor system. While a certain amount of elitism persists, and much more still needs to be done to expand citizen involvement, perhaps these findings suggest that Ann Arbor's leaders as a collective group may today be more responsive to the community than previously.

CHAPTER 9

Elite Styles and Beliefs

A recent controversy at City Hall exemplifies the different perspectives of the Democratic and Republican leaders. It concerned the adoption of the 1989 budget early that year. There were disagreements over the administrator's budget. One issue was whether a human rights investigator should be reinstated (a position promised in 1987) at a cost of $29,000. The Republicans refused. The Democrats were upset that the Republicans had backed away from an earlier commitment. A Republican councillor gave a ready explanation: "I care (about racism) *but we have different priorities*!"[1] That is the major question we are concerned with in this chapter: What are the Republicans' and Democrats' strategies and value priorities, and how do they differ?

We have discussed at length *who* the leaders are, and their social and political backgrounds. Now we are concerned with the *what* of politics. What do they consider to be the problems facing the community, and what basic orientations or values do they bring to the solution of these problems? Although one might deduce much of this from observing the actions of leaders—since actions presumably follow beliefs—systematic evidence is still necessary. To generalize with confidence about the top elite as a leadership structure (rather than speculate or talk about individual leaders only), hard data are required.

The top elite in any community has its well-developed sets of beliefs and political formulas for policy action. These belief structures need careful examination if one is to understand elite behavior, particularly if one assumes that in Ann Arbor there is not one, singular elite but competing, plural elites. Although these belief structures may change over time, the assumption is that they do have a basic continuity because they are concerned with fundamental conceptions of how politics are to be conducted, what the role of government is, and what types of policies are needed to implement development goals. In a partisan form of government, one assumes also that there is some cohesion by party in these beliefs and that the party subgroups of the top elite in power, and competing for power, will differ in certain significant ways. These propositions will be tested in the ensuing analysis.

This big question of what leaders think, perceive, and believe is a complex one. We approach it in variety of ways in this chapter. One study conducted in 1986 used a questionnaire directed to the mayor and council as well as to the heads of city departments. Since top administrators as well as mayor and council are in the elite, they were sent the questionnaire also. This effort was fairly successful, securing responses from sixteen individuals in city government. These included the mayor, Republican and Democratic councillors, the city administrator, police chief, fire chief, city clerk, director of community development, city controller, city attorney, executive director of the city housing commission, and director of the planning department. Since this included about 70 percent or better of the relevant personnel at the top leadership level, this seemed adequate. This set of leaders, then, can be considered the 1986 policy elite.

In addition, because 1986 might be considered a special year, from the previous studies over the period from 1976 to 1986, a set of thirty-two leaders was selected for whom there were interview data. These consisted of two groups: former council members and top leaders in the party organizations. This set of interviews included fifteen council members (five who had been candidates for mayor, three successful), city party chairs, and members of the party executive committees (several of whom had also run for city council). This second group is called the top political elite, 1976–86.

The demographics of the 1986 policy elite based on these studies reveal considerable diversity. There was a range in age from twenty-seven to sixty-one among councillors, thirty-eight to fifty-seven among administrators. Their occupations varied greatly, including doctor, librarian, social administrator, professor of political science, sales manager, high school teacher, homemaker, and investment analyst for the University of Michigan. The administrators had been in public service for some time, ranging from eleven to thirty-three years. Their family backgrounds, and those of the council ranged from lower and working class to upper middle class. Eighty percent had a graduate education. They were Jewish, Catholic, Lutheran, Methodist, Mormon, Church of Christ, other Protestant, and no professed religion. The administrators were mixed politically: five said they were Democrats, four Republicans, and the rest independents or refused to say. The councillors had had many years of political experience, but they usually had been exposed to local politics through the party organizations. In addition, they mentioned a great variety of local groups in which they had been active. The council consisted of three women and eight men. The administrative sample included two women. There was one black person among the top administrators and one black on council. One final introductory fact: In response to the question, "How satisfied are you with your city these days?" on a nine-point response scale ranging from "completely dissatisfied" (0) to "completely satisfied" (9), 80 percent were at the satisfied (7-8-9) end of the scale including all the administrators.

Elite Perceptions of Community Problems

The context in which these leaders perceived they were working is important to establish. The first aspect of context is what they saw as the important problems facing the city. While they were almost all personally satisfied with Ann Arbor, the study discovered that they were also realists who knew there were problems. Table 9.1 presents the data for this 1986 sample of leaders. Two major problems were cited as most serious: housing and public improvements. Three others evoked some concern from a sizable majority: the cost of local government, public

TABLE 9.1. Leaders' Perceptions of the Seriousness of Community Problems

	The Ann Arbor Elite		Comparison with a Comparable Group of 25 U.S. Cities	
	% Seeing Problem as "Very Serious" or "Somewhat Serious"	% "Very Serious"	% Seeing Problem as "Serious"	% "Very Serious"
Housing	100%	31	50	10
Public Improvements[a]	85	46	59	13
Cost of Local Government	85	15	65	23
Public Safety	77	8	55	8
Social Services and Welfare	69	15	44	5
Unemployment	54	0	68	30
Poverty	54	0	62	8
Quality of Education	54	0	45	9
Pollution	46	0	44	3
Race Relations	46	0	23	3
Economic Development	23	0	70	29
Health Services and Conditions	15	7	30	3
Recreation and Culture	8	0	25	3
Average	55.1	9.4	49.2	11.3

Source: Survey of Ann Arbor City leaders (councillors and department heads) conducted by the author in 1986. The larger study of leaders in U.S. cities was conducted in 1984 by the author in cooperation with scholars at the University of Pennsylvania, State University of California at Bakersfield, and the University of Hawaii.

[a]Includes Transportation, Streets, Water, Sewage, Sanitation.

safety, and social services. There were some leaders concerned about each of the fourteen problems put to them, but the level of concern was low for economic development, health, recreation and culture. Pollution and race relations, as well as education, unemployment, and poverty found these leaders split in their perceptions.

If we compare Ann Arbor to other cities in its population range (using data from twenty-five U.S. cities in another study we were involved in), one can see that overall the Ann Arbor elite seems to be similar to those in other cities in average level of concern for all problems (table 9.1). A closer analysis reveals that Ann Arbor's elite is clearly differentiated in certain important respects. Ann Arbor's leaders were much more concerned about the two big problems, housing and public improvements, than were leaders elsewhere. There also was more concern about social services and race relations than usual elsewhere, but there was much less concern in Ann Arbor about economic development. This supports the image of Ann Arbor as an economically successful community, concerned now about other problems: social services, race, relations, housing, and the state of public improvements. However, what must be underscored is that Ann Arbor's leaders were deeply preoccupied with a whole range of problems, more so than in other cities on the average. Eight of these problems were considered serious by over 50 percent of Ann Arbor's policy elite, five by 70 percent or more of Ann Arbor's leaders. This level of concern, comparatively quite high, is striking for a city whose image is that of a "successful" city. If successful, its leaders are still impressed with the need for action, more so than in the average American city at this population level.

While there was much consensus on the seriousness of certain problems, these general findings mask some key disagreements on priorities. One councillor felt housing was the major issue; for another, it was streets; for a third, economic development; for a fourth, health and social services. Council members were more worried than were administrators (averaging 64 percent compared to 45 percent). Democrats more concerned, Republicans and independents more sanguine (averaging, respectively, 66 percent, 40 percent, and 46 percent). When one compares the views of leaders by types of problems, a major difference between the parties emerges. Contrasting the traditional allocation and developmental problem areas (such as public improvements, public safety, and economic development) with those that deal with social welfare and social relations (such as housing, race relations, health, social services, and pollution) we find that similar proportions of Democrats, Republicans, and independents—63 percent, 56 percent, and 47 percent, respectively—report feeling that the traditional problems are serious, but far more Democrats than Republicans or independents—72 percent, 33 percent, and 44 percent, respectively—consider the social welfare problems serious.

Each person was asked two follow-up questions:

1. "Who, in your opinion, should have primary responsibility (for acting on each type of problem): the federal government, state government, local government, nongovernment agencies, or leave it to the people?"
2. "In which of these (eleven policy areas) do you think that your local government has enough power and autonomy to act effectively?"

In response, the Ann Arbor policy elite provided the responses presented in table 9.2. There was positive majority agreement concerning responsibility and power for only three problems: public improvements, recreation and culture, and crime. There was a negative consensus 80 percent or more said local government did not have power and should not have responsibility on three others: poverty, health, and unemploy-

TABLE 9.2. The Ann Arbor Elites' Perceptions of Responsibility, Power, and Action in Key Policy Areas

	Local Government Should Have the Primary Responsibility[a]	Local Government Has the Power	Effective Action Has Been or Is Being Taken
Public Improvements	85%	77	60
Recreation and Culture	62	85	73
Crime and Delinquency	100	77	40
Race Relations	46	77	20
Pollution	38	38	53
Economic Growth	46	54	53
Housing	23	54	0
Poverty	7	15	20
Health	0	15	40
Unemployment	0	0	27
Means	40.7	49.2	37.9

Source: Survey of Ann Arbor City leaders (councillors and department heads) conducted by the author in 1986.

[a]Sometimes respondents indicated local government had the responsibility with other government agencies or nongovernment actors.

ment. On four critical problems this elite was split concerning their responsibility and power to act: race relations, pollution, economic growth, and housing. Clearly there was genuine policy conflict, especially on human services and economic issues. On race, relations and housing a majority felt they had the power but a minority felt they should have the responsibility. Economic growth was a divisive issue which split the city's leaders. Actually on the critical social problems which were divisive, the division was between the Republicans and the Democrats, with the independents in between. While similar proportions of Democrats, Republicans, and independents—71 percent, 78 percent, and 73 percent, respectively—said they believed the city has the power to act upon traditional problem areas, they disagreed sharply whether the city has the power to act upon the social problem areas—92 percent of the Democrats but only 44 percent of the Republicans and 60 percent of the independents, agreed. These findings again demonstrate the differences in partisan positions. They may also represent misconceptions of city power, but it is more likely that these are projections of value positions of the party groups.

On the question of responsibility for dealing with these problems, Ann Arbor elites are similar to those in other American cities. They are inclined to reject primary responsibility for the solution of many of their problems. At the same time, they often feel these problems should be dealt with elsewhere—at federal or state levels, or that they are not the province of government at all. For the eight basically local problems as cited in table 9.2 (excluding unemployment and poverty), the views of Ann Arbor elites on responsibility are given in table 9.3 (averages for eight problems).

Ann Arbor's leaders represent a mixture of three positions: (1) split on whether local government has primary responsibility (with the Democrats most reluctant); (2) a majority say state and federal governments

TABLE 9.3. Ann Arbor Elites' Views of Responsibility for Problem Resolution

	All Leaders	Dem.	Rep.	Ind.
Local Government Responsible	41%	37	58	53
Federal and/or State Government Responsible	51	63	51	33
Nongovernmental Groups and the Public Responsible	15	9	25	13

Source: Survey of Ann Arbor City Council leaders and department heads in 1986.

Note: Percentages do not total 100 because more than one response was possible.

have a basic responsibility; and (3) a minority feel many of these problems have to be handled also, or exclusively, by nongovernmental action (true particularly of the Republicans)—on the critical social and economic problems (race, housing, pollution, economic growth), they particularly wish to deflect the responsibility elsewhere: 63 percent say state and federal government have the primary responsibility and only 37 percent admit to a basic local responsibility.

The American decentralized system of local government has much to do with such local elite perceptions. Local leaders feel ambivalent and uncertain about their own power and responsibility to deal with their problems. In addition they feel that national and state governments are failing them by not providing financial resources and other assistance and support. It appears to be an abdication of responsibility, and to a certain extent it is, but, it also is a complaint that higher government has deserted cities and has failed to assume responsibility for these problems.

The contrast with Sweden is interesting to note. In Sweden the national government maintains a direct relationship with cities, since it is a unitary not a decentralized system. The Swedish national government develops directives informing local governments of their responsibilities, develops programs under its welfare-state system for carrying out these responsibilities, and regularly provides at least 30 percent of the funds needed by cities to meet expenditures. Cities are told to develop their own tax and fee systems to raise the remainder of the funds necessary. Consequently, in the Swedish study in which these same questions were asked, it was found that the percent of local elites who said they should have responsibility for their problems was over 70 percent (80 percent for the four key social problems referred to earlier). This contrasts with 41 percent in Ann Arbor. When local governments are in a partnership with national government, as the Swedish are, there is a mutual acceptance of responsibility and the development of a mutual system of financial and administrative support. There is a more homogeneous commitment, and the Swedish city prospers. When local governments are in a confrontational-dependency-isolationist relationship with national (and state) governments, as the Americans are, there is ambivalence about capacity to perform, intergovernmental hostility, and a rejection of responsibility. With such a system, the American city suffers. (See table 9.4.)

Nevertheless, it is disturbing that a majority of Ann Arbor's top policy elite in 1986 claimed that they should not be responsible and should not have responsibility for dealing with race relations, pollution, economic growth, and housing—even though a majority admitted they had the power to act on all of these except pollution. The Republicans and independents were actually somewhat more responsibility-oriented on these problems in the 1986 study than were the Democrats, yet the Republicans were reluctant to admit they had the power to act.

Concerns deepen when perceptions of action are analyzed. Respondents were asked to "indicate whether you think effective action is being taken to deal with these problems, or whether *some* action is being taken, or *nothing* useful is being done" (emphases addes). The answers were quite revealing. Even though one might expect these elites to defend their work, and that of their predecessors, this was not necessarily the case. There were a few (three or four) euphoric types, usually bureaucrats, who were reluctant to say "nothing useful is being done." (Only 10 percent of all responses were that negative.) Yet on only four problems did a majority believe that there was really effective action: economic development, recreation, public improvements, and, interestingly, pollution (table 9.2). What is most important here is to look at their opinions concerning the problems that large proportions already said were *serious problems*. Excluded here are three serious problems—unemployment, poverty, and education—that the majority felt they had inadequate power to deal with or, in the case of education were really outside the jurisdiction of city government. On the remaining seven problems ranked high on seriousness, only 37 percent of the policy elite on the average felt that effective action was being taken (table 9.5). There was unanimity on housing: not one councillor or bureaucrat felt effective action was occurring. Race relations, social services, safety, city finance—all troubling problems for these leaders—were ranked by the majority as low in effective action. This was not basically a question of partisan affiliation—36 percent of the Democratic, 42 percent of the Republican, and 31 percent of the independents' evaluations were positive.

Ann Arbor's leaders are not much different than the leaders of other cities in their responses (table 9.6) except in one respect—Ann

TABLE 9.4. Examples of Contrasts in Elite Views about Responsibility, Ann Arbor and Sweden

% of Local Elites Who Say They Should Be Responsible For:	Ann Arbor	Sweden
Housing	23%	90
Race/ethnic relations	46	67
Pollution	38	83
Economic development	46	75

Source: Survey of Ann Arbor City Council leaders and department heads in 1986. The Swedish data are from a study conducted in 15 Swedish communes by Lars Stromberg, University of Goteborg in 1984 as part of a comparative study conducted jointly with the American study.

Arbor's leaders report that more effective action is being taken than is the norm for these cities. Even so, the percentage is low—38 percent say effective action is occurring. Here then was strong evidence of a very realistic elite, worried about a set of serious problems, though with varying degrees of concern. They for the most part admitted that the problems existed, and that they had the power to deal with them, but then said that effective action was lacking. It is indeed troubling to find elites reporting a problem as serious as housing on which no leader reports effective action: 100 percent say its serious, 62 percent say they have the power to act on it, and zero say action is being taken that effectively deals with it! Whether they, as an elite, can and will work to solve these problems is indeed the big question to be explored further.

TABLE 9.5. Evaluations by Ann Arbor Elites of the Effectiveness of Action on Seven Serious City Problems

Problem	% Saying the Problem is Serious	% Saying Effective Action Is Being Taken
Public Improvements	85%	60
Pollution	46	53
Public Safety	77	40
Social Services	69	33
Race Relations	46	20
Cost of Local Government	85	7
Housing	100	0

Source: Survey of Ann Arbor City Council leaders and department heads in 1986.

TABLE 9.6. A Comparison of Ann Arbor with 25 Other U.S. Cities on Elite Problem Perceptions[a]

Means for elites by city	Ann Arbor	Other U.S. Cities
Problems considered serious	50.8%	49.8
Local government should have the responsibility for dealing with these problems	40.7	51.7
Local government has the power to act on these problems	49.2	55.0
Effective action is being taken on these problems	37.9	25.1

Source: Survey of Ann Arbor City leaders (councillors and department heads) conducted by the author in 1986. The larger study of leaders in U.S. cities was conducted in 1984 by the author in cooperation with scholars at the University of Pennsylvania, State University of California at Bakersfield, and the University of Hawaii.

[a]For ten common policy areas.

They certainly were not blind to the existence of the problems. The issue is whether they had the will to develop a successful strategy to solve such problems.

Views of Conflict

The obstacles to the solution of problems may be numerous. One concern is the existence of social and political differences within the community. When asked whether there were "major conflicts that interfere with getting things done," 86 percent replied "yes" (compared to an average of 69 percent in twenty-five comparable-size U.S. cities) and mentioned specific conflicts. They then were given a list of eight types of differences and asked which of these divided people. The results (table 9.7) provide information on their level of awareness of conflict. Ann Arbor stands out, compared to other communities, in the degree of perceived conflict, particularly conflicts in views on political problems and on how to achieve social change. The comparable set of twenty-five other U.S. cities is, in the opinion of their leaders, *much* less conflictual.

There is considerable elite consensus on the existence of conflict, on what type of conflict is most current, disagreements in political stands on questions, no doubt a product of the fact that they as elites are in the center of a partisan conflict system. They generally agree that religion, age differences, worker-employer relations, place of residence, and education are not a source of the difficulty. Politicians and bureaucrats,

TABLE 9.7. Conflict Perceptions of Ann Arbor's Top Elite

"What types of differences divide people (here)?"	Ann Arbor Leaders		25 Comparable U.S. Cities
	Divide Very Much	Divide Somewhat	Divide Very Much
Political Views	79	21	19
Views of Social Change	57	43	17
Income Status	50	50	23
Educational Level	21	64	11
Residence (City vs. Suburbs)	21	50	18
Manager–Employee Relations	14	86	7
Age	7	93	6
Religious Beliefs	0	21	5
Average	31		13

Source: Survey of Ann Arbor City leaders (councillors and department heads) conducted by the author in 1986. The larger study of leaders in U.S. cities was conducted in 1984 by the author in cooperation with scholars at the University of Pennsylvania, State University of California at Bakersfield, and the University of Hawaii.

Republicans and Democrats, all seem to basically agree on the existence of this pattern of conflict.

One final, major, addendum to this interpretation, however: When pressed with the question "Do these conflicts come in the way of the development of the community?" only 35 percent responded "very much." The remainder were much less sure or did not think so at all. Thus, while aware of the existence of conflicts, and while seeing these as an interference, a minority felt these conflicts were really dysfunctional to community development. That corresponds to the basic theory of progress for Ann Arbor—progress *along with* conflict.

Strategies for Mobilization of Support and Information

The top elite in a democratic community like Ann Arbor develop communication relationships with other leaders in government, with each other, and with party people, interest groups, and the public. These contact networks can tell a great deal about how they conceive of their support groups in the system. Some may have rather narrow spheres of influence, as is often the case for administrators who are active in specific policy areas—planning, safety, housing, recreation, social welfare services, and others. There was indeed such a narrow interest for 70 percent of the top bureaucrats, but for only 20 percent of the council members.[2] Among council members, 80 percent said they had much influence in three or more policy areas, and all of them said they had some influence in eight or more policy areas. Therefore, their contacts with other actors in the community should be considerable. Indeed, this is what was found when they were pressed for detail on who they contacted and who contacted them.

First, there was mutual agreement that councillors and bureaucrats see each other a great deal-80 percent of each elite group report such contacts, and these are initiated by both elite groups. So this is an organizationally interactive top elite. Second, all council members are contacted by local party leaders fairly regularly, although not all of them (40 percent) initiate such party contacts. This suggests that the mayor and council are very aware of the political context in which they work. Third, neighborhood groups from time to time contact all council members (the mayor, however, with less frequency, and over half of the top administrators. Fourth, 80 percent of the top elites report either contacts with the local media or efforts on their part to approach the media. Less than half of the administrators report such contacts. Fifth, almost all the councillors and over 50 percent of the administrators report that they have their own "friends and supporters," or constituents, who contact them from time to time. These findings suggest a top elite engaged in a multiplicity of interactions and a variety of networks-in government circles, with party organization leaders, friendships, the media, and their own neighborhood constituents. In addition, some report contacts with state legislative or administrative officials, or party leaders at the state level, and occasionally with federal officials. This leaves the communitywide interest groups. As table 9.8 indicates, these group contacts are also extensive, and somewhat intransitive-that is, groups pressure the top elite more than leaders initiate contacts. The councillors are the focus of the interest groups, but administrators are by no means neglected. Over 50 percent report some pressure from these groups, the media, the parties, and friends. For councillors, it is 82 percent.

One must not lose sight of the fact that mayor and council members do establish, indeed initiate, contacts with these potential support groups. A close inspection of the data reveals that each apparently has his or her own strategy for developing support. One Republican reported that he initiated contacts with virtually every interest group listed. Another concentrated on business associations, party contacts, and neighborhood groups. A third, a Democrat, claimed to ignore the formal interest group network and worked with his own supporting circle of close friends, plus the media. Thus, each was involved in a fairly broad social and political network of contacts, but there were distinctive patterns, suggesting a latent theory of how to mobilize support (or a particular view of whom one is responsible to).

TABLE 9.8. Group Contact Frequencies of the Top Elite

	% Reported by Members of Council		Total Both Elite Groups	
% Reporting Each Type of Contact	Pressure by Group	Initiated by Elite	Pressure by Group	Initiated by Elite
Civic Groups	100%	60%	64	36
Business Groups	80	40	50	36
Ethnic or Racial Groups	80	20	36	14
Labor Union	80	20	36	7
Religious Groups	80	40	21	14
Neighborhood Groups	80	40	71	36
Employee Unions	100	40	60	20
Local Media	60	80	50	50
Close Friends	80	60	64	36
Local Party Leaders	100	40	57	29
Averages	82	44	51	28

Source: Survey of Ann Arbor City Council leaders and department heads in 1986.

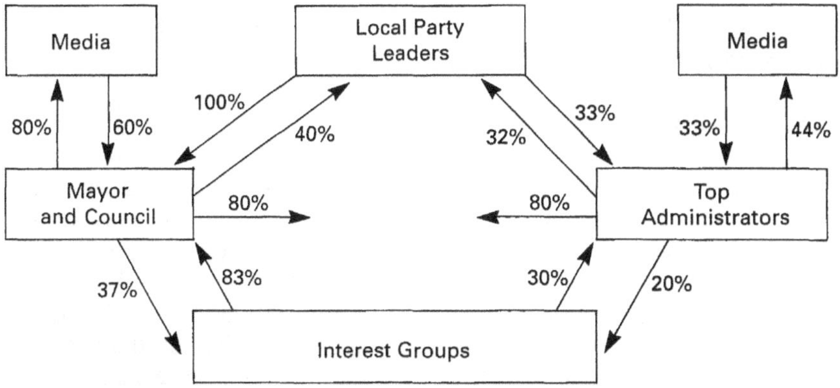

Fig. 9.1. The interaction patterns of the top elite with party, interest groups, and the media. Each percentage is a proportion of the leaders or administrators who report *initiating* contacts or *receiving* contacts from or with other specific political actors.

The overall picture of contact patterns is seen in figure 9.1. The similarity in the reported contacts for council and administrators is clear. They do work in some collaborative mode. It is notable that council and administrators report more pressure from others in every case, except the media-the council admits going to the media more than vice versa. This diagram suggests that every top elite person is in the center of a complex network of contacts. His or her decision therefore may be considered in one sense as related to these contacts, depending on what for the decision maker are the most politically useful and valid associations. Since we have seen that there is much perceived conflict in the community, this ranking by each person of the political usefulness of contacts becomes of great importance.

One should not get the impression from this analysis that Ann Arbor's top policy elite is inactive. They certainly do not see themselves that way. When asked which of ten problem areas they focus on and have influence in, they report diverse policy interests and wide influence. They are particularly active in the following areas: public safety, housing, economic development, public improvements, recreation, and city finances. Since the question asked them was whether they had "much" influence in each policy area, "some" influence, or none, it was possible to create an influence distribution index score for each respondent (table 9.9). The city counillors perceive themselves as more than unusually influential in Ann Arbor, and the administrators as clearly subordinate. The differences between the two parties in the Ann Arbor elite are negligible. It is the concentration and breadth of influence in the council that is most outstanding.

The Values of the Top Elite

In cross-national studies of local leaders we have sought in the past twenty years to determine what the value orientations of elites are in Western and non-Western societies: the United States, Sweden, India, Poland, Yugoslavia, and more recently the Netherlands.[3] We developed a set of statements by which to test the value positions of leaders and have demonstrated the usefulness, and validity, of these same statements for all these countries. In 1986, we used these same statements in our questionnaire sent to the Ann Arbor leaders. We focus here on four types of values for which we will present data. These values deal with commitment to political conflict, innovative change, political participation and economic equality. The Ann Arbor results will be presented comparatively, with results from other U.S. cities and Swedish communes (table 9.6).

The *political conflict* value position of these elites was studied by putting five statements to them and asking them to state their degree of agreement or disagreement with each statement. These statements focused on the behavior of leaders, particularly whether they should desist from policy actions that would be disruptive or divisive. Here are two examples:

> "A good leader should refrain from making proposals that divide people even if these are important for the community."
> "A leader should modify his actions to keep consensus."

TABLE 9.9. Influence Perception Scores of Elites

	Ann Arbor		U.S. Sample of 25 Cities	
	Councillors	Administrators	Councillors	Administrators
Very High Influence (Score 11–20)	80%	11	43	20
High Influence (Score 7–10)	20	44	47	48
Low Influence (Score 0–6)	0	45	11	33

Source: Survey of Ann Arbor City leaders (councillors and department heads) conducted by the author in 1986. The larger study of leaders in U.S. cities was conducted in 1984 by the author in cooperation with scholars at the University of Pennsylvania, State University of California at Bakersfield, and the University of Hawaii.

Overall, Ann Arbor's leaders were strongly "proconflict"—86 percent were. They were clearly committed to the development of community programs, even if this may seem divisive, breaks consensus, and displeases people. The political conflict value ethic is pervasive, applying equally to politicians and administrators.

Another value probed with the same technique was *innovative change*, using such items as, "The people in this community must continuously look for new solutions other than be satisfied with things as they are." The five items employed revealed a high commitment to change-on the average, 75 percent accepted the need for innovative

TABLE 9.10 Value Scales of Leaders in Ann Arbor Compared to Other U.S. Cities and Swedish Communes

Values (% Favoring)	Ann Arbor	25 Other U.S. Cities	15 Swedish Communes
Participation	78%	79%	89%
Innovative change	75	75	81
Political Conflict	86	84	79
Economic Equality	43	21	61
	N = 16	*N* = 260	*N* = 389
Examples of Items for Each Value Scale			
Participation			
"The complexity of modern day issues requires that only the more simple questions should be considered publicly"			
% agree	12%	11	5
Innovative Change			
"The people in this community must continually look for new solutions rather than be satisfied with things as they are"			
% Agree	87	87	85
Political Conflict			
"Preserving harmony in the community should be considered more important than the achievement of community programs"			
% agree	7	9	16

Source: Survey of Ann Arbor City leaders (councillors and department heads) conducted by the author in 1986. The larger study of leaders in U.S. cities was conducted in 1984 by the author in cooperation with scholars at the University of Pennsylvania, State University of California at Bakersfield, and the University of Hawaii. The Swedish data are from a study conducted in 15 Swedish communes by Lars Stromberg, University of Goteborg in 1984 as part of a comparative study conducted jointly with the American study.

Note: See appendix for all items used in these value scales.

solutions. Administrators were slightly less interested in change compared to the politicians-87 percent to 74 percent—but there was overall strong support for innovation.

A third value concerned *political participation*, again measured by a series of six items. Examples are:

> "Participation of the people is not necessary if decision making is left in the hands of a few trusted and competent leaders."
> "Only those who are fully informed on the issues should vote."

Only one of the respondents agreed to these items. Overall, 78 percent took positions endorsing the value of political participation. Again, administrators were inclined to be a bit more negative than the politicians—25 percent to 11 percent. Basically these leaders are not elitist, in their commitment to citizen involvement.

Thus, on three very critical values, Ann Arbor's top elites demonstrated high support for a commitment to "democratic" and "change" value orientations—virtually as high as in Sweden—and there is high agreement among these leaders, councillors, and administrators. This stands in contrast to elites in developing societies where there was less such commitment. On political participation, for example, only 37 percent of local political leaders in India were in favor of that value, and only 28 percent valued political conflict. Clearly different norms preoccupy local elites, depending on the political culture.

There is one value, however, that many local elites in the United States are not willing to accept—the value of *economic equality*. In the comparative study of Swedish and U.S. cities, we tested leaders with a wide variety of statements, some seen as perhaps extreme. The contrast was striking—61 percent of the Swedish leaders had positive value orientations, but only 21 percent of the U.S. leaders. Other scholars have noted the same contrast.[4] Ann Arbor leaders, however, are more egalitarian than is the norm for U.S. leaders—43 percent on the average support the value of economic equality. But their range of support on specific items is considerable (table 9.11). There is no majority favoring the poor as in Sweden. In fact, some of the items used look radically redistributive to us, but not to the Swedes: for example, "In every situation poor people should be given more opportunities than rich people." In Sweden, 64 percent of the local elites support that statement. In the United States the average for all twenty-five cities was only 3 percent. In Ann Arbor, the figure was 33 percent.

Council members are more egalitarian than administrators on our economic equality scale—52 percent to 36 percent—and Democrats are

56 percent egalitarian compared to 44 percent of the independents and 21 percent of the Republicans. This demonstrates a basic contrast by parties in value priorities. There is considerable dissensus among elites on the acceptance of this value. Nevertheless, perhaps the important point here is that Ann Arbor, again, appears rather distinctive. While the American culture does not emphasize economic equality as the Swedish social-welfare culture does, which is a major system difference, certain American cities do seem to be more inclined to an egalitarian subculture than other cities. Ann Arbor is one of them, though it still is less positive than are Swedish cities. How this liberal elite has come about is difficult to explain precisely, but the emergence of such a relatively egalitarian set of elites is the product of the recruitment and socialization process for leaders, their interactions in the community, and the norms of politics which have crystallized in certain political and social circles in the society.

Top Elites 1976–86: A Summary Interpretation

Since the special study done in 1986 of the top policy elites at that time may be considered too limited, unrepresentative, or time-restricted, the

TABLE 9.11. Elite Support of Economic Equality

Economic Equality Value Items (% agree)	Ann Arbor	25 Other U.S. Cities	15 Swedish Communes
"The government has the responsibility to see that nobody lives well when others are poor."	25	3	88
"In every situation poor people should be given more opportunities that rich people."	33	3	64
"Rich people should pay more for the support of community programs for poor people."	94	61	—
"There should be an upper limit on income so that no one earns very much more than others."	31	4	23
"Discrepancies in salaries should be continually reduced."	31	33	69
Average % Proequality, All Items	43	21	61

Source: Survey of Ann Arbor City leaders (councillors and department heads) conducted by the author in 1986. The larger study of leaders in U.S. cities was conducted in 1984 by the author in cooperation with scholars at the University of Pennsylvania, State University of California at Bakersfield, and the University of Hawaii. The Swedish data are from a study conducted in 15 Swedish communes by Lars Stromberg, University of Goteborg in 1984 as part of a comparative study conducted jointly with the American study.

results of a study of the top elites for the entire ten-year period indicated were used also. Half of the thirty-two top leaders interviewed were mayors and councillors, half were city-level party leaders, many of whom had run for council. The data are somewhat different, because the questions differed, but the evidence seems confirmatory for many of the preceding interpretations.

The key leaders in the recent period reveal in various ways their support for democratic values. Their tolerance of dissent stands out. Eighty percent do not feel a person should leave or be forced to leave a party "if you disagree with a major stand of your party." This could be called pragmatism, or it could also be tolerance, but these leaders do not believe in the monolithic party. Further, almost every one of these leaders believes that "widespread participation . . . in making party decisions" should be encouraged and they strongly believe in the role of the local party unit. An elitism scale using four statements commonly employed in U.S. surveys was used here (table 9.12). The top elites revealed (as was the case previously for precinct leaders) overwhelming rejection of elitist orientations. If one accepts their responses to these statements, one must conclude that few believe in manipulative approaches to politics and most have confidence in the capacity of voters to comprehend political issues.

Ann Arbor top elites are pragmatists, but the majority of them are also clearly in politics for ideological reasons. They also believe campaigns should present issue positions forthrightly and explicitly. They were asked why they were involved in politics—65 percent said ideological reasons were very important, while 35 percent put more emphasis on

TABLE 9.12. The Elitism Scale for Ann Arbor Elites

	The Top Political Elites, 1976–86		Precinct Leaders 1986	
Elitism Scale Items (% who disagree)	Dem.	Rep.	Dem.	Rep.
"Most people are rather easy for politicians to manipulate"	77%	100	84	72
"Only party organizations run by a few leaders are really effective"	95	100	85	53
"Arguments about policy are beyond the grasp of most voters"	82	80	100	66
"Few people know what is in their interest in the long run"	59	60	80	68
Average Rejection of Elitism	78	85	87	65

Source: Studies conducted by the author in the years indicated.

friendships, social contacts, or the fun and excitement of the political campaign. When asked whether they saw "campaign work as a way of influencing the policies of government," 68 percent of the Democrats and 70 percent of the Republicans answered in the affirmative. Campaigns, in the view of the majority, should be confrontational. For 60 percent at least, party appeals should not be vague in campaigns, and leaders should not "play down hot issues" in order to win. Thus, while some evidence of pragmatism is found, on balance three-fifths to two-thirds of these leaders reveal ideological orientations to party involvement, and as part of a partisan environment, they are willing to accept adversarial parties.

The beliefs of these top elites concerning the proper role of government in dealing with the critical social and economic issues of the day are sharply contrasted. This mirrors the findings presented in the chapter on the party organization leaders. Without reporting these results in detail again, the basic findings can be summarized, comparing the top political elites to other leaders in Ann Arbor (table 9.13 and 9.14). At the elite level, the Republican-Democratic split is consistent. The liberal section of the public (36 percent) is represented basically by the Democratic leaders; the conservative sector (20 percent) finds its expression mainly in the Republican leadership. Both parties cater to the moderates, the Republicans much more so than the Democrats. With 44 percent of the public considering themselves moderates, the Democrats have only 18 percent who are moderates to represent them, while the Republicans

TABLE 9.13. Comparison of the Ideology and Issue Positions of Different Sets of Political Leaders in Ann Arbor (By Party)

	Top Governmental and Party Elites		Interest-Group Leaders			Precinct Leaders		Ann Arbor Public
	Dem.	Rep.	Dem.	Rep.	Ind.	Dem.	Rep.	All
Ideological self-classification								
Liberal	82.0%	0.0	59.0	0.0	45.0	83.0	11.0	36.0
Moderate	18.0	80.0	35.0	61.0	35.0	17.0	61.0	44.0
Conservative	0.0	20.0	2.0	39.0	5.0	0.0	29.0	20.0
Average Liberalism on 8 specific issues	82.4	31.3	84.3	25.0	45.0	81.4	24.0	—
N	22	10	51	32	20	27	39	205

Source: Data for the top elites are based on studies in 1981 and 1986; the interest group leaders data comes from the 1983 study; the precinct leaders, 1986; the public, 1984.

have 60 percent or more. On the other hand, there are many Republican conservatives in the public (48 percent) who are in a sense not proportionately represented by the Republicans. Nevertheless, the Republican leadership appears to be closer to the public on ideological self-classification. On specific issues it is another matter. For example, on the question of government providing more aid for minorities and the poor, the Ann Arbor public in 1984 was quite liberal, compared to some of the city's elites. The public favored more governmental effort to improve the status of blacks and other minorities—at the 82 percent level. The Republican leadership's position on comparable issues was much lower white the Democratic leadership was inclined to be more supportive of the underclass. Clearly the Democrats are usually more liberal than the public, while the Republicans are less liberal on these issues. The moderate mainstream of public opinion in Ann Arbor appears to be represented by a combination of moderate Democrats, moderate Republicans (in party and interest-group leadership positions), and some independents who are active in interest groups.

Top Elites and the Party System

We come finally back to the interest in the top elites' views of the Ann Arbor party system. Here there is strong confirmation of the position that for some time now, the top elites have been proparty. When asked their evaluation of the two-party system, 70 percent say they prefer it (as do 65 percent of interest-group leaders). When asked their evaluations of the partisan system of elections, 95 percent of the Democratic top elites and 78 percent of the Republican top elites favor it (compared to

TABLE 9.14. Comparison of the Ideology and Issue Positions of Party Affiliation Groups within the Ann Arbor Public

	Dem.	Rep.	Ind.
Ideological self-classification			
Liberal	84%	1	11
Moderate	11	51	78
Conservative	5	48	11
Positions on Two Issues comparable to those for the elites			
Aid to Minorities and the Poor (% Liberal)	96	48	—
Cutting Defense Spending (% Liberal)	88	32	—

Source: Author's 1984 study.

52 percent of interest-group leaders). On a series of specific items put to them to determine specifically their feelings, the average positive evaluation of parties was 77 percent for Democratic leaders and 93 percent for Republican leaders. Consider, for example, the following statement (used in many surveys, local and national): "The parties do more to confuse the issues than to provide a clear choice on issues." In response, 52 percent of the public in Ann Arbor in 1984 disagreed with this (that is they gave a proparty response) and only 34 percent agreed. Among interest-group leaders, 53 percent disagreed (proparty) and 26 percent agreed. For the top political elites, 89 percent disagreed (proparty) and only 11 percent agreed. As one moves up to the apex of power in the Ann Arbor system, one finds an increasingly strong consensus of support for the party system.

Conclusion

Everything considered, the data on Ann Arbor's top political elites can be interpreted as revealing significant differences; yet, in many respects they are reassuring. These leaders are aware of problems and conflicts, and struggling with them. They are realistic about the extent to which action on these has been effective. They bring to their jobs not only awareness of problems, but also a rather positive set of value orientations, although only a minority really can be considered economic egalitarians in value predispositions. And they are in contact with community groups and activists in the process of resolving these problems. There is considerable disagreement, even confrontation, among these elites. They are ideologues in one sense, but pragmatists also, yet their contrasting ideologies place the two sets of party leaders often at odds, while they also compete for the moderate middle majority of the Ann Arbor public. Out of this conflict, and the struggle to mobilize support from the public, has come progress. Finally, above all, these elites are clearly committed not only to democracy, but to the type of party democracy they have in Ann Arbor.

CHAPTER 10

The Budget Decisions: Policy Payoffs of Party Conflict

There has been considerable discussion among scholars as to whether elections matter, particularly whether elections that lead to the emergence of new leadership and party turnovers have policy consequences, and if so, whether the changes in policy are significant or minor, immediate or delayed, sustained over time or reversed. One position advanced is that new leaders make a difference—indeed, that new leaders make a difference fairly soon after they take office, in an early "honeymoon" period. The contention is that there is a policy cycle: the immediate development of new policy directions in a "honeymoon" period, then a return to small and incremental change only, until new leadership again returns, leading to a different direction in policy.[1] An earlier scholarly position was that elections do not change existing policy priorities, that elections are not referenda on issues, and that forces and factors other than leadership change are responsible for new directions in policy.[2] A third group of scholars of leadership in small groups suggests that the new leaders who take control first demonstrate both their competence and their conformity to group norms, that is, cumulate "acceptance capital," then subsequently develop new policy agendas and make new policy decisions.[3]

Our theory in this study of local government is that policy decisions can change as party competition changes. Elections are therefore very important in three ways: in increasing the pressure on the party in power by intensifying the competition; in the election of new leaders with new ideas and programs for policy action; and in eventually leading to party turnovers. While party turnovers may not lead immediately to new policies, although they certainly can, it is the cumulative impact of close competition, new leaders, and eventual party turnover that will leave its mark on the content of public policy. This is the theory we now want to test by looking at forty-five years of budget decisions in Ann Arbor.

The city's budget, like other budgets, can be very revealing. It is, after all, a political document, often a partisan political document, or a document representing partisan priorities. As one scholar has put it: "Perhaps the study of budgeting is just another expression for the study of politics."[4] Budget decisions are not automatic; they don't "just happen." They are made by people, political actors, elected or appointed to make these decisions. In an earlier chapter we discussed the developmental theory or premises city leaders accepted in the early postwar period. Later these developmental goals were supplemented and modified, particularly as the two-party system evolved and the Democrats became stronger. In this chapter we analyze what specific budget decisions were adopted to implement these premises and goals. We seek here to understand the budgets in the past forty-five years in terms of the Ann Arbor system of party politics. We ask here: Do parties make a difference in "who governs" in Ann Arbor? In the previous chapters, we have described in detail what our political leaders campaigned for, what issue positions they took, what beliefs and values they were presumably committed to. Belief should be linked to action. Budget decisions are significant actions. It is in this chapter that we analyze the outcomes of beliefs, that is, policy actions.

Budget decisions are not the only important policy decisions in a community. Many nonmonetary decisions are crucial, for example: the establishment of a "self-supporting" parking system in 1949; the move from a private garbage collection system to a public one in 1950; the annexation policy of the city, forbidding city services to unannexed land; the creation of a Human Relations Commission in 1957; the Republican veto of Urban Renewal in 1959; the adoption of a Fair Housing Ordinance and the establishment of a Housing Commission in 1965; the decision to recognize a new section of the budget called human resources in 1969; the formation of the Downtown Development Authority in the early 1980s. These and many other policy actions, while not explicitly budget decisions, determined the course of the development of this city greatly. They also cost money sometimes, but they were usually not decisions requiring large allocations of funds immediately. We shall concentrate here on budget allocations and expenditures, although the nature of our theoretical argument could be tested equally well by analysis of these nonmonetary decisions.

There are different approaches one can take to understanding the budget. One can see it as an intraorganizational process in which incrementalism is the dominant characteristic. In this approach, there are standard operating procedures which usually lead to repetition from year to year in departmental allocations with, usually, small increases and no comprehensive reviews of what departmental programs are achieving. This approach relies on bureaucrats and tends to implement their priorities, although since politicians are making the decisions presumably the allocations made do accord with their priorities and preferences. The incremental approach assumes that past decisions were correct and need not be basically changed.

A second approach argues that budgets are products of economic resources. The more money a city has, the more it can and will spend. In times of recession, the city spends less and cuts down on programs. One school of political scientists (and economists) has held strongly to that position. One scholar summarized four dozen published articles as follows: "Somehow, the nature of the socioeconomic environment seems more important than the nature of community politics in shaping community policies."[5] The problem is that the "economy" does not make decisions: politicians do. If new programs are to be adopted, or current programs to be cut, a group of authoritative leaders have to do this, on the basis of their values and judgments, personal and ideological.

A third approach emphasizes the role of a variety of political forces—the pressures from citizens and interest groups, the expectations of political activists, the political preferences of the local media, and, above all, the political values and ideologies of effective political leadership. As stated earlier (chap. 1), our view is that in Ann Arbor this third approach has much validity—not that economic resources are unimportant, not that "incrementalism" doesn't exist, but political factors here are very important. Politics has an impact on the budget. It is the city's partisan system, and the partisan political actors whom that system selects to lead the city, that is important. These actors have distinctive beliefs about which city problems should be addressed, as well as about the role of government in the solution of these problems. Politicians matter. They initiate new policy and programs, debate the continuance of old policies and programs, and monitor the administrative implementation of policy. Underlying it all is the realization by leaders of the inevitability of elections and their need again to mobilize support for their positions. Budgets follow elections, and elections are indeed integral events in the politics of the budgetary process.

In the political analysis here, we will emphasize the three different political and development eras from 1945 to the present. We will focus on the relevance of the two-party system and party competition for budget decisions in each of these three periods. One key question is: Does increased party competition in elections have an impact on policy? Another key question, probably more important, is: How have the two parties together over forty years contributed to the development of Ann Arbor? Some scholars have argued that parties are ineffectual, elections irrelevant, activism a waste of time, and political actors dispensable. Is this true for Ann Arbor? If we had not had this Ann Arbor system, what would our budgets have looked like? Would they have been the same in basic allocational character, in the implementation of leadership preferences, as they have been since 1945? Without two-party government, what kind of a city would this have been? In looking at the budget over time, we get one basic view of the development of this community and the imprint of partisanism on the city.

Perspective on the Budgets

The data we use here came from the annual budget of the city, plus other financial reports, audits, and such. When available, we supplemented our information from the papers of mayors and council persons as well as the *Observer* and the *Ann Arbor News*.[6] In the presentation of the data we use different measures: actual dollars, constant dollars, and per capita dollars budgeted or spent. Despite some gaps, the data are complete enough to permit a careful analysis of the budgets from 1945 to the present.

Our analysis focuses primarily on the general fund budget of the city, but includes also the additional appropriations not included in the general fund but which are part of the total city budget. One must remember that the general fund we usually use in our discussions and analysis in this chapter was *the* budget essentially in 1945, but today it is a smaller proportion (almost exactly 50 percent in 1988 of all operating budgets). The total set of operating budgets of a city fulfill different purposes: general administration and basic services (sometimes called housekeeping), development (including planning and capital improvement), and human welfare (sometimes called redistribution).

Overall Trends

Table 10.1 provides a comprehensive look at Ann Arbor's budgets from 1945 to 1990. The total for all city budgets has grown from less than $1.5 million in 1945 to over $27 million in 1990, in constant (1967) dollars. That means the total budget is almost twenty times today what it was in 1945. In order to understand the overall magnitude and patterns of budget change, we present three different measures by decade for the 1945–90 period in table 10.1. These measures are:

1. The actual size of the budget in constant dollars.
2. The percentage change in constant dollars for the total budget, and for the general fund budget.
3. The per capita costs of government, in constant dollars.

TABLE 10.1. Ann Arbor's Budget Allocation, 1945–90: Three Measures of Change in the Total Budget Funds

	1945	1950	1960	1970	1980	1990
Total Budget (in 000s)						
Actual Dollars	$743.00	1,308.00	5,797.00	24,800.00	44,392.00	110,338.00
Constant dollars[a]	1,378.00	1,791.00	6,535.00	21,324.00	17,987.00	27,721.00
% Change in Constant Dollars		+29.9%	+260.3%	+226.3%	−15.7%	+54.1%
Per capita constant dollars	$31.40	37.30	90.70	213.20	166.60	252.00
General Fund Budget						
Actual Dollars	$743.00	1,308.00	4,044.00	12,453.00	27,232.00	56,847.00
Constant Dollars[a]	1,378.00	1,791.00	4,558.00	10,708.00	11,034.00	14,287.00
% Change in Constant Dollars		+29.9%	+154.6%	+134.9%	+3.1%	+29.5%
Per Capita Constant Dollars	31.40	37.30	67.70	107.04	102.20	130.77

Source: All tables using budget data are based on Ann Arbor city budget documents and financial reports.
[a]1967 = 100.

A careful look at table 10.1 reveals certain basic trends to keep in mind in the analysis presented here. First, the big budget increases were from 1950 to 1960 and 1960 to 1970, with a subsequent decline actually in the decade of the Seventies, and a smaller increase again in the eighties. Second, the general fund has progressively decreased in terms of its proportion of the total budget—from 100 percent during 1945–50 to 70 percent in 1960 and 51 percent since. Third, the per capita cost of government (in constant dollars) also took its largest jumps in 1960–70 and 1970–80, and has leveled off since then. The per capita general fund costs are today 52 percent of the total per capita cost of government.

These data begin to give us some insights into the reasons for the increase in the size of budgets. Obviously, inflation did not constitute the major explanation because we have controlled for that. Also, population increases, with the attendant demands for more services, cannot be held solely responsible. Our population increased—indeed, more than doubled since 1945 (from 44,000 to 109,000)—but per capita costs (in constant dollars) grew 700 percent—from $31.40 to $252.00. A summary of the change in the total budget in relation to the population increases makes this point more clear (table 10.2). Even in the two periods when the population was fairly stable (1945–50 and 1970–90) budget allocations were much higher in terms of percentage. Per capita costs as a result continued to rise in all periods with the exception of the seventies, but in the eighties the budgetary expansion momentum resumed.

The availability of local financial resources is a third explanation besides population increases and inflation, linked to increased budgets. Despite the considerable influx of funds from the federal and state governments from the mid-1960s on, the city council decided more funds were necessary to meet the increased needs of the city. It is clear that Ann Arbor's political leaders used both increased property assessments and increased tax rates to secure the money they needed to build the city

TABLE 10.2. Change in Total Budget in Relationship to Population Increases

Period	% Population Increase	% Change in Total Budget (constant $)
1945–50	9.8%	29.9%
1950–60	39.6	260.3
1960–70	48.6	226.3
1970–90	7.0	30.0

Source: Census Reports and Ann Arbor City Budget documents.

(table 10.3). The total assessed valuation of property increased 352 percent in real dollars from 1950 to 1970, the period when city hall needed the bulk of the developmental funds, when budgets were soaring by tenfold. After 1970 property assessed valuations increased much less, 40 percent from 1970 to 1990. But tax rates were also going up. After a brief decline in 1960 the rate rose from 9.16 to 14.60 mills by 1970 and then to 17.02 by 1990. Thus, the city council extracted funds from its citizens in two ways: by heavy additional assessments and by higher property tax rates. Financial resources were indeed available, or at least the city leadership made them available. To put it differently, the public tolerated—indeed, supported—a leadership over these forty five years which continuously asked citizens to invest more heavily in the expansion and development of the community.

There have been several periods of fiscal strain or crisis during the past forty years, due to recessions, declining support from the state and federal governments, reduction in allocations from the university (for fire and police services), and the like. Four of these periods are identi-

TABLE 10.3. Change in the Tax Levy and Assessed Valuations

	1950	1960	1970	1980	1990
City Tax Rate	11.94	9.16	14.60	16.70	17.02
Assessed Valuation of Property					
Actual Dollars (in millions)	$63	216	457	1008	2183
Constant Dollars[a] (in millions)	$87	244	393	408	548
Per Capita Property Assessments Constant Dollars	$1,810	3,640	3,930	3,740	4,982
	1950–60	1960–70	1970–80	1980–90	
Percent Increase in Assessed Valuation (Constant Dollars)	180%	61%	4%	34%	
	1950–70		1970–90		
	352%		40%		
Percent Increase in Per Capita Property Assessments	101%	8%	−7%	33%	

Sources: For 1950–73 data, City of Ann Arbor, *Annual Report Fiscal Year 1973–74* (Sylvester Murray, City Administrator), p. 17; For other years, city budget documents and financial reports for each year were used.

Note: The figures of 1960 and before are adjusted to their effective state equalized rates for meaningful comparisons with more recent data. In 1968, the method of determining assessed valuation changed to 50 percent of market value, from 25 percent of market value before that date.

[a]1967 = 100.

TABLE 10.4. Fiscal Crises and Budget Changes

	Decrease in the General Fund Budget (constant $, in 000s)	Change in Property Tax Rate	Change in Property Assessed Valuations[a] (constant $, in millions)	Increase in General Fund Allocation in the Year After the Crisis (constant $, in 000's)
Recent Periods of Fiscal Strain				
1970–71	– .70	+ .20	+ 14	+ 406.90
1973–75	– 398.20	+ .41	– 7	+ 422.60
1980–83[b]	– 369.80	– 2.78	+ 34	+ 793.60
1986–88	– 34.9	– 1.12	+ 22	+ 226.80[c]

Source: City Budget Documents and Financial Reports.

[a]The average yearly increases in property assessments (SEV) for these decades were (in constant dollars): 1960–70 = $14.9 million; 1970–80 = $ 1.5 million; 1980–88 = $ 6.4 million.

[b]Basically 1979 is used for calculation here.

[c]Estimated.

fied in table 10.4. The decline in general fund outlays during these periods was particularly large in the 1973–75 and 1980–83 crises. It is interesting to note that the property tax rate was lowered, or kept at a minimal level, during all of these periods, but property assessments usually increased (except for the 1973–75 period). Both parties wrestled with these fiscal crises and apparently worked collaboratively to hold down costs during them. They may have disagreed on how to meet the crisis but were responsive to the need to balance the budget, no matter how difficult. In the seventies, for example, the public turned down tax proposals in four consecutive years but somehow Ann Arbor weathered the storm. It is significant that after the crisis, recuperation in securing and appropriating funds occurred quickly. On the average, the subsequent year's budget increased by over $450,000 in constant dollars.

Departmental Allocations by Periods of City Growth

This overall picture of budgetary change obscures the relationship of city budget decisions to the stages of city development. It is necessary to segment the total postwar period into time sectors relevant to city growth, then to analyze specific departments and programs as they varied over time. This will provide a better understanding of the extent of continuity and discontinuity in council policy priorities.

We have described the magnitude of the change in the total city budget, and the general fund budget, from 1945 to the present, in rather gross terms. It is actually more useful to divide this total period into three major time segments:

1. *Initial Growth Stage* 1945–60: Population increases from 44,000 to 67,000; area of city more than doubles.
2. *Secondary Growth Stage* 1960–70: Population increases to 100,000; area of city increases from 15.0 square miles to 23.3 square miles.
3. *Stable, Minimal Growth Stage* 1970–90: Population increases by only 9,000; area of city remains virtually constant.

If we relate our data on the overall postwar change in budgets to these time periods, we find a certain pattern of linkage between expenditure decisions and city growth stages. In the initial growth stage the general fund budget increased (in constant dollars) by $211,000; in the second stage more than twice that amount—by $595,000; in the third growth stage we returned to the earlier level of expenditure—$199,000.

The major burden of development, in relative terms, fell on the budgets in the early stages.

The Chronology of Financial Decisions—
How Incremental?

The theory of incrementalism argues that year-to-year decisions on the budget are regularly made by adding small amounts to each department's allocation of the last budget, presumablywithout any serious evaluation of function.[7] It is the inertia of budget makers, the pressure of bureaucrats, the shortness of time, and the satisfaction with the past which combine, presumably, to lead to such budgetary decisions. In our analysis of Ann Arbor budgets, there is evidence that this often may not be true. Certainly, if one looks at the decision on the property tax levy from year to year, one gets the impression that the decisions are much more calculated than incremental. The adjusted tax levy changed erratically. While almost 12 mills in 1950, it declined to 9.16 in 1960 and fluctuated in the sixties until reaching 12.09 again in 1966. Subsequently, it reached 14 mills by the late sixties, then over 18 mills in the seventies, where it has remained, with some downward modifications after 1980. Clearly, city council was making very calculated tax decisions.

The route by which the general fund was increased from $743,000 to almost $57 million was far from incremental. The historical allocation patterns have been as diverse as for the tax levy. There were certain years when there was a great increase in the budget, such as 1945–46 (20 percent), 1955–57 (19 percent), 1965–66 (17 percent), 1968–69 (26 percent), and 1983–84 (11 percent). The city administrator in presenting such budgets explained them usually as accountable to "general growth and development within the community" or special needs that had arisen and had to be met. There were also many years in which the general fund rose only slightly. In fact, in seventeen of the forty-five two-year sequences, the general fund changed by relatively modest percentages (in actual dollars), less than 7 percent. (See table in appendix)

It is the irregularity of the patterns of general fund increases, however, that strikes one after close scrutiny of these data. In fact, the more one studies this forty five- year data set, the more one is inclined to characterize the budget actions of council in Ann Arbor as "splurge and decline"—large increases accompanied in a following year by a return to smaller incremental increases or even declines. Note, as an illustration, this sequence in changes in the general fund budget in recent years:

1977–78	+ 8.1 %
1978–79	+10.2 %
1979–80	+ 4.0 %
1980–81	+18.8 %
1981–82	+ 9.8 %
1982–83	− 2.0 %
1983–84	+11.3 %

During this period, the general fund budget increased on the average 7.6 percent, but changes ranged from −2.0 to +18.8. Economic conditions obviously had something to do with this pattern (for example, the 1982–83 decline), but this is obviously not the only explanation. The city council in many years was doing more than repeating the decisions of the past with incremental variations. They were splurging at times to support particular programs, responding to pressures from certain supporters, then consciously cutting back and regrouping at a lower level of allocations.

A careful look at departmental allocations from year to year reveals splurge-and-decline allocation strategy for particular departments. We find that in certain years, all departments received moderate, or even large increases. Often, however, there was a staggered pattern—large increases for one or two departments in one or two years (followed by several lean years for those departments), then subsequently large increases for other departments. It appears from the data that there was an irregular compensatory, catch-up strategy in allocating funds. (See table 10.5.) There is a special rationality that explains such patterns, but it is not incrementalism. Above all, calculations of averages obscure the reality of the year-to-year bargaining process that goes on within the bureaucracy and among council politicians as they interact with the bureaucrats. Each year's decisions seem to have a special character. Leaders do make budget decisions not randomly, not usually blindly and incrementally, but often quite purposefully.

TABLE 10.5. Variations in Departmental Budget Allocations, 1976–81

	Police	Fire	Parks	Planning
1976	5.2	8.5	13.8	12.6
1977	9.9	29.7	8.0	8.0
1978	6.5	.2	9.7	−18.1
1979	10.2	3.1	7.9	18.1
1980	13.8	22.4	21.0	1.5
1981	6.1	2.6	−6.3	−.4

Source: All tables using budget data are based on Ann Arbor City budget documents and financial reports.

The Evolution of Party Competition and the Chronology of Budget Decisions

Our central theoretical interest in the analysis of Ann Arbor's budgets is the relevance of the party system. What difference has it made in the past forty years to have had increasingly competitive elections and alternation in party control? Has party competition been facilitative, obstructive, or irrelevant? After a ten-year postwar period of one-party dominance we have had periods of high competition interspersed with periods of low competition, then a period of pluralistic three-party politics, before settling down to a period recently of continuing close competition. There are three ways we can conveniently describe and distinguish these periods from 1945 to 1990:

1. By periods of majority control of the city council. There have been five periods of Republican control, three periods of Democratic control, and a period of a split council (three parties and no party holding a majority).
2. By periods of high (or increasing) and low (or declining) competition in the party vote. In each era of development, there has been a period of low competition, a period of increasing and high competition, and in the seventies one period of very pluralistic competition (with three parties).
3. By periods of Republican or Democratic control of the mayoralty. We have had six Republican mayors and five Democratic mayors.

All three of these will be used here, but probably the first two are more theoretically useful for our purpose. Council control and electoral competition should be critical to test the theory of party relevance.

Our party conflict model suggests that the actions of political leaders will be linked to variations in party control of council and to variations in party strength at election time. This implies that these party system factors will have consequences for budget decisions. Our expectations can be briefly summarized as follows:

1. As we evolve from a one-party to a two-party system, both parties will assume mutual and alternating responsibilities for the development and maintenance of city services and programs. Over time, both parties will make significant contributions to city growth.
2. Emphases in certain types of budgetary allocations will change

as one party replaces the other in control of city government. But the changes in support for ongoing programs will be modest and minimal.

3. As party competition increases, becomes closer, there may be an acceleration of efforts by both parties to support larger budgetary allocations for needed services and developmental programs, particularly during periods of prosperity. The pressure of competition is linked to a pressure for effective development.
(One could argue the opposite position, that the parties will compete with each other to decrease budgets and cut costs, but to advocate a decrease in services and responsible development expenditures during a period of prosperity is unlikely. In a city like Ann Arbor, both parties operate in an environment of the successful and attractive city and are committed to enhancing that image—that is, if they wish to continue to win elections. The pressure from below is in that direction. Ideologically the parties will diverge in their willingness to fund certain programs, and also in the manner of providing certain services, but if the economic resources are available, both parties will press for expending the funds necessary to keep the city's services at a high level and to innovate with new programs when necessary. Political competition produces leaders at city hall who are development-conscious, not traditional types, and this means leaders willing to spend the necessary funds to accomplish their goals.)
4. The obvious exception to the previous point is that during periods of economic recession and fiscal strain, both parties in a truly competitive system will work toward a resolution of the budgetary crisis. Their proposals for holding the line and for cutting back and reducing costs may, however, differ. Indeed, they may be competitive in generating economy measures.
5. Alternation in party control will lead to the adoption of new programs, whether in areas of basic services, economic planning, improvements in the infrastructure, or social welfare programs. The parties have different constituencies as well as leaders with somewhat different political beliefs, and this leads to different types of innovative programs. Once advanced and adopted, it is the closeness of competition that preserves these programs, although changes in party control may temporarily reduce support.

A brief review of the budgetary narrative since 1945, using the general fund budget as a basis will help highlight the patterns of change.

The initial growth stage of 1945–60 began with several years of almost complete Republican dominance. While Mayor William Brown and other leaders saw the needs facing the city (chap. 1), the budgetary allocations were relatively small—an average yearly increase of $76,000 (in constant dollars) in the general fund budget from 1945 to 1950. In 1950 the Democratic vote began to increase, to 39 percent in the council vote and to 41 percent in the vote for mayor in 1951. Despite fluctuations, the Democrats continued to build until in 1957 the Democrats won the mayoralty. During this period, the budget increased sizably—an average yearly increase of $294,000 from 1950 to 1957. This was four times the budget allocation rate of the early period. Party competition appeared to stimulate budgetary activity (see table 10.6).

The secondary growth stage of 1960–70 was also divided into two parts. Party competition subsided by the early sixties—the Democratic vote dropped, and there were only one or two Democrats on the council up to 1964. The general fund allocations also dropped. In this period (1959–63) the average yearly increase in the general fund reverted somewhat to the earlier pattern: $210,000 per year. But as the Democrats recovered their strength (52.7 percent and five of the eleven seats in 1964), the budgetary allocations increased from 1964 to 1968, to a yearly average (in constant dollars) of $625,700. This was phenomenal change, the details of which will be clearer when we present departmental data. It is important to remember that during this entire period the Republicans were in control of City Hall, not the Democrats. The Republican Mayor Wendell Hulcher had a 6-to-5 or 7-to-4 council majority. It was bipartisan pressure for funding development with larger outlays, plus closer competition, that appears to have been functional to this sharp rise in general fund appropriations.

The election of 1969, a strong victory for the Democrats ushered in the last twenty-year period. This is called an era of stable, minimal growth, in so far as the change in city population and area is concerned. But this period from 1970 to 1990 was one in which the budget increased greatly—by $40 million in actual dollars and by almost $5 million in constant dollars. Much of this occurred by 1973, however—50 percent of it, to be exact—during years when the Democrats and Republicans alternated in control of council.

In the four years of the Harris administration, the general fund budget increased strikingly (for the first three years an average of $845,100), similar to the Hulcher period (an average of $700,000). But after 1973, increases leveled off. Mayor Stephenson's budget of 1973 was sizable (an increase of $839,000 for one year), but a decrease occurred in 1974. This entire period from 1972 to 1976 was complicated by Human Rights party involvement, councils with no party majority, and bitter three-party conflicts in council. Nevertheless, from 1972 to 1976 there was a net total yearly increase in the general fund budget of $212,000. Under the Belcher Republicans, the budget actually declined from 1980 until 1983 (in constant dollars). Since 1983 there has been a consistent increase (except in 1988).

TABLE 10.6. The Chronology of General Fund Increases by Political Periods

	Average Democratic % of Council Vote	General Fund Average Yearly Increase (constant $, in 000s)	Number of Years
1945–55: Republican Dominance, Low Competition	27.6%	$162.7	10
1956–58: Increasing Competition, Democratic mayor, but Republican Control of Council	47.0	329.3	3
1959–63: Republican Dominance, Low Competition	42.2	210.0	5
1964–68: Increasing Competition, but Republican Control	47.4	625.8	5
1969–71: Democratic Mayor and Control of Council, High Competition	49.6	845.1	3
1972–75: Three-party Politics, Pluralistic Competition	39.7	212.0	4
1976–79: Close Two-party Competition, Republican Mayor and Republican Control of Council	48.1	147.8	4
1980–83: Republican Dominance, Low Competition	41.0	−92.5	3
1984–90: High Competition, Alternating Party Control	51.8	373.0	7

Source: Ann Arbor City Budget Documents and Election data of the City Clerk's office.

TABLE 10.7. Party Competition and the Changes in the General Fund Budget

(Constant Dollars)	1945–60 Low Comp.	1945–60 High Comp.	1960–70 Low Comp.	1960–70 High Comp.	1970–90 Low Comp.	1970–90 High Comp.	1970–90 Three-Party Comp.
By Competition							
% Average Yearly Net Increase	6.1%	10.1	2.5	11.5	.2	2.1	1.2
Average Yearly Net Actual Increase (dollars, in 000s)	$96.0	244.0	162.0	781.0	−90.0	266.0	211.0
Overall Increases for Each Period							
% Average Yearly Net Increase	8.5%		8.2			1.9	
Average Yearly Net Actual Increase (in 000s)	$211.3		594.9			198.7	

Source: Ann Arbor City Budget Documents and Election data of the City Clerk's office.

Note: The years of low and high competition for each period are (with % of party vote): 1945–60—Low: 1945–51, average Democratic percentage 25.5, high: 1952–60, average 40.0; 1960–70—Low: 1960–63, average Democratic percentage 42.8, high: — 1964–70, average 48.0; 1970–90—Low: 1980–83, average Democratic percentage 42.6, high: 1971, 1976–79, 1984–90, average Democratic percentage 51.6; three-party period: 1972–75, average Democratic percentage 39.7, Republican 42.3, Human Rights 18.0.

The Relationship of Party Competition to Budget Allocations

What is suggested in this chronology is that the change in party strength in elections, and hence in council seats, was related to the size of budget funding decisions, for the general fund overall as well as for particular departments. To demonstrate this more precisely, we can take the three developmental periods separately (thus controlling for the three stages) and examine what happened in the periods of low competition compared to periods of high competition in each developmental period. Using two different measures and constant dollars will portray clearly the relevance of competition to budget actions of council. Table 10.7 presents these findings for the total general fund budget.

Table 10.7 is virtually self-explanatory. In all three developmental periods, we see that in the years of high competition, there was a greater increase in funds for the total budget than in periods of low competition. There was clearly more pressure from both parties for higher expenditures for development purposes and the expansion of city services. But these differentials by competition must be viewed as relative to the particular time period. Thus, in 1960–70, the average yearly increase in constant dollars was $595,000 while in 1970–90 it was only $199,000. The dollar figures reflect these differences by period—a $600,000 difference between the low and high competition periods in 1960–70 and a smaller, $360,000 difference in 1970–90. Note that during the period of three-party politics, the budget allocations were relatively quite high.

By utilizing the same approach in spending for individual departments, we can determine the relevance of party competition for increasing or decreasing support for particular functions of government. Since it is impossible to present such detail for all departments, we have selected five to test the theory of the relevance of party competition: police, parks and recreation, planning, human relations, and human services. Table 10.8 presents the data for the first three. The data for human relations and human services will be discussed in the next section. These departments received large increases over these forty five years, particularly police, parks, and planning in the two early periods of development up to 1970. Table 10.9 provides a summary: There were limited appropriations for human relations up to 1960 and for human services up to 1970; but the net yearly increases were considerable after then.

The question is, within each of these periods what was the pattern of funding by levels of party competition? As table 10.8 reveals, years of low competition are linked to significantly lower appropriations than in years when the parties competed more closely. Planning is an example of what

TABLE 10.8. The Relevance of Party Competition for Departmental Funding By Periods of Development

	1945–60		1960–70		1970–90		
(Constant Dollars)	Low Comp.	High Comp.	Low Comp.	High Comp.	Low Comp.	High Comp.	Three-Party Comp.
Police							
% Average Yearly Net Increase	8.0%	10.2	6.4	30.6	−.56	1.7	1.6
Average Yearly Allocation (in 000s)	$276	557	812	1,700	2,380	2,581	2,393
Parks and Recreation							
% Average Yearly Net Increase	1.8%	16.7	4.5	14.5	0.1	−0.1	−2.3
Average Yearly Allocation (in 000s)	$97	242	417	707	834	944	810
Planning							
% Average Yearly Net Increase	−0.3%	18.0	4.7	14.1	−3.9	2.0	−6.5
Average Yearly Allocation (in 000s)	$14	31	62	122	101	132	164

Source: Ann Arbor City Budget Documents and Election data of the City Clerk's office.

Note: The years of low and high competition for each period are (with % of party vote): 1945–60—Low: 1945–51, average Democratic percentage 25.5, high: 1952–60, average 40.0; 1960–70—Low: 1960–63, average Democratic percentage 42.8, high: 1964–70, average 48.0, 1970–90—Low: 1980–83, average Democratic percentage 42.6, high: 1971, 1976–79, 1984–90, average Democratic percentage 51.6; three-party period: 1972–75, average Democratic percentage 39.7, average Republican 42.3, Human Rights 18.0.

has happened over these forty five years as party competition ebbed or increased. It began with small allocations of $14,000 in 1945 (in constant dollars), but this support declined until 1952 when the two-party competition picked up and both parties saw the need to spend more on planning staff and their needs. Under Republican control the allocation quadrupled by 1960 to $57,000. This was just the beginning. After a slow period to 1963 the council became very interested in funding planning, and allocations for it increased greatly again. From 1963 to 1970, there was an increase of 150 percent in planning's allocation, to $164,000. Both parties contributed to this—the Republican Wendell Hulcher administration to 1969 and the Democratic Robert Harris administration from 1969 to 1971. Thereafter, funds for planning fluctuated in a downward trend, dropping from $184,000 in 1972 to $111,500 in 1990. Only during strong two-party competition was there even the semblance of strong support for planning in these later years, and even this was not consistent.

These highly suggestive findings for police and parks as well as planning indicate party competition was very relevant to increased allocations for services and development. All three departments profited greatly in the budgetary expansion up to the early 1970s. Beginning in 1972, however, the city went through ten years of ambivalence and relative decline in budgetary support for these and other functions. Even police experienced significant cuts in constant dollars after 1970. It is difficult to disentangle the several forces influencing these post 1970 changes. The decline coincided with the emergence of the Human Rights Party, but this was certainly not exclusively responsible. Short-term fiscal crises in 1973–75 and 1980–83 also contributed. The decline of party competition in the early 1980s was another factor. After 1983 closer competition was associated with increased expenditures for these

TABLE 10.9. Changes in Departmental Budget Allocations for Selected Departments 1945–90 (in constant dollars)

	General Fund % Average Yearly Net Increase in Allocations		
	1945–60	1960–70	1970–90
Police	9.4%	12.3	1.3
Parks	10.4	11.5	− .5
Planning	10.7	11.3	− .9
Human Relations	—	56.5	− 6.4
Human Services	—	—	35.0

Source: All tables using budget data are based on Ann Arbor City budget documents and financial reports.

purposes, but this, too, was erratic. It did lead, however, after 1983 to increases of over $40,000 (constant dollars) in planning by 1989, over $200,000 in parks by 1988, and over $400,000 in police by 1990.

Human Relations and Human Services Funding: The Relevance of Party Competition

A major test of the meaningfulness of the party conflict model is whether it leads to new programs when the opposition competes effectively and eventually secures power. One aspect of our model is the effect political competition has in maintaining, and increasing, support for traditional departments such as police, parks, and planning. But another aspect, as important, includes the generation of support for new ideas for meeting public needs and the mobilization of elite support for funding these new programs emanating from these ideas. The progress of a city can be described by the creative policies adopted to improve its development. Ann Arbor has had many such creative policies. One has been in the field of human relations, another in human services. We use these as specially selective cases to test our theory about Ann Arbor. In chap. 1, we described the history of the development of these programs. Here we are interested in the relationship of party competition and power sharing for these new programs.

A brief review of the budgetary history of these programs will provide the background for our analysis first, the human relations program, which was established in 1957 with the creation of the Human Relations Commission (HRC). To get support in council to fund the commission was a difficult matter at first. Although the Democrats pressed for a small budget allocation of $2,525 for 1958, the council reduced the amount to $525. There were some who felt the commission would soon be starved out of existence, but it is interesting that the budget continued to provide (small) additional funds. Under Republican Mayor Cecil Creal the appropriation finally increased to almost $6,000. Indeed, Creal spoke to council on April 11, 1960, of the need to "cooperate closely with the Human Relations Commission." When Republican Mayor Hulcher took office in 1965, the commission's funding status took a relatively big jump, to over $27,000, and increased to over $50,000 by the time Hulcher left office in 1969.

This commitment by the Republicans was very significant. It meant that a program the Democrats had initiated was gradually being accepted, defended, and supported by the opposition party. A kind of momentum had set in. A fulltime director was appointed, the commission was increased in size (to twelve), and more money was allocated.

Hulcher turned out to be a human rights liberal and in the midst of the tumultuous sixties addressed the council (April 11, 1968) about the "root causes of unrest" and what to do about them. "Social change through love and nonviolence is the key," he said, adding "We must put our money where our mouth is," recommending $100,000 more as part of an accelerated human relations program. (Such a large sum was not appropriated in 1968, however). In the meantime, the Republican party platforms in Ann Arbor reflected their conversion:

1964: "Every person regardless of race, color, or religion must be afforded an equal opportunity to . . . employment . . . the home of his choice . . . the best education available."
1968: "We feel that more should be done in the private sector . . . to continue improving human relationships. . . . We continue to support a broadly based Human Relations Commission.
1969: Ann Arbor's HRC was "a human relations program which placed Ann Arbor in front of the nation."

In Hulcher's farewell "state of the city" speech he had said: "Emphasis must be placed on human relations and equal opportunity for each of our citizens—in jobs, housing, education, recreation, and all other aspects of life." Thus we arrived at political convergence and the institutionalization of human relations in the budget, in city hall, in the Republican party—indeed, in the two-party system.

In the Harris period, 1969–72, the Democrats decided to move the support for human relations one step further: to make it a department with real power. The overwhelming Democratic victory in 1969 made that possible—they won eight out of the eleven council seats, including the mayoralty. Mayor Harris immediately proposed a new antidiscrimination ordinance creating a Department of Human Rights with broader powers: subpoena authority, cease-and-desist orders, power to seek injunctions, and power to fine violators. It included the creation of a panel of human rights examiners (to be appointed by mayor and council) and a new seven-member Human Rights Commission with an advisory function in relation to city council and an oversight function so far as all human rights programs were concerned. The explicit aim was to give the director more power to administer and enforce the law. The jurisdiction of the new department would extend to the schools, the university, even county government, according to the legal argument by the city attorney at the time. Despite some opposition and revisions the new ordinance was adopted. It broadened discrimination to include sex discrimination and increased the scope of the department to include discrimination in public accommodations and employment. In addition, the city council adopted a stronger affirmative action program which was implemented in city employment and resulted in minority group members heading the housing, human rights, model cities, and personnel departments. A new director came from Washington, D.C., to take over the administration of the program.

The financial support for the human rights program increased considerably in the Harris administration. The 1969 budget allocated $125,000, more than double that of 1968. Budgets, and expenditures, from then on ranged from $80,000 to $95,000. What is more interesting is that this new level of support continued under the next mayor, a Republican, James Stephenson. The Republican platforms now were endorsing the human relations/human rights program ardently. The 1971 Republican platform, drafted by a committee chaired by Louis Belcher, was a remarkable (and long) document. It applauded the earlier Human Relations Commission, which it said "worked constructively over the years to bring about those changes in our community's attitudes and laws required to insure equality of opportunity for all." Indeed, it claimed "the Democratic administration inherited from the Republicans an active and effective human relations program which placed Ann Arbor in front of the nation."

The history of human relations funding after 1974 (when it was funded at $94,660) has been one of modification of status, some decline in the size of allocations, but acceptance by both parties that it is an integral part of ongoing city governance. Under Democratic mayor, Albert Wheeler, funding remained high until 1977, when the human rights department lost some support. In 1978 it was combined with personnel into one department, and its appropriations remained relatively low and constant under Republican Mayor Belcher. In 1987 to 1991, there has been again a rise in dollars appropriated—but in terms of constant dollars, the funds have been more than cut in half since the seventies. There has been a shift of emphasis perhaps from human rights to human services, and the funding for the latter came to absorb much more interest and money.

In summary, the emergence of the human relations program is an illustration of what can happen under a two-party system with genuine competition; leadership with somewhat different priorities, values, and goals; and strong, durable party organizations. It illustrates the following:

1. The initiation of an entirely new program (1957)
2. The grudging support by the opposition in the early years (until 1964)

3. The gathering of momentum in financial support
4. The political conversion of the opposition (up to 1969)
5. The expansion of the program under new liberal leadership (1969–72)
6. The institutionalization of the new program as a department with real authority, and with new funding
7. The acceptance of this by both parties (1972 on)
8. The maintenance of support for this program despite a conservative reaction, as a result of pressures generated within both parties and continuing, close political competition

Party competition, as well as party turnover, was clearly related to the pattern of allocations (table 10.10). As the Democratic vote and percentage of council seats increased, the dollars were more likely to be provided—even under conditions of Republican control. There might be a decline in financial allocations, but funding was provided at a basic level of support. The peak appropriations came during the 1969–72 period of Democratic control. In the periods when the Democrats were the minority, the funding declined and never again equalled the 1969-72 peak, but it is important to note that funding continued when it could have been eliminated. This attests to the degree of bipartisan consensus, the convergence of goals, the definite incorporation of the idea of human relations funding in the city budget, and the role a strong minority-party presence on council plays.

Another New Program: Human Services

Another example of innovative funding in Ann Arbor under the two party system is in the response by the city council to the social welfare and human services needs of the community. For years after World War II there was, interestingly enough, a token allocation designated for the "poor," normally $600 or less. Thus, there was actually no real concern by the council to solve any welfare or poverty problems until the late sixties.

Under Republican Mayor Hulcher there was an expression of concern for human welfare needs, and in 1966 the city administrator's proposed budget report makes the observation that there was "an ever-increasing number of assignments from the mayor, council, and the city administrator's office to deal with situations which fall in the area of social services." They were referred to as low-income housing needs, cases of neglect, employment needs, and the like. But no money was allocated, except $10,303 in 1968 for emergency housing.

TABLE 10.10. The Linkage Between Party Competition and the Funding of the Human Relations/Human Rights Departments

Period	Description	% of Council Seats Won by Democrats	Average % of Vote Which Was Democratic (for council or mayor)	Average Allocations Yearly in Constant Dollars[a]
1945–56	Republican dominance	11.0%	33.9	$ 0
1957–63	Emergence of Democrats; Republicans held mayoralty for all but two years	18.2	44.8	3,619
1964–68	Republican control but Democratic % of vote increased gradually	44.4	47.3	39,117
1969–72	Close competition; Democrats controlled mayoralty	50.0[b]	47.4[b]	83,593
1973–77	Pluralistic three-party politics; mayoralty alternated	44.4[c]	42.7[c]	53,928
1978–83	Republican control	35.7	43.5	24,183
1984–90	Close competition; mayoralty alternated	50.6	50.6	19,396

Source: Ann Arbor City Budget documents.

[a]1967 = 100.

[b]Of the twenty-two seats, two were won by the Human Rights party in 1972. The remainder were split between the Democrats and the Republicans. The 1972 vote percentages were 35.8 Democratic, 24.4 Human Rights, and 39.8 Republican.

[c]The Human Rights party won four seats during this period. Their vote for council averaged 10.7 percent. The Republican proportion (for council or mayor) was 46.1 percent.

When Democratic Mayor Harris came into office in 1969 (with his 8–3 council majority), discussions over the need to do something about human services increased greatly. Harris at one point said he had three priorities: civil rights, civil liberties; and the war on poverty. The Democrats began at once to identify these needs. In 1969, the only relevant appropriation was $16,150 for the housing commission, which had been set up under the Hulcher administration. In the ensuing years, appropriations for what was called human resources increased quickly, and expenditures outdistanced budget allocations by a considerable margin. In 1971, the budget for human services was $75,673, but expenditures totaled $313,994. The 1972 budget allocation more than doubled, to $173,300, yet expenditures of $290,145 greatly exceeded it. In 1973, the budget fell to $74,210, but expenditures remained high at $263,034.

Once city government recognized such needs and its role in meeting some of them, the demands for funds increased greatly. Under both Democratic and Republican administrations, considerable allocations were made.

After these years of the "war on poverty" from 1970 to 1974, the spigot appeared to be turned off, beginning with the period when the Democratic Mayor Wheeler was in office and continuing during the first part of Republican Mayor Belcher's administration up to 1981. This was due to the fighting during the three-party-politics period (Wheeler chaired a council split 5–5-1), as well the defeat of a major millage proposal in June 1974 and the emergence of a national economic recession in the late seventies and early eighties. Federal revenue-sharing funds were available, but a fight ensued between Wheeler and the Republicans as to how to spend this money.

By 1981, however, an interest in human services was revived and has been strong and strongly financed ever since. Table 10.11 summarizes the change that has taken place: The general fund budget now has a separate division for human services as well as a separate one for public services (whose appropriations have ranged from $56,000 to $125,000 in the past seven years). These funds have gone for a variety of special

TABLE 10.11. Changes in Human Services Budgets 1980–90

Human Services Budgets	1980	1988	1990
Actual dollars	$13,500	$560,000	$638,319
Constant (1967) dollars	5,470	153,467	160,400

Source: All tables using budget data are based on Ann Arbor City budget documents and financial reports.

purposes (see appendix). From 1984 to 1991, the money went for housing assistance, child care, youth programs, and crisis assistance (drug programs, Ozone house, and such). In recent years there has been much continuity but also some new types of funding. It is difficult to track all the allocations because they are shifted to different rubrics, transferred to federal (CDBG) grants, or obscured under other titles, yet careful scrutiny reveals that many of the same purposes for which money was appropriated early still seem to be the purposes today.

Let us return to the basic questions we have been pursuing in this chapter: In what ways have the parties contributed to this support for human services? How has the pattern of party competition and control been linked to these budgetary and expenditure developments?

The Democratic victory in 1969 led soon to higher funding for the disadvantaged and for human services generally. Consider the eight-year sequence in general fund appropriations, 1965–72 (table 10.12). This looks like a large increase in actual dollars, and indeed it was, but in terms of the proportion of the budget, it was actually quite small—from less than 0.7 percent to 1.4 percent of the total budget. Its significance lay in its relative increase and its association with turnover in party control.

The correlation between the Democratic vote for council and the allocations for human services in recent years is interesting to observe (table 10.13). A variety of factors entered into the decisions each year, including pressures from those needing financial support, and much bargaining went on between the Republican and Democratic leadership groups which led to these funding decisions. The basic point, however, is clear: these increases in outlays for human services occurred during the period of intensified party conflict which generated the pressures for greater public support.

If we combine all our data for both the human relations and human services programs and analyze in the past twenty years how these budget decisions varied by the periods of party competition, we arrive at the

TABLE 10.12. The Relation of Party Change to Human Rights and Services Budget Allocations

	Total General Funds Appropriations		
	Human Rights	Human Services	Total
1965–68 (Republican control)	165,280	10,303	175,583
1969–72 (Democratic mayor)	391,927	309,629	701,556

Source: All tables using budget data are based on Ann Arbor City budget documents and financial reports.

overall summation presented in table 10.14. It is clear that the years of high party competition were in general linked to greater appropriations for these programs, five times as much was allocated to these programs during the high competition periods as during the low competition periods. One could well speculate at what the level of budget support would have been if there had been no significant party competition in Ann Arbor during this twenty-year period.

A final question remains: To what extent was party turnover linked to budget allocations? When the majority control of city council changed, as it did in 1969, 1971, 1973, 1976, 1985, 1988, and 1991, is there evidence that budget allocations changed? We present in table 10.15 an analysis that summarizes our data for the general fund budget and certain departments. These findings suggest that the year of a turnover does not necessarily lead to changes in the size of allocations: for police and planning

TABLE 10.13. The Correlation of the Democratic Vote and Human Services Allocations

	Democratic Vote	Human Services Outlays[a]
1980	38.7%	$5,470
1981	40.8	18,565
1982	43.6	33,430
1983	47.2	49,167
1984	49.6	56,651
1985	56.5	80,540
1986	54.5	131,221
1987	50.5	154,671
1988	51.4	153,467
1989	47.6	131,700
1990	52.6	160,400

Source: City Budget documents and Election Reports of the City Clerk
Note: Pearson Correlation: .729
[a]In constant dollars, 1967 = 100.

TABLE 10.14. The Relevance of Party Competition for Budget Allocation for Human Relations and Human Services, 1970–90

Average Yearly Allocations, in Constant Dollars[a]	Periods of High Two-Party Competition	Period of Republican Control and Low Competition	Period of Three-Party Politics
Human Relations	$98,844	24,628	52,899
Human Services	147,939	26,657	77,147
Total	246,743	51,285	130,046

Source: City Budget documents and Election Reports of the City Clerk
[a]1967 = 100.

yes, but not for parks and recreation. Likewise, the general fund budget itself does not necessarily increase greatly in the year of turnover. There are exceptions, as in 1969 with a 19.3 percent increase (but the 1968 increase had been 21.2 percent), or in 1973 (7.5 percent increase), but on the average, it was not the sudden capture of city hall and mayoralty by another party that immediately led to major new allocations for new programs. That is not to say, however, that there are no important changes. In 1991, for example, there was an interesting $17,000 increase in the human rights budget, and a $400,000 increase in community development (while parks, planning, and police, moreover, were not increased). These in a sense are important adjustments linked to a party turnover, but not major new policy directions. Nor do mayoral turnovers with no change in majority control of council lead to major changes in budgets. Rather, as our previous analysis indicated, it was the continuous and increasing pressure of party competition that was responsible for decisions by both parties and councils controlled by both parties in different time periods to make budget decisions leading to larger appropria-

TABLE 10.15. Party Turnovers as they Relate to Changes in the General Fund Budget and Selected Departments

	Year before Turnover	Year of Turnover	First Year after Turnover	Second Year after Turnover
Changes in the General Fund Budget in Years of Critical Turnovers (Changes in majority control of council; Seven cases)				
Average Net Yearly Percentage Increase in General Fund Budget (Constant dollars[a])	+6.5%	+4.9	+3.7	+2.0
Changes in Departmental Allocations in Years of Critical Turnovers				
Average Net Yearly Percentage Change in Budgets				
Police	+4.7%	+6.9	+2.6	+3.4
Planning	−.4	+4.7	+10.7	−8.7
Parks	+9.6	+4.3	−1.9	−2.3

Source: All tables using budget data are based on Ann Arbor City budget documents and financial reports.

[a]1967 = 100.

tions for the different types of development goals which over time became salient issues in the community.

General Conclusion

We have described here how our city budgets have increased since 1945, as the result of political decisions. At times the changes have been small, gradual, and incremental. They were not random, however, although they sometimes look random. Both sets of partisan leaders made calculated, purposive decisions. There was at times considerable agreement, and sometimes there was conflict, confrontation, and bargaining, but it is clear that the phenomena associated with the party conflict model, which we specified earlier, were indeed in evidence. As party competition increased and as party control changed hands, there was some revision of emphasis in budget allocations. There was also the initiation of new programs. Further, political competition produced pressure to maintain patterns of support for old programs and to continue, indeed increase, support for new programs. With the alternation in party control and closeness of electoral competition came convergence in funding perspectives, despite philosophical differences. Over the past thirty years the parties shared power, shared ideas, and debated these ideas intensely. While shifting in programmatic emphasis from time to time, the important point is that the parties shared in the development of the community through the budget decisions, both incremental and innovative, which they made. They each innovated, they each made distinctive contributions.

Our research reported in earlier chapters revealed the fluctuations in party competition and the existence of political cycles or eras of party control. The research also demonstrated the different ideological and value orientations of the Democratic and Republican leaders. When one sees such differences in attitudes, ideologies, and beliefs between party leadership groups, the natural query is—"So what?" Are there behavioral and policy consequences? This chapter seems to indicate that the financial decisions of our city leaders from time to time have indeed been derived from somewhat different commitments and value perspectives. In reality party politics does matter.

A considerable amount of policy innovation has occurred over the past forty years in Ann Arbor. If that had not been the case, this city would not have developed as it did. There are many instances of such innovation under both parties, and the two case studies presented here are only illustrative and used to test the basic party conflict theory of this book. Our basic theoretical point should be clear: a two-party system with close competition and alternating party control can lead (and has) to new policy perspectives and programs which can over time become accepted, legitimized, and institutionalized, eventually bringing political convergence and community support. Party conflict in the long run can be, and has been, productive here. The end-state of political conflict can be significant progress.

CHAPTER 11

A Summing Up: Developmental and Democratic Perspectives

The majority of American cities today are confronted with difficult economic conditions and great financial strain. The 1991 report of the National League of Cities summarized the situation for cities over 100,000 in population as follows: a per capita reduction in revenues in 1991 of 4.1 percent and a per capita increase in expenditures of 2.2 percent over 1990.[1] This imbalance has led to cuts in services, firing of employees, attempts to increase fees and taxes, and even threatened bankruptcy. The declining tax base related to population changes, the reduction in federal and state aid, the resistance to new taxes, the increase in social problems such as housing, child care, social welfare, and poverty, as well as the appearance of new problems such as solid waste disposal—all these developments have cumulated to create great pressures on the leadership in American cities.

Our problems are compounded by the decentralized nature of local government operations and finance in the United States. In a unitary system like the Netherlands, cities raise only 6 percent of their funds through local taxes and fees; in the United States it is 70 percent or more. The revenue sharing by the national government decreased dramatically during the 1980s and now cities find themselves with tasks and burdens of government heavier than ever but with less money from higher authorities to finance these needs. The basic challenge for our cities, then, is one of effective management along with, prudent, responsible, efficient, and humane leadership at a time of declining resources. As one scholar put it, the paradox of the American cities is that they are conducting more "government" than ever before (almost 60 percent of all public-sector employment was found in cities by the 1980s, compared to 50 percent in 1950), while there has been a sharp decrease in the proportion of all public sector revenues generated at the local level.[2] Presumably government revenue sharing would support the difference, however federal revenue sharing disappeared by 1987.

Ann Arbor has been weathering this storm more successfully than have most cities. Recent budgets have also been austere—a 5.9 percent average cut in department allocations in 1991, and up to twenty positions at that time were not filled. An increase in certain fees, a strong emphasis on efficiency in departmental operations, and a small increase in property assessed valuations have helped. But Ann Arbor is more on its own than it was for many years, due to cuts in federal, state, and university payments to the city. The leaders of most university cities report that university payments for police, fire, and roads are inadequate—only 40 percent report that the university pays a "fair share."[3] The University of Michigan is no different.

Yet the city of Ann Arbor has survived, and continued to thrive, reporting a $3.9 million fund balance as of February, 1992. The city continues to move ahead with both images of development, economic and infrastructural, as well as providing a variety of human services.

It is in this context that one must evaluate Ann Arbor's system of partisan government. The Ann Arbor system has undergone considerable transformation during the nineteenth and twentieth centuries, but not in the same direction as many other cities. In this century, as the Progressive Movement inveighed against "machine politics" and pressed for a variety of reforms in local government, there were several movements in Ann Arbor to alter the 1889 charter to accord with the reform model. These were all defeated, until 1956. By that time almost half the cities of Ann Arbor's size (46 percent) had adopted the council-manager system along with nonpartisan and at-large elections.[4] This trend toward the rejection of parties did not really find majority support from Ann Arbor citizens and their leaders. The council-manager concept found support but was adopted in a somewhat modified form. Ann Arbor was, thus, a deviant when it reformed its system of government in 1956. Ann Arbor kept partisan elections. Since Ann Arbor has been a success story, one may well ruminate on whether other cities have made a mistake in opting for the form of government they did.

Institutions and forms of government are important and provide the context; they do not assure good government. The working of the system in Ann Arbor, and the political cultural norms that have surrounded the working of that system, have been the focus of the analysis of this book. In our final observations now, we will first summarize the key points in the argument of this book, what we think has been demonstrated about the functioning of the Ann Arbor system. Then we will evaluate that system, asking primarily how democratic government and politics are in Ann Arbor. Finally, we will briefly discuss the proposed reforms.

Major Findings: How the Polity Has Developed

Ann Arbor's political system has been transformed over the past forty-five years, particularly since the mid-1950s. The parties have become truly competitive, with an exciting ebb and flow in party strength and party turnover. The council has developed into a real center of policy making, the mayor as a member of that council. The administrative operation of government is generally efficient, but the administration is subordinate to the council in the last analysis. In these respects the 1956 charter has been indeed implemented. Ann Arbor has a strong two-party system and a strong, well-functioning set of governmental institutions. This period of political change has had tremendous consequences for the political life of the city—campaigns are different, candidates reflect different groups and beliefs, party organizations have matured, and decision making is less patrimonial and more adversarial. It is a system emphasizing two basic dimensions or characteristics: high partisan conflict and a city council that is the decision center. This combination distinguishes Ann Arbor from many other cities.

The type of leadership, on balance quite able, that has emerged is a product of this system. Few self starters without party support or experience are successful. There have been primary contests only 13 percent of the time and in only one out of ten of these has the challenger come close. Over 60 percent of the recent top elites have had considerable party experience (compared to 7 percent in the early years), but these leaders have also had wide contacts in various types of community groups (70 percent are active in more than one group). The leaders are well educated—50 percent with graduate or professional degrees. Yet, it has not been too difficult to persuade these well-educated people to run for city office, evidence of their commitment to the city. However, it is often difficult to get them to run frequently for reelection. Only 15 percent of all candidates run more than twice, and four years in office is the norm.

There is a dynamism or liveliness to Ann Arbor's politics. Not only is there high turnover in candidacies, but also the possiblity that incumbents who try to stay on can be defeated. While typically 96 percent of members of Congress who run are reelected, this is true of less than 70 percent of incumbent mayors and councillors in Ann Arbor. Victories in recent years are often close, particularly when a new mayor is elected. In the last six mayoral turnovers, the percents for the victor were: 56.6 (1993), 53.7 (1991), 52.6 (1987), 53.1 (1985), 50.5 (1978), 50.2 (1975). This is a vibrant politics—in elections, in types of candidates, in interest group activity, in party organizational work, in council deliberations.

The public here, at least the politically alive sector of the public, seems to accept, perhaps even enjoy this type of politics. A 60 percent majority (64 percent of the voters) approve of the partisan system; and, of course, a higher percent (80 percent) of the activists do. On balance, Ann Arbor citizens support parties and partisanism at a considerably higher level than do most U.S. citizens. A majority (70 percent) also approve of the job the government is doing, although on particular problems (streets especially, or housing) there is much criticism. What is gratifying is that those who are knowledgeable are more inclined to be affirmative in their evaluations. Further, the Ann Arbor public has a higher trust in its government (at the 70 percent level) and a greater feeling of personal efficacy (89 percent do) than is true for U.S. citizens generally—a 15-to 20-point differential. To be sure, there is political alienation in Ann Arbor also. Almost 20 percent of the samples manifest some degree of negative affect for local government and politics (independents and extreme ideologues of the Right and Left particularly), but antigovernment and antisystem orientations are at a relatively low level.

Politics can become quite ideological in Ann Arbor. The data reveal to what extent this is true. When leaders and citizens are asked what they consider themselves to be—liberals, moderates, or conservatives—one finds sharp contrasts, and potential for confrontation, at all levels of the polity. In the analysis of the values of the top elites, the contrast is also seen on economic equality beliefs—56 percent of the Democrats were economic egalitarians but only 21 percent of the Republicans were.

Politics deals with "middle majority" realities, however. The ideological distribution of the Ann Arbor public generally is 36 percent liberal, 44 percent moderate, 20 percent conservative. Politicians are pragmatists, as the analysis revealed. Votes must be mobilized, which means that the Republicans and Democrats must go to that 44 percent middle. Yet, both parties are constrained by their left and right diehards. The vote mobilization realities, particularly related to low turnouts, influence campaigns and elite behavior.

This vibrant politics, this system of partisan government, linked to this type of leadership ideologically distinct but pragmatic, has had significant consequences. The analysis of the major decisions made in the past forty years, particularly the budget decisions, is fraught with interesting findings. There has been a tremendous expansion in the scope and role of government and its costs. These costs increased in all types of allocations, but particularly in infrastructural and developmental costs. Availability of resources (taxable property) and population increases were relevant, but by no means the only, explanations for increased costs. The demand, and the need, for more and new governmental expenditures increased, and political leaders responded.

Finally, what emerges as one of the virtues of partisan conflict is the initiation of new programs. We have examined two of them here: human relations (1957) and human services (1969). The history of these two programs demonstrates that politics matters, elections have consequences, party turnover can produce the funding for new programs. Party competition and the pressures generated by the two-party system played a major role.

Evaluation from a different perspective: Is this an effective democracy?

This analysis makes Ann Arbor read like a success story. But if one is objective, one must admit there are concerns for certain aspects of political life. One overriding question is: How elitist or "not-democratic" is this system? A common belief is that democratic government is associated with improvement in the welfare of humanity, and therefore, one must be concerned about the state of Ann Arbor's (and the U.S.) democracy. To address that big question in the context of the conditions of political life in Ann Arbor, one must identify certain key values or principles for democracy at the local level which are at the heart of these concerns. Each of these will be addressed briefly here, and some of the relevant evidence from the study adduced.

Competition

The idea that tolerance of, and the existence of, genuine and effective competition between political groups representing diverse, even extreme, ideologies has been accepted as a necessity of a democratic order. Schumpeter long ago articulated this conception well, although limiting his application to the electoral process: "The democratic method is that institutional arrangement for arriving at political decisions in which individuals acquire the power to decide *by means of a competitive struggle* for the people's vote."(empahsis added)[5] Other scholars have emphasized competition and political contestation also, among them Downs, Dahl, and V. O. Key.

If competition is critical for democracy, Ann Arbor today is exemplary. One could not say that before 1957—Republicans in those early years on the average had a 70 percent to 30 percent edge in the vote and controlled 89 percent of the council seats. In the decades after 1957, the vote percentage split was 55–45, and since 1969 it has been 49.5 percent

Republicans 46.5 percents Democratic and 4 percent for third parties. The competition has been close for twenty years. Further, the turnover in party control has been more frequent, and more possible. The party organizations are quite combative in campaigns, which is revealed in the reports from citizen samples about contacts from the parties. In 1984, 51 percent said there had been some contact; 24 percent report contact by both parties. The activists are almost equally active in campaigns in getting out the vote. The proportion of activists who say they get out the votes is 46 percent Republican and 55 percent Democratic in the April campaigns and from 10 to 20 percent more in the November election. This is evidence of genuine rivalry. The parties are competitive in other ways also, especially in the types of candidates they recruit. There is overlap as well as distinctiveness in the characteristics of candidates—more women and blacks for the Democrats, more persons from the business community for the Republicans. Thus, in ideology, candidacies, organizational activism, and electoral results—all the measures point to increasing political competition. Finally, the overwhelming majority of top elites at city hall believe in the value of political conflict—86 percent are proconflict, only 14 percent are not. The elites as well as a majority of the public, have lived in a climate of political conflict and apparently view it as beneficial and healthy.

The Social Bias in Elite Recruitment

One may be more concerned about the social representativeness of this leadership. "Those who rise from the general citizenry to occupy the seats of government are not a representative sample." This conclusion, by Prewitt, based on a study of the councillors in eighty-seven cities in the San Francisco Bay area, is the accepted generalization today by scholars of elites.[6] The classical scholars had long asserted the same proposition, that social status determined access to political power, and empirical research certainly has supported this observation, in Ann Arbor also. The five or six people elected each year to run the city are a distinctive breed. White, educated men with professional or business backgrounds have had over the years the greatest probabilities of becoming candidates and winners for council seats. The opportunities have opened up a bit in recent years—women now constitute 33 percent of candidates (compared to 2 percent forty years ago) and 10 percent of the candidates recently have been blacks (compared to 2 percent also in the 1940s). Further, the percentage of business managerial types who are candidates has declined sharply—from over 30 down to 17 percent in the 1980s. Nevertheless, the council is still an unrepresentative elite. For example, 86 percent are now college graduates compared to 56 percent of the Ann Arbor public age 25 or older (1980 census).

The leadership is also unrepresentative in other respects. It has become an elite with much political experience. Over 50 percent of the candidates now have held government jobs (compared to about 20 percent in the early period). In addition, the Ann Arbor leaders of today have parents who have also been active in politics in the community. Compared to the public, 22 percent of whom have had at least one parent active in community affairs, 50 percent of the Republican and 65 percent of the Democratic top elites come from homes with such parental interest in civic affairs. This may indeed be seen as fortuitous and associated with a high level of competence in, and familiarity with, public service. But it does reinforce the image of a political leadership different in basic respects from the ordinary citizenry.

One of the major arguments made is that such a special background, particularly high social status, is really irrelevant in predicting elite policy decisions and attitudes on public issues. One hears of "upper-class liberals" and "lower-class conservatives." Yet, that is not completely nor always true. In the study of Ann Arbor's elites, for example, on the question of whether "the government should do more to expand the opportunities for the poor," the following distinctions appear in the data:

> Among Democratic leaders, 92 percent feel government should do more, and the only defectors are those with higher social class. Among Republican leaders only 28 percent feel the government should do more, and they divide as follows: 38 percent from the lower class favor government action and 25 percent from the middle class are favorable. Thus, "class status" reveals some differences, although it is "party" which is more significant.

On the question of doing more for the achievement of economic equality, one finds that the top leadership with lower-class origins is more likely to provide egalitarian responses: 49 percent to 32 percent. Thus, even in Ann Arbor, a relatively liberal community, there is some evidence of the linkage of social status to elite values.

Social bias at the elite level has been mitigated and muted somewhat in Ann Arbor, but the issue is still an important one. One might be concerned about the breadth of the social base for political power. "The leadership of a society is a criterion of the values by which that society lives,"[7] it can be argued. In that sense, the narrow social base of power poses the question: Should more be done to provide opportunities for those with lower social status to seek political office?

The Responsiveness or Accountability of Elites

One democratic test of any system is the representativeness of leaders in terms of their attitudes and behavior. As Pitkin defines it, representation is leaders "acting in the interest of the represented, in a manner *responsive* to them.(emphasis added)"[8] Other writers also, such as Lasswell, argued that "the essential condition (of democracy) is accountability."[9] In one study of U.S. cities, the conclusion was reached that many city councils were not responsive; rather they were "immune to pressures emanating from the public."[10] How responsive are Ann Arbor's political leaders?

This is a very complex question—there are many interrelated conditions and factors to be considered. First is the process by which people are recruited and finally selected as candidates for city office. In Ann Arbor, the parties play a major role, and self-starters in primaries do not usually run, nor do interest groups usually pick their own representatives to run. Hence, the candidates are linked to party organizations who can be held responsible. This is the way campaigns are run also, by candidates linked to the parties, campaigns that often (but not always) result in a fairly clear articulation of candidates' and parties' views on issues. Voters can have an idea of the contrasting positions of the candidates if they are attentive to politics, which, as we have seen, is true of only one-third or fewer of Ann Arbor's citizens. The selection process is not ideal, certainly. Campaign coverage in the local newspaper has declined in recent years, and some campaigns can be rather desultory, but the conditions may be more conducive to meaningful contests for local office than in many American cities.

A second point to remember is the extent to which city leaders have maintained contacts with local party leaders, community groups, and the media. The data reveal that all elected leaders do seek to mobilize support from community groups and 100 percent report pressures on them from the leaders of five or more such groups. Particularly active in approaching councillors are business, union, neighborhood, party, and civic groups. (For only 30 percent of the administrators is this true.) There is a lively interest group involvement in politics. The elected elite also is under constant public surveillance. Leaders are attentive to public hearings each Monday evening and do keep an open ear to public appeals. Indeed, some of them complain the pressure is too intense at times.

Third, personal circulation of elected leaders has been fairly high in recent years. In the 1940s, approximately 40 percent of the elected positions on the average were filled by persons new to city hall; from 1970 on, this figure jumped to 60 percent. Put another way, since 1976, in 45 percent of the two-election sequences for city councils, a majority of councilors (six out of eleven persons on the council) have been new. This high turnover may signify developments that are beneficial but also have consequences that are not salutary. For example, this level of turnover may lead to considerable discontinuity in decision making at city hall. Such election results may or may not be relevant to the responsiveness question. Many people voluntarily stepped down. Also, the new personnel may hold the same attitudes and have the same characteristics as the old personnel. Nevertheless, the rate of the defeat of incumbents who run again (30 percent of the time), plus these personal circulation rates, do suggest that new bodies are coming into city council regularly and that the voting public does evaluate the performance of leaders, reelecting some, defeating others. There is a suggestion of dynamic renewal of city hall personnel implicit in these data, which may indeed be related to the responsiveness of city government.

In the last analysis, responsiveness has to do with the attitudes of leaders and the policies they adopt. It is clear that Ann Arbor's leaders represent both conservative and liberal elements in the community. There is continual noise from the partisans of the left and the right. On eight issues analyzed in these studies, 83 percent of the Democratic leaders took on the average liberal positions while 40 percent of the Republican leaders took liberal positions (actually none of the Republican top elites *call themselves* liberals). Thus, as representers of public opinion, two ideological configurations are arrayed against each other in the attentive public. The general public is split ideologically—35 percent liberal, 44 percent moderate, 20 percent conservative. In this context, the leaders have advanced and argued their conflicting positions, eventually settling for compromises, which seem to be satisfactory to the majority.

The public seems generally satisfied with the job done at city hall by the city council. About 70 percent also trust Ann Arbor's government "to do what is right." There are alienated citizens, to be sure, people who are very critical and negative about some aspect of city government, but on the whole, the public seems reasonably accepting. When it is not, periodically party turnover occurs and a new mayor or council majority takes office. Yet, the close partisan balance prevents landslides or revolutionary policy action. Thus many of the conditions necessary for responsiveness seem to exist; whether the outcomes are responsive depends to some extent on one's expectations. If one expects economic development, Ann Arbor has had it; orderly growth, also generally true; adequate basic services, some complaints; maintenance of streets, roads, water and sewage systems, landfill, and the like, more specific criticisms but no groundswell of revolt; adequate housing, particularly for the poor—probably not, even though this has been on the agenda for forty years! Overall, however, in the grand development perspective for Ann Arbor, its political leadership has worked hard to be aware of community needs and problems and to work consistently toward their resolution. The public has been aware of that. The discipline of organized, competitive parties has been both system-maintaining and innovative. Thus, in that sense, one can argue that this is a responsive system.

Finally, on the issue of responsiveness the question is whether Ann Arbor's government in its policies is humane enough, is concerned with the problems of the underclass. Is there inequality in the way public resources are spent, so that we do not spend enough for the poor? It has been argued that cities today face a dilemma. As one scholar has put it: cities have to spend for the purposes of economic development and "economic productivity" for which local government is responsible, and "that leaves little scope for egalitarian concerns."[11] Does Ann Arbor act as if it faces this dilemma? Considerable argument is possible on this question. Many of the liberals would like to see more redistributive policy decisions, particularly in housing and care for the needy. Yet, the competitive party system in the past twenty years has produced the kind of pressure leading to new programs for the needy, for those discriminated against, and for those with special welfare problems. The human relations and human services programs have contributed to those ends. The city now has emergency shelters, crisis help, aid for the disabled and disadvantaged, a food distribution program, and other related services. Over a half-million dollars from the operating funds of the city are allocated to such causes each year. For some, this is only a drop in the bucket, compared to economic development allocations, directly or indirectly, but clearly a move in the right direction.

Ann Arbor has been haltingly moving toward more affordable housing, but this has become a very controversial issue. If more action in that direction is necessary, availability of resources is probably one sticking point. Another is the contrasting ideological and value orientations of the top elites and their perceptions of the tolerances of the public. Only a minority of city council members can be considered advocates of policies concerned with economic equality, and only a minority (until recently) strongly advocated low-cost housing. It is argued that the public is not very liberal on this question, even though the Ann Arbor public is relatively liberal on many social issues. On the other hand, one may well argue that the strides made in this direction by the city council reflect more enlightened leadership than one might expect, given the value orientations of the elites and the state of public opinion. Competitive partisan politics has much to do with the amount of progress made, but many activists feel much more needs to be done.

Participation

The precondition for effective democratic life has long been considered to be citizen participation. For John Stuart Mill, it was participation of *all* citizens.[12] We long ago gave up such utopian expectations (although in some European countries, 80 percent or higher voting turnout, even in local elections, does occur). There has been much debate on many aspects of the participation question. As Verba and Nie remind us, this debate is related to how we evaluate "the quality of American political life."[13] As applied to voting participation, key issues such as the following emerge:

1. How high do the numbers have to be—at what levels of voting turnout is democracy threatened? Is 23 percent for example, enough?
2. If voting turnout is low, are there mitigating conditions (such as the characteristics of those who vote and who stay home) that lead to less concern?
3. Is there a link between voting and the way the system functions? A *perceived* link (perceived by citizens), and a *real* link (between voting and leaders' decisions)?
4. Is high turnout associated with more democracy, or, to put it negatively; does low turnout lead to no democracy? One scholar has argued in his recent study of American cities that "nonvoting has reached crisis proportions which question the very legitimacy of elections."[14] Does low turnout also threaten the legitimacy of local government?

Keeping these issues in mind, what about nonvoting in Ann Arbor? Is there enough participation to make democracy effective? Or is the amount of participation irrelevant to the functioning of democracy?

There is a real participation puzzle in Ann Arbor. Some of the participation statistics look good and some look bad. Consider these facts about Ann Arbor adults taken from the 1984 study:

1. This is a fairly educated community—56 percent have a college education; 76 percent read the local newspaper (46 percent say they read the local political news); 45 percent reveal considerable knowledge of local politics.
2. A relatively high proportion reveal some involvement in local politics—35 percent say they belong to one or more political groups; 37 percent say they attend coffee hours for candidates; 35 percent claim to have contributed money to the parties or candidates for office; 20 percent report engaging in some activity during the campaign; 39 percent report being contacted by both parties during the campaign.
3. In national presidential elections (such as 1984), 60 percent of this eligible voting population voted, far above the national norm.
4. In the April election in 1984, 16 percent voted (19 percent in 1989).

Added to this is the fact that in the April elections of the seventies, participation was higher—over 40 percent voted (43.7 percent in 1973).

These statistics are somewhat disheartening. In the past also this city experienced low voting turnout—as low as 2.5 percent of those eligible in 1946. High participation in local elections was never a tradition, or a norm in Ann Arbor. Even when the city adopted a new charter in 1956, only 25 percent voted in that election. Turnout improved—to a peak of 44 percent in 1973—then subsided to the present low levels of less than 20 percent. The city, like other cities, seems mired in deep voting apathy. Some 60,000 adults do not vote in April, chronic nonvoters—a stunning reality.

What causes people to participate; what causes them to ignore their opportunities to participate? The studies of Ann Arbor used here attempted to explain low turnouts (chap. 7). Three approaches were used to get at the reasons for low turnout: citizen integration in the community, citizen attitudes toward the political system, and citizen exposure to parties and campaigns. It seems clear that in this community of many educated, affluent, professionals and successful businesspeople, politics can be very peripheral. For many people, their interests, values, and commitments lie elsewhere—at least on election day in April. Community integration is positively related to voting, true, but by itself is not enough to lead to high political involvement. Positive attitudes toward parties and toward city government also help, but, again, are not adequate to bring large numbers of people to the polls. Party effort is linked to higher turnout, but still many people who are heavily canvassed by both parties stay home on election day.

Certain, possibly encouraging, observations, however, stand from our data. First, people who are very knowledgeable about local politics are much more likely to vote than are the ignorant (a 50 percent differential). Second, homeowners and those with long residence have a higher turnout compared to renters and those in town who arrived only recently (a 25 to 30 percentage point differential). Third, those contacted by the parties turn out much more than those not contacted (a 23 point differential). Fourth, those who have a sense of trust in relation to local government are also more participative (a 20-point differential).

These may be seen as mitigating findings, and may tend to make one feel better about the voting performance of citizens. But should they? Less than 50 percent of those with adequate knowledge vote; 78 percent of homeowners stayed home in 1980 and 54 percent in 1984; despite valiant efforts by the parties, almost 60 percent of those contacted did not vote; and a majority with high trust in local government refused to vote. It appears from the data that many Ann Arbor citizens are giving certain messages, among which are:

> "Local government is not important to me; national government *is* important."
> "Voting in local elections was important to me in the past, but not today."
> "I think city government is doing a good job, so I really don't see the need to vote."
> "I think city government is doing a poor job, despite elections, so why vote?"
> "Politics is something I know nothing about locally and I cannot take the trouble to become informed."
> "Politics is fun to talk about—but let others do the voting."
> "The parties have contacted me, but I am skeptical of these people—a plague on both parties!"
> "I personally am just too busy with my personal goals and problems to be able to spend time on local politics."

And so on. Underlying all of these negative orientations is one basic one: "I do not believe that I have any personal responsibility as a citizen to participate in the local political process," followed by, "I personally do not feel such participation would in any way enrich my personal life." This type of negation of responsibility is chronic here (not in Europe, however, where 60 percent or more of the adults [80 % in Sweden] vote in local elections).

There is a dual problem. On the one hand, there has been a decline in the traditional idea of voting as a key component of the local democratic culture. This still obtains at the national level, but for fewer than 50 percent of the adults in national elections (although 60 percent vote in Ann Arbor). One might argue that despite the low voting record in city elections, there is actually a lively involvement of citizens in Ann Arbor politics, through other channels and groups than parties and elections, and which does link citizens meaningfully to the political life of Ann Arbor. The data suggest one should doubt this, that such other activity affects at most one-third of adults and then appears to be only superficially linked to the decisions of politics. On the other hand, many citizens do not see the linkage between voting and the achievement of policy goals. As we have argued throughout this study, elections have consequences—in selecting leaders who stand for particular issue positions or ideologies, in replacing one party with another in the mayoral position, and in the monetary and nonmonetary decisions made by these leaders. Eighty percent of Ann Arbor's adults don't understand this, or feel it is irrelevant for them. They do not accept the proposition that the leaders we elect make crucial decisions which affect their lives and the community welfare.

One wonders whether the 60,000 Ann Arbor adults who have withdrawn from politics have any sense of identification with the city as a political community. For them it is perhaps a bedroom community, or a marketplace, or a place to earn an income, or a playground, or a cultural center. It has utilitarian value for them but no political value. It is difficult, then, to see this as a real community, which shares an identity, which shares democratic values. The abdication of democratic obligations in relation to the local politics level seems a bit overwhelming.

It is clear from much research that political participation, including voting, has consequences. Verba and Nie's study of participation strongly demonstrated this. The analysis in this book reveals a close proximity in views of top elites and the organizational activists as well as the loyal partisans in the public. There is a strong suggestion in the data that as voting turnout increases, party competition is closer, and that has policy implications. There is clear evidence also in voting on referenda. A good example is the affordable housing vote in April 1987. After all the debate, only 21 percent voted on that millage issue—6,903 for and 11,709 against. But when the street repair bonding issue was voted on earlier, 35 percent turned out and 60 percent voted favorably.

The implications for democracy in Ann Arbor are complex, and not altogether clear. Ann Arbor has minority government—the not-completely-representative few make the decisions in elections for the many. Certain social sectors are not represented adequately in April elections: young people, recent residents, renters, those with low incomes, those with high school educations or less, and others. The leaders who run for office and win are aware of who their constituents are, particularly who will probably vote in the next election, and perhaps make their policy decisions accordingly. To say, however, that this is not a democratic system would also be improper. What Ann Arbor has is a highly competitive, two-party democracy with a very narrow popular base, consisting of approximately 20,000 to 25,000 adults who perform, or attempt to perform, the democratic chores for all the rest. These regular voters are a diverse set of people—Democrats, Republicans, and independents, also split ideologically. While this is a type of democracy one does not necessarily hope for or approve, it is a democracy one can (and probably have to) live with. It is a party-competitive, minority-based democracy, which has been progressive and has contributed to the development of the community. The saving grace of the system is intense party competition. In its absence and with low turnout, Ann Arbor would have an unnatural consensual system dominated by one political ruling class. They had that back in the 1940s, and many probably would say, hopefully never again.

Are Reforms Necessary?

Such reflections on the problems of democracy in Ann Arbor have a twofold, reciprocal relevance. On the one hand, they are revealing about the citizens, not all of which is reassuring. On the other hand, they have import for the system and how well it is working. The impact of politics on the role of citizens in Ann Arbor may be disquieting. It is of little reassurance to know that nonpartisan systems on the average have 10 percent less turnout than Ann Arbor has, or that those who do participate are usually knowledgeable and committed. The fact remains that most of the citizens are withdrawn from involvement in local politics. What should be done to try to change that? What other suggestions can be made aimed at other, structural, features of the Ann Arbor system?

Periodically the cry for reform is heard, usually rationalized on the basis that "the city has changed" now, major problems have emerged, and "the charter is, after all, quite old." The recent discussions by the Ann Arbor Charter Revision Committee echo these concerns. What should be the reaction to the desire to reform the Ann Arbor system? The response could be a partisan one (indeed, it is often inclined to be that), or a more detached and objective assessment of the needs and problems of the Ann Arbor system of politics. Following the latter approach used here, it would be wise to keep in mind the character and goals, the desiderata, of Ann Arbor's system. These are: genuine partisan competition; a city council that effectively controls policy making; strong grass-roots party organizations; active interest groups concerned about city offices and in contact with city political elites and party organizations; a more inclusive and representative politics both in candidate selection and policy making; a desire to have leaders who will work with both types of developmental perspectives the economic and the humane. At least for some, the goal also might be the expansion of the size and quality of the voting electorate, while maintaining a high level of political participation in campaigns and political groups.

Keeping such goals in mind, emanating as they do from the basic character of Ann Arbor's political culture as it has matured over these past forty-five years, what specific types of changes might be considered? Rather than take an advocate's role, one can state some of these proposed changes hypothetically. That is, we can ask the reader to reflect on what the consequences would be if a particular reform were pursued. Thus, what if . . .

> . . . The party organizations became more inclusive in their recruitment of workers so that more minorities and those less economically advantaged were encouraged to take precinct positions?
> . . . the parties self-consciously recruited as candidates for city council those now effectively excluded (as the data in this study reveal)?
> . . . the party organizations did a more extensive and continuous job of communicating with the public (not just with their loyal supporters) about politics?
> . . . The *Ann Arbor News* revised its policy on covering Ann Arbor politics, particularly campaign politics, so that it would again have the intensive and continuous coverage and visible role it had in the fifties, and occasionally since then?
> . . . community groups and the schools made a greater commitment to programs to educate citizens about Ann Arbor's government and its parties and made more people conscious of their obligations and opportunities as citizens for participating in political decision-making processes?

If these changes occurred, would Ann Arbor's political system be strengthened? There will be no attempt to answer this question here. Yet the data in this study suggest that these are relevant "what ifs." These hypothetical proposals are only a short list. They are presented on the dual assumptions that there is a desire to improve the democratic process and that the primary aim would be to strengthen the present system, not basically to revise it. It assumes that Ann Arbor's citizens want to keep partisan government and a council-manager form of government. It avoids special questions like the desirability of the ward system, the November vs. April date for city elections, or the term of offices. These are not the basic issues. The basic issues are maintaining a strong party government, improving representative government, and broadening the electoral base for leadership decisions.

The puzzle about low voting participation in Ann Arbor is indeed a perplexing one. The components of that puzzle have been described and analyzed in detail in this study. It is a multicausal phenomenon. Many different types of people stay home from April elections, for a variety of reasons: hearty satisfaction with city government, alienation from city government, indifference to city government, inertia, ignorance, inconvenience, a limited and weak democratic conscience. Would that this study could discover a dramatic cure for voter apathy! Short of a revolutionary change in people's attitudes toward local government and a resocialization to the meaning of electoral democracy at the municipal level, not much change will occur. It is easy to say, "change the registration system," but 70,000 to 80,000 adults are already regularly registered in Ann Arbor; or, "hold the election on another day," but citizens should be involved in local politics per se, not incidentally to national politics. There is no dramatic cure which is a real cure (even if we would take the right to vote away from the 50,000-plus who never vote). The system can only change if leaders, parties, the press, and civic groups generate a real interest in voting and a real awareness of the value of the vote and its importance for the local citizen and the local community.

What Ann Arbor and almost all American cities need is a dialogue—in the parties, in the interest groups, in the press, in the schools, in private circles—on the virtues and vexations of this system. Ann Arbor has defied the doomsayers who predict the inevitable decline of the city. Those who talk only about "city limits" and "the decline" of urban politics find their rebuttal in Ann Arbor. This is a model which generally combines good politics with good economics to lead to the development of an attractive community. It is an example of how much communal good can emerge from much political conflict. But there is obviously an agenda for improvement of the system also. Even mature democracies have to continue to develop. People need to work continuously to make the local governmental system work better, to broaden its popular base, to bring more of the public into an understanding of the system that helps garner support for it; and above all, to educate them in the importance of their involvement. Politics matters in Ann Arbor, but it could matter more, to more people.

Appendixes

Appendix A

TABLE A.1. Ann Arbor Election Results: April Elections for Mayor and Council

Year	Estimated Eligible Voting Population[a]	Total Vote		Democratic Percentage of Vote		Republican Percentage of Vote		Other Candidates Percentage of Vote	
		Cast	Turnout[b]	Mayor	Council	Mayor	Council	Mayor	Council
1946	24,429	627	2.5%		27.8		72.2		
1947	25,560	3,339	13.1	0.0	4.9	100.0	95.1		
1948	26,690	1,992	7.5		28.9		71.1		
1949	27,820	5,977	21.6	29.8	30.9	67.2	67.3	3.0	1.8
1950	28,951	5,385	18.6		38.6		61.4		
1951	29,985	7,535	25.1	41.0	27.4	59.0	72.6		
1952	31,020	7,353	23.9		36.9		63.1		
1953	32,056	7,139	22.2	35.8	33.6	64.2	66.4		
1954	33,091	6,312	19.1		37.2		62.8		
1955	34,126	8,090	23.5	45.7	29.3	54.3	70.7		
1956	35,161	6,219	17.4		46.4		53.6		
1957	36,196	11,437	31.4	53.1	45.7	46.1	54.3	0.8	0.0
1958	37,231	7,047	18.9		48.9		51.1		
1959	38,266	11,814	30.8	43.1	39.4	56.9	60.6		
1960	39,296	10,194	25.6		43.3		56.7		

TABLE A.1—*Continued*

Year	Estimated Eligible Voting Population[a]	Total Vote		Democratic Percentage of Vote		Republican Percentage of Vote		Other Candidates Percentage of Vote	
		Cast	Turnout[b]	Mayor	Council	Mayor	Council	Mayor	Council
1961	41,458	13,021	31.4	40.1	43.4	59.9	56.6		
1962	43,620	8,313	19.3		44.1		55.9		
1963	45,782	16,325	35.6	40.9	40.7	59.1	59.3		
1964	47,944	14,089	29.4		52.7		47.3		
1965	50,106	18,537	37.0	39.9	43.7	60.1	56.3		
1966	52,268	17,405	33.1		50.8		49.2		
1967	54,430	16,403	29.6	44.5	43.3	55.5	56.7		
1968	56,592	15,084	26.7		48.6		51.4		
1969	58,754	21,121	35.9	51.4	51.7	48.6	48.3		
1970	60,916	19,592	32.1		45.0		55.0		
1971	63,078	27,117	42.9	58.6	52.2	41.4	47.8		
1972	74,122	30,035	40.5		35.8		39.8		24.4
1973	75,778	33,118	43.7	36.6	38.7	47.0	45.2	16.4	16.1
1974	77,434	30,619	39.5		43.2		38.5		18.3
1975[c]	79,090	29,449	37.0	40.2	41.1	49.0	45.8	10.8	13.1
1976	80,746	20,993	25.3		44.6		52.1		3.3
1977	82,402	21,683	25.9	49.2	48.2	49.2	49.1	1.7	2.7

1978	84,058	28,516	33.9	49.5	49.8	50.5	50.2		
1979	85,714	19,399	22.6	48.3	49.8	51.7	50.2		
1980	87,372	9,301	10.7		38.7		61.3		
1981	87,015	15,931	18.3	37.1	40.8	62.9	59.2		
1982	86,658	10,857	12.5		43.6		56.4		
1983	86,301	23,204	26.6	47.7	47.2	51.1	52.8	1.2	0.0
1984	85,944	13,774	16.0		49.6		50.4		
1985	85,587	19,085	22.3	53.1	56.5	46.9	43.5		
1986	85,230	17,146	20.1		54.5		45.5		
1987	84,841	19,407	22.9	47.4	50.5	52.6	49.5		
1988	84,500	24,150	28.6		51.4		48.6		
1989	84,500	17,024	20.1	43.6	47.6	55.3	51.6	1.1	0.8
1990	84,500	23,461	27.8		52.6		47.4		
1991	84,500	20,686	24.6	53.7	56.4	44.5	41.0	1.8	2.6
1992	85,000	12,768	15.1		50.4		47.7		1.9
1993, April	85,000	17,318	20.4%	40.8	47.0	56.6	49.1	2.6	3.9
1993, November	85,000	11,324	13.3%		59.0		33.6		7.4

Source: Election Documents, Ann Arbor City Election office; U.S. Census Reports.

[a]Figures based on percentage of population 21 years of age or older (1972 on, 18 years of age); intercensal estimates used. "Total vote" is largest vote cast mayor or council.

[b]Indicates the percentage of eligible voting population voting.

[c]In 1975, when the preference vote system was in effect for the mayoral election, the original vote was as is reported here. After the allocation for second preference (from those who voted for the Human Rights party first), the vote was: Wheeler (D)—14,684 (50.2 percent), Stephenson (R)—14,563 (49.8).

TABLE A.2. **Some Major Referenda in Ann Arbor**

	Vote			
	Yes	No	Total Vote	Percentage of Eligible Electorate Voting
Vote to proceed with charter revision (1953)	4,604	519	5,123	16.0%
Adoption of city charter (April 1955)	6,548	2,207	8,755	25.6
Charter tax rate limitation increase (1957)	3,406	5,471	8,877	24.4
Liquor dry line (1963)	7,641	8,233	15,874	34.6
Liquor dry line (1964)	7,909	5,676	13,585	28.4
Retirement system (1966)	2,551	3,138	5,689	30.0
City treasurer and assessor under administrator (1966)	10,093	4,470	14,563	27.8
Municipal court (1969)	15,527	2,210	17,737	29.3
Income tax advisory referendum (1969)	6,516	10,301	16,817	28.7
Bonding of $3,500,000 for acquiring parklands (1971)	17,260	7,034	24,294	38.6
Highway bonds for Ashley-First bypass (1972)	8,266	19,524	27,790	37.6
Income tax referendum (1972)	5,626	8,022	13,648	18.4
Tax for public transportation system (1973)	19,495	12,548	32,043	42.3
Rent control (1974)	12,878	18,208	31,086	40.4
Preferential voting change (1974)	17,405	15,715	33,120	42.8
Five-dollar marijuana fine (1974)	16,047	14,809	30,856	39.8
Repeal of preferential voting (1976)	13,451	8,095	21,545	26.6
Tax for street and bike path repair (1976)	9,320	12,048	21,368	26.3
Fair rental information (1978)	17,346	8,850	26,196	31.1
Bonding of $525,000 for street repair (1979)	18,464	11,877	30,341	35.4
Major street and intersection general obligation bonding, $850,000 (1982)	7,760	5,136	12,896	14.8
Landlords weatherization and renovation (1983)	9,550	13,199	22,749	26.1
Additional ½ mill tax for parks (1983)	14,412	8,294	22,774	26.1
Repeal of marijuana fine (1983)	8,660	13,977	22,640	26.1
Bonding in constructing Huron River dam (1983)	14,812	6,662	23,474	27.0
Street repair (1986)	10,077	6,510	16,587	19.1
Central America (1986)	10,190	6,544	16,734	19.2
Expansion of city hall, $3,200,000 (1987)	7,244	10,839	18,083	21.3
Affordable housing millage (1987)	6,903	11,709	17,612	20.8

TABLE A.2—*Continued*

	Vote			
	Yes	No	Total Vote	Percentage of Eligible Electorate Voting
Rent control (1988)	8,015	16,652	24,667	29.2
Parkland Acquisition millage (1988)	15,161	9,097	24,258	28.7
Parks tax increase (1989)	10,946	5,450	16,396	19.4
Headlee waiver (1989)	4,194	11,719	15,913	18.8
Pot law fine change to $25 (1990)	12,901	11,419	24,320	28.8
Zone of reproductive freedom (1990)	15,698	8,578	24,276	28.8
Solid waste bonds (1990)	18,866	5,601	24,467	28.8

Source: Election documents, Ann Arbor City Clerk's office.

TABLE A.3. Candidates for Mayor in Ann Arbor

	Republican	Percentage of Vote	Democratic	Percentage of Vote
1947	William Brown	100.0	no candidate	0.0
1949	William Brown	66.9	Leslie Wikel	29.8
1951	William Brown	59.0	Lewis Reiman	41.0
1953	William Brown	64.2	Jesse Ormondroyd	35.8
1955	William Brown	54.2	Albert Logan	45.7
1957	William Brown	46.1	Samuel Eldersveld	53.1
1959	Cecil Creal	56.9	Lloyd Ives	43.1
1961	Cecil Creal	59.9	Dorothea Pealey	40.1
1963	Cecil Creal	59.1	Albert Schneider	40.9
1965	Wendell Hulcher	60.1	Eunice Burns	39.9
1967	Wendell Hulcher	55.5	Edward Pierce	44.5
1969	Richard Balzhiser	48.6	Robert Harris	51.4
1971	Jack Garris	41.4	Robert Harris	58.6
1973[a]	James Stephenson	47.1	Frank Mogdis	36.6
1975[b]	James Stephenson	49.1	Albert Wheeler	40.1
1977[c]	Louis Belcher	49.1	Albert Wheeler	49.2
1978	Louis Belcher	50.5	Albert Wheeler	49.5
1979	Louis Belcher	51.7	James Kenworthy	48.3
1981	Louis Belcher	62.9	Robert Feber	37.1
1983	Louis Belcher	52.3	Leslie Morris	47.7
1985	Richard Hadler	46.9	Edward Pierce	53.1
1987	Gerald Jernigan	52.6	Edward Pierce	47.4
1989	Gerald Jernigan	55.3	Raymond Clevenger	43.5
1991	Gerald Jernigan	44.5	Elizabeth Brater	53.7
1993	Ingrid Sheldon	56.6	Elizabeth Brater	40.8

Source: Election documents, Ann Arbor City Clerk's Office.

[a]Human Rights party candidate 1973 Benita Kaimowitz received 16.3 percent of the vote.

[b]Human Rights party candidate 1975 Carol Ernst received 10.8 percent of the vote.

Under the preferential ballot in use, Wheeler won with a final total vote of 14,684 over Stephenson, who had 14,563 votes.

[c]Human Rights party candidate 1977 Diana Leigh Slaughter received 1.7 percent of the vote.

Appendix B

TABLE B.1. Budget Allocations and Changes, 1945–91

	Actual Dollars General Fund Budget (in 000s)	Percentage Increase Actual Dollars	Total Constant Dollars in Budget (in 000s)	Per capita Constant Dollars	Percentage Increase in Constant Dollars
1945	743	—	1,378	31.40	—
1946	893	20.2	1,552	34.65	12.6
1947	996	11.9	1,622	35.52	4.5
1948	1,180	19.0	1,822	39.16	12.3
1949	1,236	4.8	1,805	38.14	−0.9
1950	1,308	4.5	1,791	37.30	−0.8
1951	1,520	17.7	1,954	38.95	9.1
1952	1,886	24.1	2,373	45.57	21.5
1953	1,967	4.3	2,456	45.51	3.1
1954	2,105	6.9	2,615	46.79	6.4
1955	2,409	14.5	3,005	53.72	14.9
1956	2,876	19.4	3,534	59.18	17.6
1957	3,243	12.7	3,847	62.43	8.9
1958	3,458	6.6	3,993	62.85	3.8
1959	4,018	16.2	4,603	70.34	15.3
1960	4,044	.6	4,558	67.70	−1.0
1961	4,458	10.2	4,976	71.37	9.2
1962	4,343	−2.6	4,793	66.48	−3.3
1963	4,625[a]	6.5	5,043	67.42	5.2
1964	4,991	8.0	5,372	69.17	6.5
1965	5,301	6.2	5,610	68.83	4.4
1966	6,211	17.2	6,390	75.78	13.9
1967	6,726	8.3	6,726	76.21	5.3
1968	8,515	11.7	8,172	88.65	21.2
1969	10,707	25.7	9,752	101.46	19.3
1970	12,453	16.3	10,708	107.04	9.8
1971	13,063	4.9	10,707	106.22	−0.0[b]
1972	13,924	6.6	11,114	109.36	3.8
1973	15,909	14.3	11,953	116.71	7.5
1974	17,267	8.5	11,691	113.28	−2.2
1975	18,626	7.8	11,555	111.10	−1.2
1976	20,421	9.6	11,977	114.29	3.7
1977	21,967	7.6	12,103	114.62	1.1
1978	23,757	8.1	12,158	114.28	0.4
1979	26,187	10.2	12,046	111.53	−0.9
1980	27,232	4.0	11,034	102.20	−8.4

TABLE B.1—*Continued*

	Actual Dollars General Fund Budget (in 000s)	Percentage Increase Actual Dollars	Total Constant Dollars in Budget (in 000s)	Per capita Constant Dollars	Percentage Increase in Constant Dollars
1981	32,365	18.8	11,881	110.01	7.7
1982	35,564	9.8	12,301	113.90	3.6
1983	34,840	−2.0	11,676	108.10	−5.1
1984	38,793	11.3	12,469	115.46	6.8
1985	41,071	5.9	12,437	115.16	−0.3
1986	43,676	6.3	13,300	123.11	6.9
1987	45,320	3.8	13,314	123.28	0.1
1988	48,241	6.8	13,220	122.41	−0.7
1989	52,620	9.1	13,583	124.60	2.7
1990	56,847	8.0	14,287	130.77	5.2
1991	61,191	6.8	14,733	135.10	3.1

Source: Ann Arbor City Council Proceedings, City Budget documents, Annual Reports, and other financial reports.

[a]Estimated.

[b]Actual figures = −0.0001.

TABLE B.2. Departmental Expenditures, Ann Arbor: 1945–91[a]

	Police	Fire	Health	Parks and Rec.	Planning
1945	113	102	24	54	8
1946	131	127	28	66	8
1947	188	142	30	60	10
1948	192	142	32	59	9
1949	200	146	35	60	10
1950	209	147	35	60	10
1951	249	187	45	78	11
1952	291	215	48	88	11
1953	317	240	51	95	12
1954	327	251	42	114	12
1955	374	291	46B	146	16
1956	419	342	52B	225	18
1957	585	405	57	255	31
1958	617E	384E	58	260E	40E
1959	631B	440	62	299	46
1960	651	458	51B	343	51
1961	647	490	77B	360	53B
1962	758	562	78	366	34E
1963	804	630	82	410	60
1964	869	620	84	436	73
1965	933	680	88	457	91
1966	1,126	773	92	534E	100
1967	1,376	977	107	560	124B
1968	1,738	1,061	134	805	142E
1969	2,307	1,289	152	1,107	169

TABLE B.2—*Continued*

	Police	Fire	Health	Parks and Rec.	Planning
1970	2,649B	1,470B	170B	1,288	191
1971	2,783	1,627	175	1,058	220
1972	2,725	1,515	188B	1,014	231
1973	3,303	1,784	207	1,120	234
1974	3,689	2,086E	168E	1,177	231
1975	3,891B	2,281B	108B	1,278	223
1976	4,093	2,475	229	1,455	250
1977	4,498	3,111	183	1,573	270
1978	4,791	3,117	138B	1,725	221
1979	5,279	3,214	92	1,862	262
1980	6,007	3,944	46	2,252	266
1981[b]	6,372	4,047	—	2,110	265
1982	6,760	4,383	—	2,316	275
1983	7,178	4,201	—	2,524	340
1984	7,489	4,468	—	2,750	320
1985	8,280	5,698	—	3,221	338
1986	10,247	5,513	—	3,439	457
1987	9,897	5,941	—	3,951	523
1988	10,054	5,957	—	3,663	467
1989	10,719	6,280	—	3,643	570
1990	11,494	6,732	—	3,800	434
1991	11,353B	6,720B	—	3,625B	433B

Source: Ann Arbor City Council Proceedings, City Budget documents, Annual Reports, and other financial reports.

Note: B = Budget, E = Estimated, because final data were not available.

[a]Actual dollars spent, in 000s.

[b]The Health Department allocations were discontinued in 1981 as part of an agreement with the county.

TABLE B.3. Human Relations/Human Rights Allocations in the General Fund Budget, 1945–91

	Actual Dollars	Constant Dollars[a]
1945–57	no allocations	—
1958	$ 525	$ 606
1959	1,275	1,461
1960	2,275	2,565
1961	4,385	4,894
1962	5,224	5,766
1963	5,891	6,424
1964	27,441	29,536
1965	29,543	31,263
1966	41,149	42,234
1967	44,047	44,047
1968	50,541	48,503
1969	125,709	114,563
1970	80,450	69,175
1971	90,150	74,320
1972	95,618	76,316
1973	97,562	73,300
1974	94,660	64,090
1975	81,870	50,788
1976	55,000	32,260
1977	52,000	28,650
1978	51,186	26,190
1979	55,905	25,260
1980	60,096	24,290
1981	65,116	23,900
1982	71,861	24,860
1983	75,324	25,240
1984	78,188	25,130
1985	57,729	17,910
1986	58,476	17,810
1987	87,952	25,840
1988	83,809	22,970
1989	50,500	13,300
1990	53,935	13,560
1991	71,059	17,250

Source: Ann Arbor City Council Proceedings, City Budget documents, Annual Reports, and other financial reports.

Note: The Human Relations Commission (HRC) was established in 1957 and received its first funds in the 1958 budget. In 1970 a Human Rights Department and Human Rights Commission replaced the earlier HRC. In 1978 human rights was combined with personnel department. This has made it difficult to determine the exact funds allocated to human rights. We have estimated the amounts by looking at the human rights designated personnel in the joint department and attempting to determine the proportion properly considered human rights. The personnel department chair, Robert Scott, has provided assistance in making these estimates from 1978 on.

[a]1967 = 100.

TABLE B.4. Allocations for Human Welfare/Human Services in the General Fund[a]

	Actual Dollars	Constant Dollars[b]
1968	10,303	9,858
1969	16,150	14,708
1970	44,506	38,268
1971	75,673	62,385
1972	173,300	138,309
1973	74,210	55,755
1974	77,000	52,133
1975	0	0
1976	12,495	7,328
1977	7,970	4,400
1978	8,500	4,350
1979	8,500	3,909
1980	13,500	5,470
1981	50,570	18,565
1982	96,645	33,430
1983	146,714	49,167
1984	176,240	56,651
1985	259,500	80,540
1986	430,930	131,221
1987	526,500	154,671
1988	560,000	153,467
1989	500,000	131,700
1990	532,500	133,900
1991	569,775	138,400

Source: Ann Arbor City Council Proceedings, City Budget documents, Annual Reports, and other financial reports.

[a]Apart from human relations or human rights departments.

[b]1967 = 100.

Appendix C: Indices Used in the Analysis

Political Alienation Index

As explained in chapter 6, we combined responses to thirteen questions, dealing with trust in local government, sense of efficacy about involvement in local politics, evaluation of the job city government is doing, general (diffuse) support for political parties, specific support for parties (in functional terms and in personal terms), and general level of satisfaction with life in Ann Arbor. Maximum score possible (high alienation): 55. The scores range from 2 (nineteen respondents) to 40 (two respondents), and the median score was 5.

Index of Community Integration

Four variables were used: length of residence in the city, home ownership or rental, regular readership of the *Ann Arbor News*, and the discussion of politics with three best friends. Maximum score possible was 10 (owned home, resident over ten years, *News* reader, discussion of politics with all three friends). Of our sample, 35 percent scored 8–10, 40 percent scored 5–7, 25 percent scored 0–4.

Political Exposure Index

As explained in chapter 6, three types of information were used: level of knowledge about local government (which party controlled council, the name and party of the mayor), whether respondent had ever been contacted by the political parties in the recent campaign or previously, and the number of activities the respondent participated in in the campaign (out of ten possible activities). Maximum score possible was 9 (for activities 4, for knowledge 3, for party contact 2). Scores ranged from 0 (ten cases) to nine (twenty-five cases) with a median of 5.

The Value Scales

The four scales (political participation, innovation, political conflict, and economic equality) were developed from a set of agree-disagree items (thirty-one in all) which have been tested and validated in studies in the past twenty years in many countries, including Sweden, the Netherlands, India, Poland, Yugoslavia and the United States. The percentages are averages of the agree (or disagree) responses for each set of items for each value scale.

The specific agree-disagree items used in the elite questionnaire in 1986 to determine value orientations were taken from the international study of elite values in 1966 and used again, and validated, in the 1984 study in the United States and Sweden and in the 1989 Netherlands study. The response options were strongly agree, agree, disagree, or strongly disagree.

Participation Scale:

The complexity of modern day issues requires that only the more simple questions should be considered publicly.

Widespread participation in decision making often leads to undesirable conflicts.

Most decisions should be left to the judgment of experts.

Only those who are fully informed on the issues should vote.

Participation of the people is not necessary if decision making is left in the hands of a few trusted and competent leaders.

Only those who are competent on an issue should speak about it.

Innovative Change

The people in this community must continually look for new solutions rather than be satisfied with things as they are.

Changes are desirable even if they do not seem to contribute as much as one might expect.

A community should not accept programs which upset the settled ways of doing things.

There is nothing inherently superior in the past.

If society is to progress, newer solutions to problems are essential.

Political Conflict

If there is disagreement about a program, a leader should be willing to give it up.

Public decisions should be made by unanimous consent.
Leaders who are overconcerned about resolving conflicts can never carry out community programs successfully.
Preserving harmony in the community should be considered more important than the achievement of community programs.
A good leader should refrain from making proposals that divide the people even if these are important for the community.
A leader should modify his actions to keep consensus.
It is important for a leader to get things done even if he must displease people.

Economic Equality

See chapter 9, table 9.11.

Index of Attitudes toward Political Parties

There were eight commonly used agree-disagree statements included in this index. Respondents were asked to indicate the strength of their agreement or disagreement with these statements, using a seven-point scale. Hence, this was both a directional and intensity measure. Respondents were scored for each item on whether their response was proparty or antiparty and on whether they strongly (or not strongly) agreed or disagreed. They were then classified by their mean agreement scores. Total scores could range from 8 (strong agreement on all items—proparty) to 56 (strong disagreement on all items—antiparty). Ten percent of our respondents were found at each of the extremes, very strong proparty and very strong antiparty.

Influence Distribution Index

The influence distribution index used in chapter 9 is a simple scoring of responses to the question: "How much influence do you feel you have on what is accomplished in your city in the following areas (A great deal of influence, only some influence, or none at all)?" Using scores of 0 (no influence) to 2 (a great deal of influence) for ten relevant policy areas resulted in an index ranging from scores of 0 to 20.

Appendix D: Students Who Participated in the Collection and Analysis of the Data in This Book

All of these students were undergraduates in the Department of Political Science, University of Michigan.

Jennifer Adolph	David Hart
Merileen Agatep	Ann Hartman
Scott Almquist	Steven Helme
Peter Angelas	Michael Herman
Kristen Bamford	Rebecca Hoffman
Elizabeth Barbour	Beth Hyman
Susan Biddle	Carolyn Jereck
Harry Binder	Paul Josephson
David Bowers	Christina Junior
Cynthia Brown	Nicholas Kabcenell
Lori Burrington	June Kirchgatter
Richard Charlton	Matthew Lane
Stephen Brzezinski	Teresa Ledoux
Heidi Cohen	Winston Lee
Keith Cunningham	Kerry Leibowitz
Timothy Damschroder	Ann Luvera
Sharlene Deskins	Steven Lynch
Paula Drury	Sandra Macauley
Daniel Egeler	Joseph Malenfant
David Egeler	Maura Malone
Dean Etsios	Margaret Maly
Michael Freeman	Laura Marcus
Charles Fritz	Elizabeth Mazza
David Geiss	Donald McCann
Maryalyce Glionna	Dawn McLoud
Lisa Greenfield	Mary McCafferty
Douglas Greenhart	Claire McMurtrie
Michael Hansen	John McNabb

Douglas Mervis
Ann Miller
Kathy Myalls
Donna Napiewocki
Michael Neitach
Patrick O'Keeffe
Shari Odenheimer
Josephine Ortisi
Jeanne Phillips
Jeffrey Parness
Mark Perrin
Erik Post
Michael Redstone
George Reindel
Alan Rice
Leslie Richter
Mark Rose
Denise Rossman
Daniel Salliotte
Mark Sellinger
Jeffrey Seller
Sheri Silber
Steve Sugarman
Frederich Tipton
Jackie Vestevich
Irene Wassel
Nancy Webster
Robert Wilens
Ann Witkowski
Kenneth Wittenberg
Catherine Wycoff
Nicole Yakatan
Dina Zarin
Colin Zick
Allison Zousmer

Notes

Introduction

1. *Municipal Year Book*, 1988. See Arthur B. Gunlicks, "Local Government in the U.S.: Diversity and Uneven Development," in *Local Government and Urban Affairs in International Perspective* ed. J. J. Hesse(Baden-Baden: Nomos Verlagsgesellschaft, 1991).

2. Paul E. Peterson, *City Limits* (Chicago: University of Chicago Press, 1981), 12

3. Robert Fried, *Comparative Urban Performance* (Los Angeles: UCLA Press, 1972).

4. Edward C. Banfield, *Big City Politics* (New York: Random House, 1965), 3; Heinz Eulau and Kenneth Priwitt, *Labyrinths of Democracy* (Indianapolis: Bobbs-Merrill, 1973), 519; Terry N. Clark, ed., *Urban Policy Analysis* (Beverly Hills: Sage Publications, 1981), 94; Ted Gurr and Desmond S. King, *The State and the City* (Chicago: University of Chicago Press, 1987), 190

5. L. J. Sharpe and K. Newton, *Does Politics Matter?* (Oxford University Press, 1984), 19.

6. James March and John A. Olsen, "The New Institutionalism: Organizational Factors in Political Life," *American Political Science Review*, 78, no. 3 (1984): 747.

7. Michael A. Pagano, "City Fiscal Conditions in 1991," National League of Cities Research Report, July 1991.

8. *New York Times*, December 18, 1991.

9. *Detroit Free Press*, April 28, 1987.

10. M. Gottdiener, *The Decline of Urban Politics* (Beverly Hills: Sage Publications, 1987), 13

11. Theodore J. Lowi, "The State of Cities in the Second Republic," in *Fiscal Retrenchment and Urban Policy* ed. John P. Blair and David Nachmas (Beverly Hills: Sage Publications, 1979), 47.

12. Gurr and King, 75–76.

Chapter 1

1. Peterson, Paul E . 69.

2. See, for example, Gottdiener, 86—93.

3. For a discussion of early planning in U.S. cities based on a report of 800 cities, see Arthur Bromage, *Municipal Government and Administration*, 2d ed. (New York: Appleton, Century, Crofts, 1957), 408.

4. Bent F. Nielsen, speech before the American Municipal Congress in Miami, reported in the *Ann Arbor News*, August 10, 1964.

5. Ibid.

6. Guy Larcom, , "Planning for the Future," speech to the Ann Arbor Chamber of Commerce," January 14, 1965.

7. *Ann Arbor News*, February 16 and March 1, 1987.

8. Council Minutes, April 11, 1960, 4.

9. See the excellent review of the Human Relations Commission in this early period by Cal Samra in the *Ann Arbor News*, November 24, 1969.

10. See the *Ann Arbor News*, November 18, 1964, for a report on these two early studies.

11. *Ann Arbor News*, January 1, 1967.

12. Memorandum to City Council dated April 11, 1968.

13. See Lynn W. Eley and Thomas W. Casstevens, *The Politics of Fair Housing Legislation* (San Francisco: Chandler Publications, 1968), pp. 353—82. Eley was a councillor in Ann Arbor at the time and a major figure in the movement to fair housing.

Chapter 2

1. March and Olsen, 734–49.

2. The actual charters are available in the Bentley Historical Library or the Ann Arbor Public Library.

3. Council-Manager Government for Ann Arbor Citizens' Committee for Charter Revision,(pamphlet, 1948), quoted in Bromage, 262.

4. Robert Dahl, *Who Governs?* (New Haven: Yale University Press, 1961), 86.

5. See Eulau and Prewitt, 176.

6. Robert Dahl, *Pluralist Democracy in the U.S.* (Chicago: Rand-McNally, 1967), 261.

7. Ralf Dahrendorf, "Die Functionen Sozialer Konflikte," in, *The Nature of Human Conflict* ed., Elton B. McNeil (New York: Prentice Hall, 1965), 104.

8. V. O. Key, Jr., *Southern Politics in State and Nation* (New York: Alfred A. Knopf, 1949), 299—309.

9. Paul J. Quirk, "The Cooperative Resolution of Policy Conflict", *American Political Science Review*, 83 no.3 (1989): 905–22. See also Robert Axelrod, *The Evolution of Cooperation* (New York: Basic Books, 1984).

10. Hugh Heclo and Henrik Madsen, *Policy and Politics in Sweden* (Philadelphia: Temple University Press, 1987), 31.

11. *Ann Arbor News*, April 27, 1987.

12. *Municipal Yearbook*, 1982.

13. Eulau and Prewitt, 75–77.

14. Arthur H. Miller, et al., *Voter Participation in Ann Arbor*, Report prepared for the Ann Arbor Citizens' Council, 1981, 49–54.

15. *Ann Arbor News*, January 27, 1991.

16. *Municipal Yearbook*, 1977.

17. For discussions of the nature and meanings of political culture see: Gabriel Almond, "Comparative Political Systems," *Journal of Politics*, 18 no.3, (1956): 396. James Q. Wilson, ed., *City Politics and* Public Policy (New York: John Wiley and Sons, 1968), 12; Samuel H. Barnes, *Politics and Culture* (Ann Arbor, Center for Political Studies, University of Michigan, Ann Arbor, 1988): 2–3, 28; Michael Thompson, Richard Ellis, and Aaron Wildavsky, *Cultural Theory* (Boulder, Colo.: Westview Press, 1990).

Chapter 3

1. *Ann Arbor News*, March 3, 1950.

2. See for a discussion of these views and approaches, Russell J. Dalton et al., *Electoral Changes in Advanced Industrial Democracies* (New Haven: Princeton University Press, 1984).

3. Arthur M. Schlesinger, Jr., *The Cycles of American History* (Boston: Houghton-Mifflin, 1986), especially 23–24.

4. Figures supplied by the editor of the *Ann Arbor News*.

5. Miller et al., 44. In 1984 a second sample survey revealed that 63 percent were readers.

6. Ibid., 46.

7. Ibid., 47.

8. For the period 1947–87, we tabulated for the two-week period before each April election: (1) the articles dealing with parties, candidates, their meetings, and issue positions; (2) other articles about the election—proposals on the ballot, registration, turnout, and other information; (3) the political advertisements of each party or other community groups.

9. The *News* has changed its policy from time to time. In 1966 a memo from the newspaper was sent to all political candidates describing a new policy. It said that the previous "coverage of the coffee-hour type of meetings" has "proved unsatisfactory." They said that henceforth a column of comment would be printed each day, Monday through Friday, one day for each ward, each statement limited to 250 words.

10. Donald E. Stokes and G. R. Iversen, "On the Existence of Forces Restoring Party Competition," *Public Opinion Quarterly* 26 (Summer 1962): 159–171. See also S. J. Eldersveld, *Political Parties in American Society* (New York: Basic Books, 1982), 37–43.

Chapter 4

1. V. O. Key, *Political Parties and Pressure Groups*, see also his *Southern Politics in State and Nation* (New York: Knopf, 1949), chap. 14.

2. See the appendix for a detailed description of these surveys.

3. For a detailed analysis of these data see S. J. Eldersveld, "The Party Activists in Detroit and Los Angeles: A Longitudinal View, 1956–1980," in *Political Parties in Local Areas,* ed. William Crotty (Knoxville: University of Tennessee Press, 1986).

4. For a brief review of some of this research, see Eldersveld, *Political Parties in American Society* , 289–90.

Chapter 5

1. Floyd Hunter, *Community Power Structure* (Chapel Hill: University of North Carolina Press, 1953); Robert Dahl, *Who Governs?*

2. Peterson, 116–117.

3. Another 10 percent belonged to groups interested in school or library affairs. Overlapping with these were those active in church groups (29 percent), sports clubs (13 percent), hospital and nurses associations, or charitable groups (12 percent).

Chapter 6

1. This figure is based on U.S. Bureau of the Census reports. It can be argued that this inflates the size of the eligible electorate because of residence requirements, and in a university town this may be more true (especially since 1972, when the voting age dropped to 18) because of the difficulty students have in proving residence. With the increased possibilities for student registration recently, this reduces somewhat the strength of that argument. Before 1972 of course students were not calculated in the "eligibles" because most students were not yet 21 years of age. Yet, there is also the possibility that the figure is inflated. The base figure of the eligible electorate of voting age which is used here, then, may be too high, but it is the only figure available by which to standardize calculations. It is impossible, for example, to get the number of registered citizens for each of the past forty years, certainly not back to 1946.

The census figures sometimes vary considerably, particularly the figure on the percentage of the population of voting age. For example, in 1960 it was 60.4. In 1972 (when 18-year-olds first could vote) the percentage was 74.2; by 1980, it was 80.9; in 1987 it dropped to 78.6.

2. The figure for registered citizens is for April. The number can vary, during an election year. In 1972, for example, the April figure from the city clerk's record was 57,942. By August this had increased to 61,088 and by November to 72,878, based on the administrator's annual report. The 26th Amendment no doubt was responsible for this special case of the dramatic increase in the number of registered voters. In 1988 also there was a great change in registration: from 76,746 in April to 96,698 in November, a figure hard to believe. By April 1990 it had dropped again to 77,267, because the city clerk's office "purged" the rolls; but by that November it was up to 80,919.

3. See Miller, a study which did a great deal of the preliminary work leading to our surveys of 1980 and 1984.

4. Gottdiener, 20.

Chapter 7

1. There is an extensive literature on political socialization. Many scholars have done pioneer research in this area, leading to the theories presented in this section. I am particularly grateful to my colleagues Kent Jennings and Kenneth Langton, who are among the leading scholars in this field and whose studies have influenced this presentation greatly.

Chapter 8

1. See Kenneth Prewitt, *The Recruitment of Political Leaders* (New York: The Bobbs-Merrill Company, 1970); also T. B. Bottomore, *Elites and Society* (Baltimore: Penguin Books, 1964).

Chapter 9

1. *Ann Arbor Observer*, July 1989, 19.

2. We asked: "How much influence do you have on what is accomplished (in Ann Arbor) in the following areas?" We listed ten policy areas.

3. These studies have been reported in a variety of publications. See Eldersveld, *Political Elites in Modern Societies* (Ann Arbor: University of Michigan Press, 1989). and Philip Jacob, ed., *Values and the Active Community* (New York: Free Press, 1971).

4. Sidney Verba and Gary R. Orren, *Equality in America* (Cambridge: Harvard University Press, 1985).

Chapter 10

1. Valerie Bunce, *Do New Leaders Make A Difference?* (Princeton: Princeton University Press, 1981).

2. See a review and criticism of these studies in Bunce, 14–16

3. Edwin P. Hollander, "Leadership and Power," in *The Handbook of Social Psychology*, 3rd ed. Vol. 2, ed. Garner Lindzey and Elliot Aronson(New York: Random House, 1985), 485–537. See also Sidney Verba, *Small Groups and Political Behavior: A Study of Leadership* (Princeton Princeton University Press, 1961), 20.

4. Aaron Wildavsky, "Political Implications of Budgetary Reform", *Public Administration Review* 21 (Autumn 1961); 190. See also his *The Politics of the Budgetary Process* (Boston: Little, Brown, 1974), 4–5.

5. Robert Fried, quoted in L. J. Sharpe and K. Newton, *Does Politics Matter?* (Oxford: Oxford University Press, 1984), 11.

6. The annual budget document in the early years, from 1945 to almost 1960, was not a separate report but was incorporated in the minutes of the city council each year. The budget document in later years was not always readily available. The city clerk's office and the public library's collections are not complete, nor is that of the university. The Bentley Library has certain years, as part of the collection it has for certain mayors. Thus, it is difficult to get complete budget data for all departments for each fiscal year. Ideally, one would like three types of date: proposed budget, approved budget, and actual expenditures. But these are not always available (actual expenditures for the early years are difficult to find now). Hence, budgets are sometimes used in place of actual expenditures, and estimates are sometimes necessary.

7. Wildavsky, *The Politics of the Budgetary Process,* 15.

Chapter 11

1. Pagano, 5.

2. Thomas Anton, *American Federalism and Public Policy* (Philadelphia: Temple University Press, 1989), 134. In 1929, locally generated revenues represented 47 percent of all public sector revenues; by 1980 the figure was 15 percent.

3. Matt Kane, "Issues and Opportunities for University Communities," Research Report of the National League of Cities, 1989, 16.

4. Bromage, 304. On home rule generally and in Michigan, see 117–122.

5. Joseph A. Schumpeter, *Capitalism, Socialism and Democracy*, 2d ed. (New York: Harper and Row, 1950), 269.

6. Kenneth Prewitt, *The Recruitment of Political Leaders: A Study of Citizen Politicians* (Indianapolis: Bobbs-Merril, 1970), 49.

7. Harold Lasswell, Daniel Lerner and C. Easton Rothwell, *The Comparative Study of Political Elites,* Hoover Institute Studies (Stanford: Stanford University Press, 1952), 1.

8. Hannah Pitkin, *The Concept of Representation* (Berkeley: University of California Press, 1967), 209.

9. Lasswell et al., 11.

10. Eulau and Prewitt, 542–43. They found 44 percent of the eighty-seven city councils in the San Francisco Bay area to be unresponsive.

11. Peterson, 69.

12. John Stuart Mill, *Representative Government* (London: J. M. Dent and Sons, 1954), 185–202. See a commentary on this by Erik Allardt "Representative Government in a Bureaucratic Age," *Daedalus*, Winter 1984, 170 ff.

13. Sidney Verba and Norman H. Nie, *Participation in America* (New York: Harper and Row, 1972), 1.

14. Gottdiener, 49.

Bibliography

Allardt, Erik. "Representative Government in a Bureaucratic Age." *Daedalus* 113, no. 1 (Winter 1984): 169–97

Almond, Gabriel. "Comparative Political Systems." Journal of Politics 18, no. 3 (1956): 391–409.

Anton, Thomas. *American Federalism and Public Policy.* Philadelphia: Temple University Press, 1989.

Axelrod, Robert. *Evolution of Cooperation.* New York: Basic Books, 1984.

Banfield, Edward C. *Big City Politics.* New York: Random House, 1965.

———. *City Politics and Public Policy.* New York: John Wiley and Sons, 1968.

Barnes, Samuel H. *Politics and Culture.* Ann Arbor: Center for Political Studies, University of Michigan, 1988.

Bottomore, T. B. *Elites and Society.* Baltimore: Penguin Books, 1964.

Bromage, Arthur. *Municipal Government and Administration.* 2d ed. New York: Appleton, Centrury, Crofts, 1957.

Bunce, Valerie. *Do New Leaders Make a Difference?* Princeton University Press, 1981.

Clark, Terry N., ed. *Urban Policy Analysis.* Beverly Hills: Sage Publications, 1981.

Crotty, William. *Political Parties in Local Areas.* Knoxville: University of Tennessee Press, 1986.

Dahl, Robert. *Pluralist Democracy in the United States.* Chicago: Rand-McNally, 1967.

———. *Who Governs? Democracy and Power in an American City.* New Haven: Yale University Press, 1961.

Dahrendorf, Ralf. "Die Functionen Socialer Konflikte." In *The Nature of Human Conflict,* edited by Elton B. McNeil. New York: Prentice-Hall, 1965.

Dalton, Russell J., et al. *Electoral Changes in Advanced Industrial Democracies.* Princeton: Princeton University Press, 1984.

Eley, Lynn W., and Thomas W. Casstevens. *The Politics of Fair Housing Legislation.* San Francisco: Chandler Publications, 1968.

Eldersveld, Samuel J. *Political Parties in American Society.* New York: Basic Books, 1982.

———. "The Party Activist in Detroit and Los Angeles: A Longitudinal View, 1956–1980." In *Political Parties in Local Areas,* edited by William Crotty. Knoxville: University of Tennessee Press, 1986.

———. *Political Elites in Modern Societies*. Ann Arbor: University of Michigan Press, 1989.

Eulau, Heinz, and Kenneth Prewitt. *Labyrinths of Democracy*. Indianapolis: Bobbs-Merrill, 1973.

Fried, Robert. *Comparative Urban Performance*. Los Angeles: University of California Press, 1973.

Gottdiener, M. *The Decline of Urban Politics*. Beverly Hills: Sage Publications, 1987.

Gunlicks, Arthur B. "Local Government in the U.S.: Diversity and Uneven Development." In *Local Government and Urban Affairs in International Perspective*, edited by J. J. Hesse. Baden-Baden: Nomos Verlagsgesellschaft, 1991.

Gurr, Ted, and Desmond S. King. *The State and the City*. Chicago: University of Chicago Press, 1987.

Heclo, Hugh, and Henrik Madsen. *Policy and Politics in Sweden*. Philadelphia: Temple University Press, 1987.

Hollander, Edwin P. "Leadership and Power." In *The Handbook of Social Psychology*. 3d ed., vol.2, edited by Gardner Lindzey and Elliot Aronson. New York: Random House, 1985.

Hesse, J. J. *Local Government and Urban Affairs in International Perspective*. Baden-Baden: Nomos Verlagsgesellschaft, 1991.

Hunter, Floyd. *Community Power Structure*. Chapel Hill: University of North Carolina Press, 1953.

Jacob, Philip, ed. *Values and the Active Community*. New York: Free Press, 1971.

Kane, Matt. "Issues and Opportunities for University Communities," *National League of Cities Research Report*, 1989.

Key, V.O., Jr. *Political Parties and Pressure Groups*, 5th ed. New York: Crowell, 1964.

———. *Southern Politics in State and Nation*. New York: Crowell, 1964.

Lasswell, Harold, Daniel Lerner, and C. Easton Rockwell. *The Comparative Study of Political Elites*. Hoover Institute Studies. Stanford: Stanford University Press, 1952.

Lowi, Theodore J. "The State of Cities in the Second Republic." In *Fiscal Retrenchment and Urban Policy*, edited by John P. Blair and David Nachmas. Beverly Hills: Sage Publications, 1979.

March, James, and John A. Olsen. "The New Institutionalism: Organizational Factors in Political Life." *The American Political Science Review* 78, no. 3 (1984): 734–49.

Mill, John Stuart. *Representative Government*. London: J. M. Dent and Sons, 1954.

Miller, Arthur H., et al. *Voter Participation in Ann Arbor*. Ann Arbor Citizens Council, 1981.

Pagano, Michael A. "City Fiscal Conditions in 1991." *National League of Cities Research Report*, July 1991.

Peterson, Paul E. *City Limits*. Chicago: University of Chicago Press, 1981.
Pitkin, Hannah. *The Concept of Representatives*. Berkeley: University of California Press, 1967.
Prewitt, Kenneth. *The Recruitment of Political Leaders: A Study of Citizen Politicians*. New York: Bobbs Merrill, 1970.
Quirk, paul J. "The Cooperative Resolution of Policy Conflict," *American Political Science Review* 83, no. 3 (1989): 905–22.
Schlesinger, Arthur M., Jr. *The Cycles of American History*. Boston: Houghton-Mifflin, 1986.
Schumpeter, Joseph A. *Capitalism, Socialism, and Democracy*. 2d ed. New York: Harper & Row, 1950.
Sharpe, L. J., and K. Newton. *Does Politics Matter?* New York: Oxford University Press, 1984.
Stokes, Donald E., and G. R. Iversen. "On the Existence of Forces Restoring Party Competition." *Public Opinion Quarterly* 26 (Summer 1962) 151–71.
Thompson, Michael, Richard Ellis, and Aaron Wildavsky. *Cultural Theory*. Boulder, Colo.: Westview Press, 1990.
Verba, Sidney. *Small Groups and Political Behavior: A Study of Leadership*. Princeton: Princeton University Press, 1961.
Verba Sidney, and Norman H. Nie. *Participation in America*. New York: Harper and Row, 1972.
Verba, Sidney, and Gary R. Orren. *Equality in America*. Cambridge: Harvard University Press, 1985.
Wildavsky, Aaron. "Political Implications of Budgetary Reform," *Public Administration Review* 21 (Autumn 1961): 185–97.
———. *The Politics of the Budgetary Process*. Boston: Little, Brown, 1974.
Wilson, James Q., ed. *City Politics and Public Policy*. New York: John Wiley and Sons, 1968.

Index

www.ingramcontent.com/pod-product-compliance
Lightning Source LLC
Chambersburg PA
CBHW020658270326
41928CB00005B/179
9780472065622